THE CIVIL RIGHTS MOVEMENT

The Civil Rights Movement

MARK NEWMAN

Westport, Connecticut
London

12-05

Published in the United States and Canada by
Praeger Publishers, 88 Post Road West, Westport, CT 06881
An imprint of Greenwood Publishing Group, Inc.
www.praeger.com

English language edition, except the United States and Canada,
published by Edinburgh University Press Ltd., Great Britain

First published in 2004

U.S. CIP information is on file at the Library of Congress

ISBN: 0-275-98529-6

Printed in Great Britain

Contents

Abbreviations

AAA	Agricultural Adjustment Administration
ACMHR	Alabama Christian Movement for Human Rights
AFL	American Federation of Labor
BSCP	Brotherhood of Sleeping Car Porters
CAP	Community Action Program
CBC	Congressional Black Caucus
CCC	Civilian Conservation Corps
CCCO	Coordinating Council of Community Organizations
CDGM	Child Development Group of Mississippi
CFM	Chicago Freedom Movement
CIC	Commission on Interracial Cooperation
CIO	Congress of Industrial Organizations
CNO	Committee on Negro Organizations
COFO	Council of Federated Organizations
CORE	Congress of Racial Equality
CREB	Chicago Real Estate Board
DRUM	Dodge Revolutionary Union Movement
EEOC	Equal Employment Opportunity Commission
FBI	Federal Bureau of Investigation
FEPC	Committee on Fair Employment Practice
FOR	Fellowship of Reconciliation
FSA	Farm Security Administration
FTA	Food, Tobacco, Agricultural and Allied Workers Union
HEW	Department of Health, Education and Welfare
ICC	Interstate Commerce Commission
LCCMHR	Lowndes County Christian Movement for Human Rights
LCFO	Lowndes County Freedom Organization
MFDP	Mississippi Freedom Democratic Party
MIA	Montgomery Improvement Association
MOWM	March on Washington Movement

NAACP	National Association for the Advancement of Colored People
NCC	National Council of Churches
NCLC	Nashville Christian Leadership Council
NNC	National Negro Congress
NRA	National Recovery Administration
NUL	National Urban League
NYA	National Youth Administration
OEO	Office of Economic Opportunity
OFCC	Office of Federal Contract Compliance
PDP	Progressive Democratic Party
PUSH	People United to Save Humanity (later renamed People United to Serve Humanity)
PWA	Public Works Administration
RNA	Republic of New Africa
SCEF	Southern Conference Educational Fund
SCHW	Southern Conference for Human Welfare
SCLC	Southern Christian Leadership Conference
SNCC	Student Nonviolent Coordinating Committee
SRC	Southern Regional Council
STFU	Southern Tenants Farmers' Union
TVA	Tennessee Valley Authority
UAW	United Auto Workers
UFT	United Federation of Teachers
UMW	United Mine Workers of America
UN	United Nations
UNIA	Universal Negro Improvement Association
US	United States
VEP	Voter Education Project
WPA	Works Progress Administration
WPC	Women's Political Council

Chronology

1896 In *Plessy* v. *Ferguson*, the Supreme Court upheld the separate but equal doctrine.
1909 NAACP established.
1911 NUL organised.
1915 *Guinn* v. *United States* outlawed the grandfather clause.
1917 *Buchanan* v. *Worley* declared residential segregation ordinances unconstitutional.
1925 BSCP organised under A. Philip Randolph.
1928 Oscar DePriest elected the first African American to serve in Congress since 1901.
1935 NNC organised.
1936 Development of a 'Black Cabinet' of African-American federal government appointees who advised the president.
1938 SCHW established.
    Missouri ex rel. Gaines v. *Canada* rejected state provision of out-of-state tuition grants for African-American graduates to study subjects unavailable in state.
1939 NAACP Legal Defense and Educational Fund, Inc. created.
1940 *Alston* v. *Board of Education of the City of Norfolk* rejected racial differentials in the payment of African-American and white teachers' salaries.
1941 A. Philip Randolph inaugurated the MOWM.
    FEPC established by President Franklin D. Roosevelt's Executive Order 8802.
1942 CORE founded.
1943 Race riots in Detroit and Harlem.
1944 SRC organised.
    Smith v. *Allwright* outlawed the white primary.
    Gunnar Myrdal's *An American Dilemma: The Negro Problem and Modern Democracy* published.

1946 *Morgan* v. *Virginia* outlawed segregated interstate transport.
President Harry Truman's Executive Order 9808 established the
President's Committee on Civil Rights.

1947 CORE organised the Journey of Reconciliation.
Jackie Robinson desegregated major league baseball.
Release of *To Secure These Rights*, by Truman's Committee on
Civil Rights, calling for an end to segregation and other forms of
racial discrimination.

1948 Truman called unsuccessfully on Congress to enact legislation
against the poll tax and lynching, and to create a permanent Fair
Employment Practice Commission.
Shelley v. *Kraemer* ruled that racial covenants were unenforceable.
Truman's Executive Order 9980 barred discrimination in federal
employment; and Executive Order 9981 began gradual desegre-
gation of the armed forces, completed under the Eisenhower
administration.
Truman won the presidential election, despite the defection of the
Dixiecrats and Henry Wallace's Progressives from the Democratic
Party.

1950 In *McLaurin* v. *Oklahoma State Regents for Higher Education* and
Sweatt v. *Painter*, the Supreme Court ruled that separate but equal
facilities in graduate education did not guarantee equal educational
quality, and in *Henderson* v. *the United States* it held that segregation in railway dining cars violated the Interstate Commerce Act.

1951 Harry T. Moore, former Florida NAACP executive director,
murdered.

1953 An African-American boycott of Baton Rouge buses achieved
improvements within segregation.

1954 *Brown* v. *Board of Education of Topeka, Kansas* declared segregated
state schools unconstitutional.
First Citizens' Council established in Indianola, Mississippi.

1955 *Brown II* called for desegregation of state schools 'with all
deliberate speed' but at a pace to be decided by federal district
courts.
Murders of NAACP activist George W. Lee, Lamar Smith, and
fourteen-year-old Emmett Till in Mississippi.
The 381-day Montgomery bus boycott began.

1956 Autherine Lucy failed in her attempt to desegregate the University
of Alabama.

Southern Manifesto issued.

Browder v. *Gayle* outlawed segregated buses in Montgomery, ending the boycott.

1957 SCLC formed.

Little Rock school desegregation crisis.

Civil Rights Act passed.

1958 *Shuttlesworth* v. *Birmingham Board of Education* upheld the legality of pupil placement plans.

1959 Some Virginia schools closed to avoid desegregation.

1960 Sit-in movement began.

Civil Rights Act passed.

SNCC founded.

New Orleans school desegregation crisis.

Boynton v. *Virginia* outlawed segregation in interstate transportation terminals.

1961 University of Georgia desegregated after a riot.

Executive Order 10925 directed federal agencies and departments to cease racial discrimination in hiring, and created the President's Committee on Equal Employment Opportunity.

Freedom Rides began.

Herbert Lee murdered in Liberty, Mississippi, for assisting SNCC.

Albany campaign inaugurated.

1962 COFO reorganised.

VEP started.

Violence failed to stop desegregation of the University of Mississippi.

1963 Birmingham demonstrations.

Peaceful desegregation of the University of Alabama.

Murder of Medgar Evers, field secretary of the Mississippi NAACP.

March on Washington for Jobs and Freedom.

1964 SCLC campaign in St Augustine, Florida.

MFDP founded.

Murder of three civil rights workers in Neshoba County, Mississippi.

Mississippi Summer Project.

Civil Rights Act passed.

Race riots broke out in New York and some other northern cities, as they were to do during the next three summers.

1965 Malcolm X murdered.

Selma demonstrations.
Voting Rights Act passed.
Watts Riot.

1966 The SCLC's Chicago campaign began.
During the Meredith March in Mississippi, Stokely Carmichael called for Black Power.
Black Panther Party founded.

1967 Thurgood Marshall became the first black Supreme Court justice.
The FBI began applying its Counter Intelligence Program (COINTELPRO) against some civil rights and black nationalist groups.

1968 Report of President Lyndon B. Johnson's National Advisory Commission on Civil Disorders (Kerner Commission).
Martin Luther King, Jr's murder in Memphis, Tennessee, followed by riots in over 100 cities.
Civil Rights Act passed.
Green v. *New Kent County Board of Education* mandated the creation of a unitary school system.
Poor People's Campaign led by Ralph Abernathy.

1969 *Allen* v. *State Board of Elections* ruled that the Voting Rights Act applied to racial discrimination in all aspects of the electoral process.
The Nixon administration's Philadelphia Plan adopted affirmative action for minorities.
Alexander v. *Holmes County Board of Education* ordered an immediate end to school segregation.

1971 *Griggs* v. *Duke Power Co.* determined that employers would have to prove that racial discrimination did not account for an unrepresentative level of minority employment in their businesses.
Swann v. *Charlotte-Mecklenburg Board of Education* sanctioned busing to achieve desegregation in state schools.
Jesse Jackson left the SCLC and founded PUSH.

1972 National Black Political Convention held in Gary, Indiana.

1974 *Milliken* v. *Bradley* ended interdistrict busing to achieve school desegregation.
White resistance to busing in Boston.

1978 *University of California Regents* v. *Bakke* rejected racial quotas.

1979 *United Steelworkers of America* v. *Weber* upheld affirmative action programmes for minorities.

1980 *City of Mobile* v. *Bolden* ruled that plaintiffs challenging voting
laws had to prove they had been adopted with intent to discri-
minate against minorities.
Riot in Miami.
Fullilove v. *Klutznick* upheld federal minority set-aside programmes.
Ronald Reagan elected president.

1982 Voting Rights Act extended for a further twenty-five years.

1983 Reagan signed a bill making Martin Luther King, Jr's birthday a
federal holiday.

1984 Jesse Jackson finished third in the Democratic presidential
nomination race.

1988 Jesse Jackson finished second in the Democratic presidential
nomination race.
Civil Rights Restoration Act.

1989 Reagan left the presidency after serving two terms.
City of Richmond v. *Croson* severely restricted the use of minority
set-aside programmes.

CHAPTER I

Prerequisites for Change

America's pre-eminent social movement of the twentieth century, the civil rights movement, overturned *de jure* racial segregation and African-American disfranchisement in the South, enhanced black pride, and helped open up economic, political and cultural opportunities for many blacks across the nation. The movement also influenced the development of other protest movements against discrimination within and beyond the United States (US), such as women's movements, and the civil rights movement in Northern Ireland. In America, the movement failed to achieve more than token residential, social and school integration or to eliminate poverty. *De facto* segregation persisted in the North and replaced *de jure* segregation in the South, while a third of African Americans suffered from poverty with little prospect of upward mobility.

Although historian Clayborne Carson has argued that the term 'civil rights movement' should be displaced by the term 'the black freedom movement' to recognise the continuity and longevity of the African-American struggle for equality, this study, like contemporaries in the 1950s and 1960s, will refer to the civil rights movement.[1] The movement sought to secure equality under the law and to enable African Americans to enjoy equal access to and an equitable share in education, economic prosperity and political life, while fostering within them an assured sense of self-worth. Multifaceted and decentralised, the movement was black-led and dominated, but, to some degree, it was also interracial and assisted by white allies. The movement included national, regional and local organisations that at times worked together in various degrees and combinations, but also possessed their own particular, and changeable, emphases and approaches.

Some popular studies and documentary histories, the television documentary series *Eyes on the Prize*, and the exhibits at the National Civil Rights Museum in Memphis, Tennessee, focus on the 1950s and 1960s, with a brief acknowledgement of the movement's precursors in

I

previous decades.[2] After a succinct summary of earlier developments, Harvard Sitkoff begins his history of the civil rights struggle in 1954 with the Supreme Court's *Brown* v. *Board of Education of Topeka, Kansas,* ruling that declared state school segregation unconstitutional, followed by the successful 1955–6 Montgomery, Alabama, bus desegregation protest that made Martin Luther King, Jr, a civil rights leader.[3] Sociologist Aldon D. Morris locates the movement's origins in the ten years between the Baton Rouge, Louisiana, bus boycott in 1953 and the Birmingham, Alabama, civil rights campaign in 1963.[4] Historian Robert Weisbrot devotes fifteen pages to the period before 1960. He concentrates the bulk of his movement history on events between the sit-in protests of 1960, that marked the emergence of mass direct-action protest in the South, and King's assassination in 1968 and subsequent passage of a civil rights bill.[5]

Implicit in this choice of dates, bookended by major events, is a conception of the movement as being dominated by regional and national civil rights organisations and their leaders, and by federal actions. By relying on presidential and federal archives, the records of major civil rights groups and the written and spoken memoirs and personal papers of prominent figures, much of the scholarship published in the 1970s and into the 1980s encouraged an essentially top–down understanding of the movement.[6]

However, beginning in the 1980s some scholars produced local studies that pushed the movement's origins back into the 1930s and 1940s, and suggested that local movements often had their own dynamics and history. In a sophisticated account that drew on interviews as well as traditional written sources, William H. Chafe carefully charted the struggle for civil rights in Greensboro, North Carolina, between 1945 and 1975.[7] In his study of Tuskegee, Alabama, between 1870 and the 1960s, Robert J. Norrell argued that the town's civil rights movement began in 1941. Norrell contended that in the 1930s and 1940s, the South witnessed 'not just a few tantalizing moments of protest but a widespread, if not yet mature, struggle to overthrow segregation and institutionalized racism'.[8] However, the movement 'had a different experience in each place', and Norrell cautioned that only when many of the region's communities had told their stories could the movement be 'well understood'.[9]

In the past two decades, local studies have investigated not just southern communities, but also some northern, western and border state cities.[10] Further research may lead scholars to regard the movement less as an essentially southern phenomenon, and more as a national, or at least border and southern state, development.

Since the 1990s, historians have increasingly sought to understand the interaction between local, regional and national civil rights groups and events. Glenn T. Eskew's detailed study of the Birmingham campaign in 1963 revealed tensions between Martin Luther King and local activist Fred Shuttlesworth over tactics, and divisions within Birmingham's African-American leadership.[11] Studies of the movement in Georgia, Louisiana and Mississippi have contributed to the 'interactive model' that historian Steven F. Lawson saw emerging in 1991.[12] They have demonstrated that the movement involved a complex mix of local, regional and national groups and events. Patient and painstaking grass-roots organising and leadership were as important to the movement's development as prominent national leaders, federal action and well-publicised direct-action protests. While leaders, such as King, were important in the movement, so too were many local leaders and activists.

State and local studies have found that women played key roles in the movement's activities, not only as foot soldiers but often also as civil rights leaders, and organisers. Women performed important functions in many local National Association for the Advancement of Colored People (NAACP) chapters and in some NAACP state conferences, as well as in the Student Nonviolent Coordinating Committee (SNCC), citizenship education programmes, and many local groups and activities.[13]

Scholars have also found that local and state NAACP organisations did not necessarily fall into line between the NAACP's often cautious national leadership, and that there was a degree of reciprocal influence, as well as some disagreement, between the NAACP's local, state and national bodies. Furthermore, local and state NAACP groups were often far more diverse in their membership than their reputations as preserves of the black elite suggest, and their approaches to the black struggle for equality ranged from timidity and caution, to voter registration and litigation efforts, and even direct-action campaigns. The NAACP's chapters underpinned the civil rights struggle in much of the South between the 1940s and 1970s, in addition to the national NAACP lobbying Congress and taking cases through the courts in cooperation with local people.[14]

Studies of Georgia and Louisiana by Stephen G. N. Tuck and Adam Fairclough have not only traced the movement's history back to the 1930s and 1940s, they have also extended it beyond the mid-1960s. Work by Frank R. Parker, Akinyele Omowale Umoja and Mark Newman find the struggle continuing in Mississippi in the 1970s and 1980s, albeit in a much-diminished form.[15]

Historians are divided over whether continuity or discontinuity marked the civil rights struggle. August Meier and Elliott Rudwick argued in 1976 that the roots of African-American protest in the 1960s 'lay not in any past tradition of nonviolent direct action, but in the changing context of race relations which had emerged by the middle of the twentieth century'.[16] Emphasising discontinuity, Sitkoff claimed that the mass direct action movement of the 1960s was 'hardly ... just an extension, a continuation, of previous civil rights reform efforts'.[17] For Eskew, 'the civil rights movement began when local black activists in the South organized new indigenous protest groups in the 1950s and 1960s' which 'marked a departure in black protest as the new leaders appealed to a mass base by refusing to accommodate' segregation.[18] Eskew accuses historians who find continuity in African-American protest as operating 'within a cloud of relativism that borders on ahistoricism'.[19]

Despite Eskew's protestations, local and state studies have largely found continuity in the civil rights struggle.[20] Fairclough argues that advocates of discontinuity have exaggerated 'the extent of the mass mobilization that took place during the 1960s' and 'neglected the importance of litigation and drawn too sharp a distinction between litigation and direct action'.[21] In Louisiana, he finds 'a moderate, legal-istic, incrementalist movement'.[22] Charles M. Payne's study of Mississippi contends that 'the well-known movement of the early sixties was predicated on the activism of an earlier, socially invisible generation'.[23]

As in all social movements, most of those the civil rights movement sought to help held aloof from involvement. The African-American community, like other American communities, was diverse in opinion, and riven by class, colour and gender divisions. Nevertheless, partici-pation in the movement occurred in many forms, from demonstrations and voter registration to more discreet involvement, such as economic boycotts, and the movement often, although not always or easily, overrode black divisions in pursuit of common goals.

African Americans constituted 11.1 per cent of the nation's population in 1970, and in 1967 they formed a majority in 110 counties, all located in the rural South.[24] The movement's strategies at the national, regional and local levels were in consequence partly conditioned by its perception of the actions and response of the white majority. Early work on the response of whites to the civil rights movement, notably Numan V. Bartley's study of massive resistance, and Neil R. McMillen work on the Citizens' Councils, concentrated on the movement's most committed opponents.[25] Beginning in the 1980s, scholars, such as Chafe, began to focus on the often subtle ways in which some white political and economic leaders made token concessions to placate blacks, while retaining the substance of racial discrimination and white domination.[26]

In the first half of the 1960s, direct action comprised a great deal of movement activity, but a majority of northern and southern whites opposed civil rights demonstrations. However, southern white violence against the movement outraged many northern whites, including many of those who had not initially supported the protesters' demands. Not surprisingly, most southern whites opposed the movement's tactics and aims.

However, studies by David L. Chappell and Newman have demonstrated that southern white opinion was far from monolithic. White southerners were divided between a sizeable minority of militant, unyielding segregationists, a moderate segregationist majority that was prepared to accept racial change as the price of maintaining lawful order and economic progress, and a small minority of integrationists. Aware of fissures in national white opinion, civil rights protesters tailored their tactics accordingly.[27]

This study is an introductory survey of civil rights history that also familiarises readers with historiographical issues in a developing field of scholarship that lacks distinct interpretive schools. In line with recent research, the book traces the civil rights movement's emergence to the 1940s, discusses movement activities within and outside the South, emphasises the movement's diversity and complexity, acknowledges the long-term contribution of the NAACP, and argues that women were central to the movement. Attention is also paid to the various ways in which whites, nationally and in the South, responded to the movement and African-American demands for equality. Historiographical issues are integrated into the text as they arise in the course of the narrative, with endnotes for readers who wish to explore them further. The book's chronological arrangement is designed both to provide context for the historiography and to enable those less concerned with historiographical issues to bypass them and still gain an understanding of the movement's development, composition and impact.

Chapter 1 examines the establishment of *de jure* segregation and disfranchisement in the South in the late nineteenth century, racial discrimination in the North and the development of the civil rights movement's preconditions. Chapter 2 examines the emergence of the movement in the 1940s, its escalating challenge to discrimination, southern white resistance and the southern movement's efforts to survive and surmount the attacks upon it. Chapter 3 discusses the movement's mass direct-action phase which successfully pressured the federal government to end *de jure* segregation of public accommodations in the South and black disfranchisement. Chapter 4 explains the disintegration of the national civil rights coalition that had emerged in the first half of the 1960s, the re-emergence of northern protests against discrimination and a resurgence in black nationalist ideas. Chapter 5 considers federal civil rights policies from Richard Nixon to Ronald Reagan, assesses the long-term impact and durability of the southern civil rights movement, and charts the decline of many black nationalist and radical groups in the 1970s. Chapter 6, the book's conclusion, provides an analytical overview of the civil rights movement.

The Nature of Racial Discrimination

The history of African Americans, since their first recorded arrival in colonial Virginia in 1619, has, in large part, been one of struggle against discrimination. While the North successfully fought the Civil War (1861–5) to preserve the Union in the face of southern secession, the war also had the unanticipated consequence of ending black enslavement as slaves forced the issue of emancipation on to the political agenda by escaping to Union lines. The US Congress made the eleven states of the defeated Confederacy accept the Thirteenth, Fourteenth and Fifteenth Amendments to the Constitution, which abolished slavery, accorded citizenship to African Americans, and attempted to guarantee universal adult male suffrage by outlawing disfranchisement based 'on account of race, color, or previous condition of servitude'.[28] The efforts made by the federal government to enforce the amendments and to create a genuine biracial democracy in the South lasted fitfully until 1877. Known as the Reconstruction period, they foundered on the strength of southern white resistance and defiance, and growing northern white indifference to the plight of southern blacks, who formed over 90 per cent of America's black population.

With neither land nor money, former slaves, particularly in the cotton-growing areas of the Deep South, remained dependent on white planters for employment. Lacking sufficient funds to pay their workers but reliant on their labour, planters developed the sharecropping system in a compromise with their workforce. Sharecroppers grew cotton and enjoyed relative autonomy in their work. They paid the planter rent for land and farming equipment by giving the landowner around half of the crop at harvest time. African Americans who could afford their own tools and stock worked as tenant farmers. Tenants rented land by giving the owner roughly a quarter of the crop. Both sharecroppers and tenants also gave a lien or mortgage on the crop to planters or merchants who provided them with food and other supplies during the year. Worldwide overproduction of cotton drove its price down in the 1880s and 1890s, while high charges for supplies, and often outright fraud, ensured that sharecroppers and tenants became trapped in a cycle of debt to planters and merchants that kept blacks tied to the land. Tenants often found themselves reduced to sharecropping as they sold off their tools to reduce their arrears. The preference of southern and northern industrialists for white labour, except in the most unappealing jobs, also helped to confine many southern blacks to agriculture, while *de facto* racial segregation in the North and other forms of racial discrimination also limited opportunities for black northerners.

Beginning in 1881 and continuing into the 1940s, southern states and localities adopted a series of laws mandating racial segregation in virtually every aspect of life, and even death. Known as Jim Crow, after a northern minstrel song, these laws were primarily an urban phenomenon that codified existing custom and behaviour, imposed primarily by whites. Like many whites, many African Americans did not desire interracial association or integrated housing, but they objected to the inferior status and inferior facilities that Jim Crow enshrined in law. Despite segregation, interracial contact remained commonplace if only because most African Americans worked for whites in agriculture, or as domestics. The anonymity of urban living and the racial equality implied by shared use of new forms of public transportation led whites to segregate the races by law, so that previously established but unwritten 'rules' governing behaviour between the races received legal sanction. However, segregation, in some respects, replaced black exclusion from public accommodations and thereby marked an improvement in the lives of African Americans.[29]

Jim Crow inevitably meant that, when available to blacks, separate facilities were inferior to those whites enjoyed. Consequently, some

African Americans challenged segregation through the courts. The Supreme Court ruled in *Plessy* v. *Ferguson* (1896) that separate facilities were constitutional, providing that they were equal. Although southern states never afforded blacks equal facilities, state and local governments enacted further segregation legislation without judicial interference.

Unwilling to accept subordination, many southern African Americans had left white churches and denominations in the late 1860s and 1870s to found their own. The development of black urban churches fostered ministers who, unlike their rural counterparts, were independent of white financial control. The urban black community financed churches' expenses and pastors' salaries. Segregation, whether *de jure* or *de facto*, also helped ensure the development of an urban black middle class in both halves of the country. Its members provided services, such as banking, barbering, insurance, funeral homes and merchant stores, that white business people often would not offer African Americans. Despite having significant conservative elements, the black middle class later proved to be crucial in the development of the civil rights movement.

Like the rest of the black population, the southern black middle class lost the vote in the 1890s and early 1900s. Planter elites supported disfranchisement of blacks and poor whites after the Populist movement raised the prospect of a biracial alliance of the agricultural poor. Concerned with ridding politics of venality, urban middle-class Progressives also favoured black disfranchisement in the belief that corrupt white politicians manipulated African-American voters to keep themselves in office. To evade the Fifteenth Amendment, southern states required voter applicants to pay poll taxes, pass literacy tests, satisfy residency requirements, or, in the case of the grandfather clause, have a relative who had voted prior to the enfranchisement of blacks during Reconstruction. With few exceptions, most blacks soon lost the vote. The Democratic Party ensured the exclusion of the few remaining black voters from political influence by conducting white primary elections for office. With the vast majority of whites committed to the Democratic Party, its primaries effectively chose the South's officeholders at every level of the political system.

The development of scientific racism in the late nineteenth century helped provide ideological support for segregation and disfranchisement. Proponents of scientific racism, such as Madison Grant, held that humans could be classified hierarchically according to race, with whites deemed more genetically advanced than nonwhites and those of mixed race.[30] The growing assertiveness of a new generation of post-slavery African Americans led some whites to use violence as a means of control. Lynching of blacks reached its peak between 1882 and 1901, as whites sought to coerce African Americans into accepting subordination. While white men typically claimed that lynching punished black rapists of white women, in the majority of cases its victims had been accused of murder or attempted murder, rather than sex crimes.

Confined to inferior facilities by segregation, mostly excluded from the political system, subject to random white violence and largely dependent on whites for employment, African Americans had few realistic opportunities in the South to protest against discrimination. Although black boycotts of segregated buses may be thought of as a feature of the 1950s, they occurred in every state of the former Confederacy during the first decade of the twentieth century. A relatively risk-free strategy for participants that was orchestrated by members of the growing urban black middle class, the boycotts failed as whites refused to concede and the judiciary accepted the constitutionality of Jim Crow. While African Americans created some cultural space for themselves through their families, churches and civic clubs, and segregation unwittingly encouraged the growth of black businesses, white domination severely restricted black autonomy in the South.

Booker T. Washington, America's pre-eminent black leader from 1895 until his death in 1915, urged blacks to accept segregation, de-emphasise voting rights, and focus on education, industrial training and self-help as means of advancement. President of the Tuskegee Institute in Alabama, Washington, himself born in slavery, had the ear of Republican presidents and decisive influence over black appointments to federal office. While Washington and other black middle-class champions of racial uplift endured criticism for seeking white approval and acquiescing in white supremacy, Washington, at least, privately financed unsuccessful court cases against segregation and discrimination. However, it was from the North that African Americans began a sustained, open challenge to racial discrimination.

The Great Migration

W. E. B. Du Bois, a northern-born social scientist, emerged as Booker T. Washington's foremost critic. Du Bois argued that the black elite, 'The Talented Tenth', should lead African Americans in a struggle for equal rights and justice. In 1905, Du Bois organised the Niagara movement, a group of prominent influential blacks who called for complete racial equality. He and other members of the Niagara movement joined with prosperous, sympathetic northern whites to establish the NAACP in 1909.

From its headquarters in New York City, the NAACP challenged discrimination through the courts and conducted a national publicity campaign against lynching. In 1915, the NAACP achieved its first success, when the Supreme Court outlawed the grandfather clause in *Guinn* v. *United States*. However, the ruling had little impact on black disfranchisement because white registrars had a battery of other discriminatory devices to employ. Nevertheless, the NAACP's efforts attracted both middle- and working-class African Americans to its membership. Du Bois edited the organisation's newspaper, the *Crisis*. In 1916 the NAACP had sixty-seven branches, six of them in the South. By the end of 1919, the Association had a total of 300 chapters and 88,448 members, with 155 branches and 42,588 members in the South.[31] Women formed a significant minority of the membership, and they often played important roles in developing local chapters.

Some of those who joined the NAACP's northern branches were southern black migrants. To escape segregation, disfranchisement and violence, nearly 200,000 African Americans migrated to the North between 1890 and 1910.[32] Yet even in 1910, 89 per cent of America's black population lived in the South.[33] However, the next few years and especially the First World War marked the beginning of the Great Migration of blacks from the rural South to the urban South, and from the South to the urban North. Over half a million African Americans went north between 1910 and 1920, the bulk of them during the war, followed by nearly 750,000 more during the 1920s. Ravages to the cotton crop rendered by boll weevil infestations and floods, and falling cotton prices, pushed blacks away from southern agriculture. At the same time, increased wartime industrial production and the cessation of European immigration created a labour shortage that pulled African Americans northward.[34] By 1920, 34 per cent of African Americans lived in urban centres, compared with 27.4 per cent in 1910, and by 1930, only 78.7 per cent of blacks lived in the South.[35]

Rural black migrants to the urban South often took jobs as unskilled labourers or domestics. Although their income was low, collectively it contributed to the growth of black businesses and the urban church, thereby enlarging the black middle class. African-American migrants to the North sometimes benefited from the efforts of the National Urban League (NUL), which, unlike the NAACP, was not a membership organisation. Founded by northern blacks and whites in 1911 to help black migrants, the NUL located jobs and housing, and tried to ease migrant adjustment to northern life. Eschewing the more confrontational strategy of the NAACP and avoiding civil rights issues, the Urban League relied on persuading and conciliating white employers. From its headquarters in New York City, the NUL rapidly spread to other northern industrial and southern cities as the Great Migration unfolded.

Just as earlier black rural to urban relocation had led to white mob violence against African Americans between 1898 and 1908 in Wilmington, North Carolina, New York, New Orleans, Atlanta, and Springfield, Illinois, so further migration led to riots in more than twenty cities across America during the First World War and its aftermath. The worst riot occurred in East St Louis, Illinois, in July 1917. Motivated primarily by exaggerated fears of African-American competition for employment, a white mob attacked and killed blacks on the streets and in their homes. Thirty-nine African Americans and nine whites died in the conflagration, but few rioters faced prosecution or punishment.

White hostility to black servicemen also led to racial violence. Confined to segregated units, mostly commanded by white officers, African Americans suffered frequent acts of discrimination. Black soldiers at Camp Logan in Houston, Texas, reacted so strongly to police harassment that seventeen whites died in a race riot in September 1917. Many of the race riots of 1919 were triggered by white fears that returning black servicemen were planning to revolt against discrimination. Both northern and southern whites used violence in an attempt to ensure black subordination.

The First World War and black migration, then, brought no respite from white racism. White landlords in both northern and southern cities habitually refused to rent homes to African Americans beyond certain areas. Similarly, residential segregation ordinances confined black home buyers to particular zones. Although the NAACP persuaded the Supreme Court to outlaw these devices in *Buchanan* v. *Warley* in 1917, they were quickly replaced by restrictive covenants in which whites agreed not to sell their homes to nonwhites.

Residential segregation was most marked in northern cities. By contrast, some older southern urban areas, such as Montgomery,

Alabama, had developed with something of a hotchpotch of black and white housing. To be sure, racially defined ghettoes existed in southern cities, but they were especially prevalent in northern cities, partly because of the recent rapid arrival of thousands of African Americans. Ghetto residents faced exorbitant rents for dilapidated housing, and, even in the North, black children experienced segregated education in inferior schools, despite the absence of Jim Crow legislation.

However, persistent racial discrimination and their close proximity and burgeoning numbers helped give urban blacks an increased sense of racial identity. Marcus Garvey, a Jamaican who arrived in the United States in 1916 to undertake a thirty-eight-state speaking tour, quickly attracted a mass following with his message of racial unity and black pride. Garvey's all-black Universal Negro Improvement Association (UNIA) soon had members across the US, including the South, and a greater membership than the NAACP. Garvey preached black separatism, self-help and the right to armed self-defence. He also maintained that God was black, created a black religious denomination, and developed elaborate pageantry to boost racial pride. The UNIA advocated a partial and symbolic return to Africa, purchased ships for trade across the black diaspora, and organised the Black Star Steamship Line. Garvey's separatist message and the competition for black allegiance the UNIA provided were anathema to the NAACP. Each organisation vehemently denounced the other. Socialist A. Philip Randolph, who was to found the all-black Brotherhood of Sleeping Car Porters (BSCP) in 1925, also denounced Garvey for urging blacks to undercut white workers' wages and for advocating capitalism. Alarmed by the UNIA's teachings and encouraged by hostile African-American leaders, the federal government convicted and jailed Garvey for mail fraud in 1923 and again, after a failed appeal, in 1925, before deporting him in 1927. Without his presence, the UNIA collapsed.

There was some interaction between the Garvey movement and the Harlem Renaissance, a literary and artistic movement which developed in New York City in the 1920s. Like the UNIA, the renaissance celebrated black culture and African origins, and was also short-lived. The Stock Market crash of 1929 and subsequent Great Depression led wealthy whites who sponsored many Harlem Renaissance writers and poets to withdraw their patronage, while the economic collapse also deprived black creative talent of support from the relatively small African-American middle class.

Just as their concentrated numbers in the urban North provided fertile ground for the UNIA and encouraged black cultural expression, so it also enabled African Americans to gain political influence there since they had access to the ballot. Needing their support, white municipal politicians appealed to African Americans by improving pavements, street lighting and sanitation in the ghettoes. Blacks also began winning local office in cities where they were most concentrated, such as Chicago, Cleveland, Detroit, New York City and Philadelphia. In 1928, Oscar DePriest won election to Congress from Chicago's South Side, the first black congressmen since 1901 and the first from the North.

Even some white congressmen began to respond to black voters. In 1920, Republican Representative Leonidas C. Dyer of St Louis, Missouri, whose district had a large African-American population, introduced a bill to make lynching and failure to protect a prisoner from a lynch mob a federal offence. The NAACP, which began to make anti-lynching a centrepiece of its efforts, lobbied for the bill in Washington DC. It also investigated and publicised lynchings in an attempt to rally public opinion against them. Although the Dyer bill passed the House in 1922, it was blocked in the Senate by a filibuster as the bill's southern opponents prevented the bill coming to a vote using obstructive tactics. Committees in both houses held hearings on anti-lynching bills in 1925, but it took a decade before another bill came to a vote on the floor of either house.

A fear that Congress might pass an intrusive anti-lynching bill helped reduce the number of lynchings after 1919, when eighty-three were recorded, to single figures by 1932. The anti-lynching efforts of some southerners also played a part in the reduction. In 1919, black and white southerners formed the Commission on Interracial Cooperation (CIC), which created state and local committees across the South. The committees acted to stop lynchings by contacting local leaders and officials. In Georgia, they helped to indict twenty-two accused lynchers and secure four convictions in 1923. The CIC tried to ameliorate racial tension whenever it appeared. Formed under CIC auspices in 1930, the Association of Southern Women to Prevent Lynching, led by Texan Jessie Daniel Ames, gathered thousands of signatures on anti-lynching petitions, and the organisation's members repeatedly intervened to prevent lynchings. However, most southern white anti-lynching campaigners refused to endorse a federal anti-lynching law, claiming that it would be counterproductive and undermine states' rights. They also did not challenge Jim Crow.

Although lynching declined, southern blacks remained subject to white violence, disfranchised and segregated, with inferior schools and facilities. African Americans continued to migrate to the North, which offered them better economic opportunities and some political influence but also ghettoes, discrimination and white hostility. However, the onset of the Great Depression in the 1930s closed off many of the opportunities that had drawn blacks north. At the same time, falling crop prices and federal government policies that encouraged planters to evict tenant farmers and sharecroppers forced two million African Americans from southern agriculture. A time of economic catastrophe, especially for black Americans, the 1930s also witnessed key developments that aided the emerging civil rights movement.

The New Deal

Inaugurated as president in March 1933, Franklin D. Roosevelt's priority was to revive an economy that had over twelve million unemployed and had seen industrial output and agricultural prices more than halve under his Republican predecessor, Herbert Hoover.[36] Roosevelt promised the American people a New Deal of economic recovery, relief and reform. Already disproportionately poor, blacks suffered during the Depression far more than whites, who, to some extent, displaced them from employment as jobs became scarce. Federal agricultural and industrial policies unwittingly encouraged white employers to dispense with many African-American workers. Yet, the majority of black voters deserted the Republican Party for Roosevelt's Democrats in federal elections, grateful for their inclusion in the New Deal's relief and welfare measures.

In its early stages, the New Deal's economic recovery measures proved to be particularly damaging to African Americans. The National Recovery Administration (NRA) excluded agriculture and domestic labour, which absorbed at least 75 per cent of employed blacks, from its wage codes. Industrial employers responded to NRA codes that increased pay, either by downgrading their black employees' job classifications and hence their wages, or by replacing thousands of them with white workers. In the tobacco and steel industries, NRA codes allowed employers to pay white workers higher wages than blacks. In the oil, cotton and textile industries, the NRA allowed no pay rise or lessening of hours for unskilled workers, nearly all of them African American. With justice, blacks bitterly assailed the NRA as standing for 'Negro Removal Administration'.[37]

Designed to raise crop prices, the Agricultural Adjustment Administration (AAA) paid planters to reduce acreage under cultivation. In control of local AAA boards, white planters refused to share payments with their tenants and sharecroppers as the federal government intended, and instead evicted them from the land, especially when Washington began insisting that farm workers receive direct payment.[38]

Local white administrative control ensured that racial discrimination pervaded the Tennessee Valley Authority (TVA), which sought to revive the region's economy by developing cheap hydroelectric power, and flood and soil erosion control. At first, TVA excluded African Americans from clerical jobs and from living at its model village in Norris, Tennessee. TVA also segregated its workforce and confined blacks to lower-paid jobs, while denying them skills training. Jim Crow pervaded the Authority's offices and housing.[39]

Similarly, local white officials, particularly in the South, ensured that African Americans received limited assistance from the New Deal's early relief measures. For the most part initially excluded from the Civilian Conservation Corps (CCC), blacks faced segregation when eventually admitted, and they were denied training. In response to white anger at such relief benefits as blacks received, the Federal Emergency Relief Administration and the Civil Works Administration soon reduced the minimum wage for relief work and ensured that relief rates would not outstrip local pay scales.[40]

Complaints to the Roosevelt administration by the Joint Committee on National Recovery, comprising predominantly black organisations such as the NAACP and the NUL, along with pressure from sympathetic New Dealers, brought some easing of New Deal racial discrimination. However, much depended on the disposition of the heads of individual federal agencies, and the perennial problem of discrimination by local white administrators, especially in the South, remained. Nevertheless, the percentage of African-American CCC enrollees steadily rose from 3 per cent in 1933 to over 11 per cent five years later. By the time the Corps ended in 1942, 350,000 young black men had participated, approximately 14 per cent of the total number of enrollees, and over 40,000 blacks had benefited from literacy education.[41] TVA also increased its black workforce significantly to around 11 per cent but maintained segregation.[42]

Secretary of the Interior Harold Ickes, head of the Public Works Administration (PWA) and his white Georgian assistant Clark Foreman, ensured that from 1934 the agency included a quota for black employment in its building contracts. The quota reflected African-American representation in the 1930 occupational census. Implemented with some success, it led to some desegregation of white construction unions in the South and boosted the income of a limited number of skilled southern black workers. The US Housing Authority and the Federal Works Agency also later adopted quotas. African Americans benefited significantly from PWA spending on black schools, hospitals, libraries and housing projects. With incomes substantially below those of whites, African Americans occupied approximately one-third of the housing built by the PWA and the US Housing Authority. However, the new buildings largely perpetuated racial segregation in both halves of the country.[43]

Harry Hopkins worked assiduously to prevent racial discrimination in the Works Progress Administration (WPA), inaugurated in 1935. Outside the South, African Americans tended to receive equal treatment. However, local southern white administrators often thwarted the WPA's rules against racial discrimination in the jobs and wages which the programme provided. Nevertheless, the agency helped many southern blacks to survive the Depression. By 1939, nearly 750,000 southern black families chiefly depended on WPA income.[44]

Headed by Aubrey Williams, a white Alabamian sympathetic to black problems, the National Youth Administration (NYA) aided approximately 300,000 African Americans. Although the NYA tolerated separate black projects in the South, it ensured that they employed black administrative assistants, and refused to differentiate wages on the basis of race or region. Furthermore, the agency required that aid to black secondary and college students at least matched their proportion in the population, but poverty and inferior educational opportunities significantly limited the number of black students.[45]

Belatedly, the New Deal tried to offset some of the damage that it had inflicted on southern rural African Americans. The Resettlement Administration and its successor the Farm Security Administration, headed by Will Alexander, the former director of the CIC, provided aid to southern black farmers, but local administrators limited the value and the number of loans that African Americans received. The agencies also funded 141 supervised model farming communities to enable tenants and sharecroppers to become landowners. Thirteen of the projects catered for 1,151 African-American families in nine southern states, and another 1,117 black families received farming land under the scheme in nineteen integrated southern projects. These efforts produced a small new group of independent black landowners. In some locations, such as Mileston, Mississippi, the farmers and their offspring became a mainstay of local civil rights activity in the 1960s.[46]

Whatever the disposition of New Deal agency heads, Roosevelt steered clear of supporting anti-discrimination legislation. Concerned primary with economic recovery, he was not willing to endanger New Deal legislation and funding by risking certain opposition to civil rights bills from southern Democrats, who chaired over half of all House and Senate committees by virtue of seniority. The president also did not wish to offend southern white voters, who traditionally supported the Democratic Party. Yet at the same time, continued black migration to the North made northern Democrats and Roosevelt increasingly conscious of the importance of black votes in local, state and federal elections. Under the impact of the New Deal, most African Americans switched from the Republican to the Democratic Party, which, in turn, took its first tentative steps against racial discrimination. In defeating Chicago incumbent Oscar DePriest for the House in 1934, Arthur W. Mitchell became the Democratic Party's first African-American congressman. Departing from their historic support for the party of Abraham Lincoln, the 'Great Emancipator', a majority of black voters switched to the Democrats in that year's election, and two years later roughly two-thirds of them voted for Roosevelt.[47]

Although Roosevelt had avoided legislative commitments against racial discrimination, he and his officials moved against discrimination on several fronts. They employed significant numbers of African Americans, tripling their number in federal employment during the 1930s. Administration officials began desegregating federal offices and facilities in Washington DC and they recruited over 100 African Americans to administrative positions.[48]

Roosevelt also appointed black professionals and civil rights leaders to prominent, if secondary, advisory positions in cabinet and federal departments and agencies. Chief among them was educator Mary McLeod Bethune, who became director of the NYA's Division of Negro Affairs. Roosevelt also made William H. Hastie the first African-American federal judge. Calling themselves the Federal Council on Negro Affairs or 'Black Cabinet' in 1936, African-American government appointees met regularly in Bethune's home, and they increased government awareness of black problems. Black officials and Walter F.

White, the Atlanta-reared secretary of the NAACP, also pressed their concerns on the president, his administration and the Democratic Party by conveying them through the president's sympathetic wife, Eleanor.[49]

Eleanor Roosevelt frequently met with and addressed civil rights groups. During her husband's second term, she called for federal legislation to end the poll tax. In 1938, the president's wife defied Jim Crow by sitting in the black section of the first meeting of the Southern Conference for Human Welfare (SCHW) in Birmingham, Alabama, and then relocated her chair between the meeting's black and white sections when threatened with arrest. A year later, she condemned the Daughters of the American Revolution for barring black singer Marian Anderson from performing at Constitution Hall in Washington DC and, along with White and Harold Ickes, arranged for Anderson to sing in front of the Lincoln Memorial.[50]

President Roosevelt exhibited growing sympathy for African-American demands in the second half of the 1930s but without committing his prestige to them. He invited black leaders to the White House, and he also publicly declared his opposition to the poll tax and lynching. While he supported the principle of federal legislation against such discrimination, Roosevelt would neither propose it, nor push for its enactment. Influenced by Roosevelt and by the need to attract African-American voters, the Democratic Party admitted its first black convention delegates in 1936. The same convention also abolished the two-thirds rule for presidential nominations, which had given the South a veto over them for more than a century. Four years later, Roosevelt appointed the first black army brigadier general, Benjamin O. Davis, in what remained a Jim Crow military, and his party's platform promised 'to strive for complete legislative safeguards against discrimination in government service and benefits, and in the national defense forces'.[51]

Notwithstanding such advances, historians generally accept that New Deal programmes were frequently riven with racial discrimination, did not go far enough in helping African Americans, and did nothing to tackle de jure segregation, disfranchisement and lynching.[52] Nevertheless, historians such as Anthony J. Badger and Sitkoff also justly praise Roosevelt and the New Deal for giving blacks unprecedented assistance and recognition, and enabling them to survive the Depression.[53]

Historians disagree about the approach of New Dealers who opposed racial discrimination. John B. Kirby contends that white New Dealers, such as Ickes and Foreman, naïvely believed that racial prejudice among whites would diminish as federal policies improved the economic and educational levels of impoverished African Americans, and enabled them to join the American mainstream. By urging blacks to be patient in the expectation that white racism would decline, Kirby argues, white reformers helped prolong it, and they blunted the more radical tendencies of black New Dealers.[54] By contrast, Patricia Sullivan celebrates the efforts of reform-minded southern white and black New Dealers and sympathisers. She argues that they sought to tackle what they regarded as the interrelated problems of economic distress and racial discrimination. However, their efforts were often thwarted by Roosevelt's and his party's concern to placate conservative southern Democrats.[55]

Whatever the criticisms of historians, the black electorate over-whelmingly welcomed the New Deal. New Left historian Barton Bernstein contends that African-American and other marginalised people were 'seduced' by the administration's rhetoric and by symbolic gestures that obscured a lack of achievement.[56] However, Sitkoff attributes black support for Roosevelt to the New Deal's symbolic and substantive achievements, and its efforts to promote equality.[57] Nancy Weiss concedes that Roosevelt's rhetoric and appointments gave African Americans a sense of inclusion, but she claims that 'blacks became Democrats in response to the economic benefits of the New Deal ...'[58]

Trying to disentangle the administration's symbolism and rhetoric from the economic benefits it accorded African Americans as determinants in black voting patterns is a difficult, if not impossible, task. However, Sitkoff and Weiss are correct in arguing that the New Deal probably achieved as much for African Americans as circumstances permitted. The disproportionate power of southern Democratic congressmen, the primacy of improving the economy, the US tradition of decentralisation and states' rights, the opposition of white southerners to civil rights and the indifference of white northerners limited what could be achieved. Ostensibly unconnected to civil rights, the New Deal's labour legislation also had important, though unintended and unforeseen, consequences for advancing them.[59]

Challenges to Injustice in the South

With some exceptions, relations between organised labour and African Americans had traditionally been hostile. The American Federation of Labor (AFL) comprised craft unions that mostly excluded blacks or confined them to segregated locals, while many unskilled workers were unorganised. For decades, northern employers had used African Americans as strike-breakers in coal mines, docks and stockyards, and in the railway, iron and steel industries. Black strike-breakers, for their part, welcomed opportunities for better, albeit temporary, pay. They were also suspicious of the union movement, which generally discriminated against them. However, unlike many AFL unions, the United Mine Workers of America (UMW), founded in the late nineteenth century, accepted African-American membership despite opposition from many white miners. In the South, the UMW sometimes challenged racial discrimination in pay and promoted interracial collaboration. It foreshadowed a more widespread opening of industrial unionism to blacks in the 1930s.

By guaranteeing the right to collective bargaining and allowing the closed shop, the National Labor Relations Act of July 1935 encouraged the rapid spread of industrial unions, spearheaded by the newly-formed Congress of Industrial Organizations (CIO). To maximise their size, effectiveness and influence, CIO unions sought African-American recruits while organising previously neglected sectors, such as steel and meat, which had a significant black workforce. Of necessity and often from conviction, CIO unions assumed an equalitarian position. The United Auto Workers (UAW) and the Steel Workers Organizing Committee, for example, sought to avoid racist practices within their ranks. However, the racism of white workers, especially but not exclusively in the South, often undermined efforts by national and state leaders and organisers of CIO unions to promote genuine interracial unionism. White workers repeatedly insisted on protecting their seniority rights and restricting blacks to unskilled or dead-end jobs, thereby perpetuating racial inequality. Local CIO union leaders, particularly in the South, frequently capitulated, rather than lose members or potential recruits to the AFL.

New Deal protection for unions saved the BSCP from near fatal decline and allowed it to increase its membership, which had fallen dramatically during the Depression. In 1937, the revitalised union, led by A. Philip Randolph, won its long-standing battle for recognition by the Pullman Company, having secured an international charter from the AFL two years before by threatening to withdraw from the Federation.

Unions most committed to equal rights tended to be left-led, and many were communist influenced. They usually had integrated leadership and substantial black membership. The United Packinghouse Workers of America, which organised meatpackers in Chicago, Fort Worth, Texas and other cities, included many blacks and had a significant communist presence. Communists led the International Union of Mine, Mill and Smelter Workers of America, and the almost exclusively southern Food, Tobacco, Agricultural and Allied Workers Union (FTA). Both unions had large black majorities in the South. In Alabama, members of the Mine Mill union promoted voter registration and campaigned against lynching and the poll tax, while the FTA in Durham, North Carolina, also worked for civil rights in the 1940s.

Leftists generally had an ideological commitment to racial equality, and they believed that working-class solidarity was essential to achieve social change. In 1928, the Sixth Congress of the Communist International called for African-American self-determination, including the creation of an autonomous black nation in the American South. The Congress hoped that if white Americans came to accept blacks' right to self-government and, in so doing, overcame their racism, then eventually the working class could unite across racial lines in revolutionary struggle. In the meantime, communists sought to organise black industrial and agricultural workers in the belief that their oppression gave them revolutionary potential. Much to the chagrin of the NAACP, the Communist Party USA gained some black support by aiding the Scottsboro boys, nine African-American youths arrested and, all bar one, convicted for allegedly raping two white women in Alabama in 1931. Southern black communists combined Christianity with Marxist class struggle. Communists enjoyed some success in organising black sharecroppers in Louisiana and Alabama, but planter violence, harassment arrests and evictions defeated the unions and the strikes they organised.

During the Great Depression, impoverished African-American workers accepted communist aid in predominantly northern hunger marches, eviction protests and rent strikes, but only a small minority of blacks joined the party or shared its ideology. Most blacks wanted to be included in the American system, and the benefits accorded by the New Deal also blunted any potential for radicalism.[60] When thousands of African Americans rioted and looted in Harlem in March 1935, it was not a sign of revolutionary insurgency but a spontaneous response to a false rumour that white police had killed a black child found stealing from a department store, and frustration at persistent racial discrimination and economic deprivation.[61]

A small number of white southerners took active steps to relieve the suffering of the poor. Socialism motivated white Arkansan Henry L. Mitchell to help impoverished black and whites organise the Southern Tenant Farmers' Union (STFU) in 1934. The union tried unsuccessfully to improve conditions in Arkansas, Oklahoma and Missouri. Virginian Howard Kester, a Christian socialist, spent the 1930s helping Tennessee coal miners, NAACP lynching investigations and the STFU. Influenced by Danish folk schools, seminary-trained Myles Horton co-founded the Highlander Folk School in his native state of Tennessee in 1932. Highlander focused primarily on trying to create a racially-integrated labour movement in the South. Black and white southern liberals and moderates organised the SCHW in 1938, which sought to revive the southern economy, eliminate southern poverty, and end the poll tax, primarily through public-awareness campaigns. African Americans comprised a third of the group's membership.[62]

In organisations in which they predominated, blacks mounted a more direct challenge to racial discrimination, working with allies in the labour movement, religious groups and sympathetic whites. Convinced that the NAACP's strategy of pursuing racial integration in concert with white allies had failed given entrenched white racism, W. E. B. Du Bois wrote in the *Crisis* during 1934 that blacks should adopt 'voluntary segregation', build cooperatives and create a self-sufficient community.[63] Supported by the NAACP board, Walter White attacked Du Bois's change of mind as defeatist, and he reiterated the NAACP's integrationist policy. His position rendered untenable, Du Bois resigned.

White believed that the NAACP's successful effort four years earlier to deny Judge John J. Parker Senate confirmation to the Supreme Court justified the Association's approach. Parker, a North Carolina Republican, opposed black enfranchisement and supported company unions. The NAACP mobilised black community organisations in a national campaign against Parker, while the AFL also worked against the confirmation which southern Democrats opposed for partisan reasons.

The NAACP also found white allies for its long-standing anti-lynching campaign. Idealism and a partisan desire for black votes led Democratic Senators Edward P. Costigan of Colorado and Robert F. Wagner of New York to introduce an NAACP-drafted anti-lynching bill in 1934. Opposition from southern senators stymied the effort, and blocked anti-lynching bills passed by the House in 1937 and 1940. Although their pressure had failed to move the Senate, some liberal

Protestant, Catholic and Jewish groups had supported the NAACP's lobbying efforts. Furthermore, the prospect of legislation and the efforts of lynching's southern white opponents helped reduce the number of its victims from eight in 1936 to three in 1939, following a resurgence in the early years of the Depression.[64]

On the faculty of Howard University, a black institution in Washington DC, radicals Abram L. Harris, E. Franklin Frazier and Ralph J. Bunche urged the NAACP to broaden its attempts to create a civil rights coalition by forging an alliance with the white working class. Their influence, combined with concern at the Communist Party's ability to mobilise impoverished blacks in some areas, led reluctant NAACP leaders to attend some meetings of the National Negro Congress (NNC), although the Association itself held aloof. Envisaged primarily as a means of uniting black organisations, the NNC elected A. Philip Randolph as its first president in 1936. The Congress also attracted other BSCP leaders, members of several black groups, black intellectuals, sympathetic whites and both black and white communists. The Congress shared a similar programme to the NAACP but advocated greater militancy, including economic boycotts and picketing, and closer links with white labour groups. Hostile to communism and distrustful of a what it perceived as a competitive rival, the NAACP was relieved when the NNC disintegrated as communists became dominant within it. Resolutely anti-communist, Randolph declined re-election as Congress president in 1940.[65]

Although committed to integration, the NAACP came firmly under black control in 1935 as its white board chairman, Joel Spingarn, stepped aside, and the Association created a legal department under Charles H. Houston, a Harvard-trained black lawyer. Houston's appointment reflected White's desire to end the NAACP's reliance on unpaid white lawyers for its leading cases, and to use black lawyers at each level of the judicial process. Committed to using the law for social change, Houston had overseen the improvement of the law school at Howard University prior to joining the NAACP as special counsel. Thurgood Marshall, a Houston protégé, joined the NAACP staff in 1936. He became the first director of the NAACP Legal Defense and Educational Fund, Inc., created as a separate entity in 1939 to take advantage of new tax laws.

Houston and Marshall implemented an innovative strategy of challenging black exclusion from southern professional and graduate schools. They also worked to equalise the facilities of black state schools and the salaries of their teachers, who earned less than half the pay of their white counterparts. Adopted with the intention of forcing the abandonment of segregated education by making it too expensive, the strategy focused initially on urban areas in border and Upper South states because of the relative availability of local lawyers willing to assist and the region's closeness compared to the Deep South.

The NAACP soon benefited from Roosevelt's liberal appointments to the Supreme Court. Of the president's eight appointees, only James F. Byrnes of South Carolina did not become sympathetic to civil rights. Rejection of scientific racism by biologists and social scientists in the 1930s also encouraged some justices, intellectuals and opinion makers to reject discrimination, and, to some extent, helped ease acceptance of the court's rulings. In the early twentieth century, anthropologist Franz Boas had begun refuting the idea of a genetically determined racial hierarchy. Boas's students and other academics contributed to the development of a scholarly consensus that stressed environmental, rather than genetic, factors in determining people's actions.

In June 1935, Houston, assisted by Marshall, secured an order from the Baltimore City Court for the University of Maryland School of Law to admit its first African-American student, Donald Gaines Murray, a ruling that the Maryland Court of Appeals upheld the following January. In *Missouri ex rel. Gaines* v. *Canada* (1938), the Supreme Court rejected out-of-state scholarships for black graduates to study subjects unavailable to them in their home states and ordered the University of Missouri Law School to admit Lloyd L. Gaines. In an attempt to satisfy the court, the state hastily created a separate law school for blacks, but Gaines disappeared, leaving the NAACP unable to challenge the school's quality.

The NAACP also made progress towards equalising black teachers' salaries. Faced with an NAACP lawsuit, in 1937 the governor of Maryland promised progress towards equalisation. Further suits in Maryland produced a limited victory in Arundel County in 1939, and out-of-court settlements elsewhere. In neighbouring Virginia, the Fourth Circuit of Appeals supported equal teachers' pay in *Alston* v. *Board of Education of the City of Norfolk* (1940). The Supreme Court acquiesced in the decision. However, extensive pressure and litigation proved necessary to secure compliance across Virginia. Following further court victories in the South by the NAACP, other border and Upper South states also moved towards equalisation.

Pressure from African Americans hurt by the Depression, racial discrimination in New Deal programmes and opportunities provided by New Deal labour legislation encouraged the NAACP to address economic issues. With varying degrees of success, it pressed federal agencies to eliminate discrimination. In 1934, the NAACP picketed the AFL convention, while A. Philip Randolph spoke inside attacking union discrimination. Wary of communist leadership among some CIO unions and sharing traditional African-American suspicion of unions, the NAACP held back from the CIO, which gravitated to the more militant NNC. However, an enduring alliance between the NAACP and the CIO developed with the demise of the NNC, and following the NAACP's willingness to dissuade black strike-breaking during the Ford strike of 1941 in exchange for a UAW agreement to cease racial discrimination.

The NAACP's national leaders conceded that their organisation lacked mass appeal, drew the bulk of its membership from the black elite, and, in much of the South, needed leadership, organisation and finance. The national office did not appoint a full-time field secretary in Mississippi until 1954, despite the presence of NAACP branches in the state since 1918. The NAACP's national membership held up remarkably well during the 1930s after the Depression brought an initial decline. Its revival, centred in the urban North, owed much to the efforts of female branch officers and to women on the national staff, such as Juanita E. Jackson, who worked with black youth.

Concerned with litigation and lobbying, the NAACP's national leaders primarily regarded local branches as sources of funds and potential test cases, although they also intended that their victories would stimulate community activism. Some NAACP branches made important local contributions, with and without support from the national office. They helped create and support some of the first manifestations of the civil rights movement, including direct-action protests in northern and Upper South cities. Local civil rights groups and activities also emerged independently of the NAACP.

The civil rights movement developed in Tuskegee, Alabama, in the late 1930s, and in Louisiana had its origins in NAACP, labour and left-wing activism during that decade. Lawyer A. P. Tureaud was foremost among a group of otherwise predominately working-class men, who gained control of the New Orleans NAACP from an inactive elite leadership in 1941 after two years of effort. They revitalised the branch and some of them remained active into the 1960s and 1970s. NAACP

indifference led attorney William Howard Flowers and young professionals to establish the Committee on Negro Organizations (CNO) in
Arkansas during 1940, which subsequently coordinated statewide poll-
tax drives to boost black voter registration.

Meier and Rudwick persuasively argue that the 'era of the Depression
marked a watershed in Afro-American direct action', which reached a
peak not 'equaled or surpassed until the late 1950's and 1960's'.[66] The
NAACP supported school boycotts in several northern cities against *de
facto* segregation during the Depression decade. Between 1929 and 1941,
African Americans, occasionally with NAACP backing, also picketed
and boycotted retailers in thirty-five cities, a third of them in southern
and border state areas. The campaigns sought guarantees of black
employment, and, in a few cases, to protest ill-treatment of black
customers by white clerks. Aside from these efforts, African Americans
beyond the Deep South protested in some cities against public
accommodations that excluded them, and they participated in protests
directed at relief offices, rent strikes, anti-eviction demonstrations and
hunger marches.[67] Rather than being a phenomenon of the 1960s,
nonviolent direct action, Meier and Rudwick contend, has had a long
history in the African-American community, rising and falling 'in
response to shifting patterns of race relations and the changing status of
blacks in American society'.[68]

By 1940, a small inchoate civil rights movement had begun to develop
in parts of the South. The NAACP had earned several victories in the
courts and local movements had developed in various places, from both
within and outside the NAACP's ranks. Consumed by the everyday
struggle for survival and fearful of white retribution, most African
Americans were not part of the nascent movement, which was to expand
its numbers, organisation and influence significantly during the Second
World War and its aftermath.

Notes

1. Clayborne Carson, 'Civil Rights Reform and the Black Freedom Struggle', in
    Charles W. Eagles (ed.), *The Civil Rights Movement in America* (Jackson and
    London: University Press of Mississippi, 1986), p. 27.
2. Juan Williams, *Eyes on the Prize: America's Civil Rights Years, 1954–1965* (New
    York: Viking Penguin, 1987); Clayborne Carson, David J. Garrow, Gerald Gill,
    Vincent Harding and Darlene Clark Hine (eds), *The Eyes on the Prize Civil Rights
    Reader* (New York: Penguin, 1991); Peter B. Levy (ed.), *Let Freedom Ring: A
    Documentary History of the Modern Civil Rights Movement* (New York, Westport,

CT, and London: Praeger, 1992); Amy Wilson, 'Exhibition Review: National Civil Rights Museum', *Journal of American History* 83 (December 1996), pp. 971–6.

3. Harvard Sitkoff, *The Struggle for Black Equality, 1954–1992*, rev. edn (New York: Hill and Wang, 1993), pp. 3–54.

4. Aldon D. Morris, *The Origins of the Civil Rights Movement: Black Communities Organizing for Change* (New York: Free Press, 1984), pp. vi, ix–x, xiii, 229–74.

5. Robert Weisbrot, *Freedom Bound: A History of America's Civil Rights Movement* (New York and London: W. W. Norton, 1990).

6. Steven F. Lawson, 'Freedom Then, Freedom Now: The Historiography of the Civil Rights Movement', *American Historical Review* 96 (April 1991), pp. 456–7. Examples include August Meier and Elliott Rudwick, *CORE: A Study in the Civil Rights Movement, 1942–1968* (1973; Urbana, Chicago and London: University of Illinois Press, 1975); Steven F. Lawson, *Black Ballots: Voting Rights in the South, 1944–1969* (New York: Columbia University Press, 1976); Carl M. Brauer, *John F. Kennedy and the Second Reconstruction* (New York: Columbia University Press, 1977); David J. Garrow, *Protest at Selma: Martin Luther King, Jr., and the Voting Rights Act of 1965* (New Haven: Yale University Press, 1978); David L. Lewis, *King: A Critical Biography* (New York: Praeger, 1970); David L. Lewis, *King: A Biography*, rev. edn (Urbana: University of Illinois Press, 1978); Robert Fredrick Burk, *The Eisenhower Administration and Black Civil Rights* (Knoxville: University of Tennessee Press, 1984); David J. Garrow, *Bearing the Cross: Martin Luther King, Jr., and the Southern Christian Leadership Conference* (New York: William Morrow, 1986); Adam Fairclough, *To Redeem the Soul of America: The Southern Christian Leadership Conference and Martin Luther King, Jr.* (Athens and London: University of Georgia Press, 1987).

7. William H. Chafe, *Civilities and Civil Rights: Greensboro, North Carolina, and the Black Struggle for Equality* (1980; Oxford and New York: Oxford University Press, 1981).

8. Robert J. Norrell, *Reaping the Whirlwind: The Civil Rights Movement in Tuskegee* (1985; Chapel Hill and London: University of North Carolina Press, 1998), p. x.

9. Ibid. p. ix.

10. David R. Colburn, *Racial Change and Community Crisis: St. Augustine, Florida, 1877–1980* (1985; Gainesville: University of Florida Press, 1991); Alan B. Anderson and George W. Pickering, *Confronting the Color Line: The Broken Promise of the Civil Rights Movement in Chicago* (Athens and London: University of Georgia Press, 1986); Richard A. Couto, *Lifting the Veil: A Political History of Struggles for Emancipation* (Knoxville: University of Tennessee Press, 1993); Peter B. Levy, 'Civil War on Race Street: The Black Freedom Struggle and White Resistance in Cambridge, Maryland, 1960–1964', *Maryland Historical Magazine* 89 (Fall 1994), pp. 291–318; Sandy M. Shoemaker, '"We Shall Overcome, Someday": The Equal Rights Movement in Baltimore, 1935–1942', *Maryland Hisorical Magazine* 89 (Fall 1994), pp. 261–89; Charles M. Payne, *I've Got the Light of Freedom: The Organizing Tradition and the Mississippo Freedom Struggle* (Berkeley, Los Angeles and London: University of California Press, 1995); Christopher Robert Reed, *The Chicago NAACP and the Rise of Black Professional Leadership, 1910–1966* (Bloomington and Indianapolis: Indiana University Press, 1997); Glenda Alice Rabby, *The Pain and the Promise: The Struggle for Civil Rights in Tallahassee, Florida* (Athens and London: University of Georgia Press, 1999); Daniel Crowe, *Prophets of Rage: The Black Freedom Struggle in San Francisco, 1945–1969* (New York: Garland, 2000);

Jack E. Davis, *Race against Time: Culture and Separation in Natchez since 1930* (Baton Rouge: Louisiana State University Press, 2001); Gretchen Cassel Eick, *Dissent in Wichita: The Civil Rights Movement in the Midwest, 1954–72* (Urbana and Chicago: University of Chicago Press, 2001); John A. Kirk, *Redefining the Color Line: Black Activism in Little Rock, Arkansas, 1940–1970* (Gainesville: University Press of Florida, 2002).

11. Glenn T. Eskew, *But for Birmingham: The Local and National Movements in the Civil Rights Struggle* (Chapel Hill and London: University of North Carolina Press, 1997).

12. Steven F. Lawson, 'Freedom Then, Freedom Now', p. 457; John Dittmer, *Local People: The Struggle for Civil Rights in Mississippi* (Urbana and Chicago: University of Illinois Press, 1994); Adam Fairclough, *Race and Democracy: The Civil Rights Struggle in Louisiana, 1915–1972* (Athens and London: University of Georgia Press, 1995); Stephen G. N. Tuck, *Beyond Atlanta: The Struggle for Racial Equality in Georgia, 1940–1980* (Athens and London: University of Georgia Press, 2001).

13. Michael L. Gillette, 'The Rise of the NAACP in Texas', *Southwestern Historical Quarterly* 81 (April 1978), pp. 394–7, 409, 411–14; Raymond Gavins, 'The NAACP in North Carolina during the Age of Segregation', in Armstead L. Robinson and Patricia Sullivan (eds), *New Directions in Civil Rights Studies* (Charlottesville and London: University Press of Virginia, 1991), pp. 105, 108–10, 112; Vicki L. Crawford, Jacqueline Anne Rouse and Barbara Woods (eds), *Women in the Civil Rights Movement: Trailblazers and Torchbearers, 1941–1965* (1990; Bloomington and Indianapolis: Indiana University Press, 1993); August Meier and John H. Bracey, Jr, 'The NAACP as a Reform Movement, 1909–1965: "To reach the conscience of America"', *Journal of Southern History* 59 (February 1993), pp. 19–20; Dittmer, *Local People*, pp. 126–7, 332; Fairclough, *Race and Democracy*, p. xvi; Peter J. Ling, 'Local Leadership in the Early Civil Rights Movement: The South Carolina Citizenship Education Program of the Highlander Folk School', *Journal of American Studies* 29 (December 1995), pp. 399–422; Payne, *I've Got the Light of Freedom*, pp. 194, 265–83; Joanne Grant, *Ella Baker: Freedom Bound* (New York: John Wiley & Sons, 1998); Belinda Robnett, *How Long? How Long? African-American Women in the Struggle for Civil Rights* (New York and Oxford: Oxford University Press, 1997); Peter J. Ling and Sharon Montieth (eds), *Gender in the Civil Rights Movement* (New York: Garland, 1999); Merline Pitre, *In Struggle against Jim Crow: Lula B. White and the NAACP, 1900–1957* (College Station: Texas A & M University Press, 1999); Linda Reed, 'The Legacy of Daisy Bates', *Arkansas Historical Quarterly* 59 (Spring 2000), pp. 76–83; Flora Bryant Brown, 'NAACP Sponsored Sit-Ins by Howard University Students in Washington, D.C., 1943–1944', *Journal of Negro History* 85 (Fall 2000), pp. 276–80; Bettye Collier-Thomas and V. P. Franklin (eds), *Sisters in the Struggle: African American Women in the Civil Rights-Black Power Movement* (New York and London: New York University Press, 2001); Lynne Olson, *Freedom's Daughters: The Unsung Heroines of the Civil Rights Movement from 1830 to 1970* (New York: Scribner, 2001); Merline Pitre, 'Building and Selling the NAACP: Lula B. White as an Organizer and Mobilizer', *East Texas Historical Association Journal* 39 (Spring 2001), pp. 22–32; Tuck, *Beyond Atlanta*, pp. 248–9; Kirk, *Redefining the Color Line*, pp. 30, 47–8, 71, 72–3, 98, 106–32 passim, 138, 159–60, 171. See also the special edition of the *Journal of Black Studies* 26 (May 1996) on women in the civil rights movement.

14. Dittmer, *Local People*, pp. 29–34, 36–7, 41–5, 49–52, 77–9, 119, 157–69, 274–5, 312–13, 339; Fairclough, *Race and Democracy*, pp. xii-xvi, 48–50, 69–73, 107–9, 112–19, 153–6, 275, 279–80, 282–3, 296, 336, 384–5, 401, 402–8; Tuck, *Beyond Atlanta*, pp. 3, 154–5, 198–9, 245–6; Gavins, 'The NAACP in North Carolina', pp. 105–20; August Meier, 'Epilogue: Toward a Synthesis of Civil Rights History', in Robinson and Sullivan (eds), *New Directions in Civil Rights Studies*, pp. 212–16, 221–3; Eick, *Dissent in Wichita*, pp. 208, 209–11; Rabby, *The Pain and the Promise*, pp. 4, 6–7; Kirk, *Redefining the Color Line*, pp. 3–4, 9, 10, 30; Mark V. Tushnet, *The NAACP's Legal Strategy against Segregated Education, 1925–1950* (Chapel Hill and London: University of North Carolina Press, 1987), pp. 140–1, 148–53, 155.
15. Tuck, *Beyond Atlanta*; Fairclough, *Race and Democracy*; Frank R. Parker, *Black Votes Count: Political Empowerment in Mississippi after 1965* (Chapel Hill and London: University of North Carolina Press, 1990), pp. 103–209; Akinyele Omowale Umoja, '"We Will Shoot Back": The Natchez Model and Paramilitary Organization in the Mississippi Freedom Movement', *Journal of Black Studies* 32 (January 2002), pp. 271, 291–2; Mark Newman, *Divine Agitators: The Delta Ministry and Civil Rights in Mississippi* (Athens and London: University of Georgia Press, 2004), pp. 145–8, 172–4, 176, 178, 197–209.
16. August Meier and Elliott Rudwick, 'The Origins of Nonviolent Direct Action in Afro-American Protest: A Note on Historical Discontinuities', in August Meier and Elliott Rudwick (eds), *Along the Color Line: Explorations in the Black Experience* (Urbana, Chicago and London: University of Illinois Press, 1976), p. 307.
17. Harvard Sitkoff, 'African American Militancy in the World War II South: Another Perspective', in Neil R. McMillen (ed.), *Remaking Dixie: The Impact of World War II on the American South* (Jackson: University Press of Mississippi, 1997), p. 92.
18. Eskew, *But for Birmingham*, pp. 14–15.
19. Ibid. p. 14.
20. Norrell, *Reaping the Whirlwind*, p. x; Tuck, *Beyond Atlanta*, pp. 2, 3, 244–6.
21. Fairclough, *Race and Democracy*, p. xiv.
22. Ibid. p. xix.
23. Payne, *I've Got the Light of Freedom*, p. 4.
24. Paul S. Boyer, Clifford E. Clark, Jr, Joseph F. Kett, Neal Salisbury, Harvard Sitkoff and Nancy Woloch, *The Enduring Vision: A History of the American People*, 5th edn (Boston and New York: Houghton Mifflin, 2004), p. A–19; Stokely Carmichael and Charles V. Hamilton, *Black Power: The Politics of Liberation in America* (New York: Vintage, 1967), p. 166.
25. Numan V. Bartley, *The Rise of Massive Resistance: Race and Politics in the South during the 1950's* (1969; Baton Rouge: Louisiana State University Press, 1999); Neil R. McMillen, *The Citizens' Council: Organized Resistance to the Second Reconstruction, 1954–64* (1971; Urbana and Chicago: University of Illinois Press, 1994).
26. Chafe, *Civilities and Civil Rights*; Elizabeth Jacoway and David R. Colburn (eds), *Southern Businessmen and Desegregation* (Baton Rouge and London: Louisiana State University Press, 1982).
27. David L. Chappell, *Inside Agitators: White Southerners in the Civil Rights Movement* (Baltimore and London: Johns Hopkins University Press, 1994), pp. xxi-xxv; Mark Newman, *Getting Right with God: Southern Baptists and Desegregation, 1945–1995* (Tuscaloosa and London: University of Alabama Press, 2001), pp. 20–34.
28. US Constitution, Amendment XV.

29. Howard N. Rabinowitz, 'From Exclusion to Segregation: Southern Race Relations, 1865–1890', *Journal of American History* 63 (September 1976), pp. 325–50; Howard N. Rabinowitz, *Race Relations in the Urban South, 1865–1890* (1978; Athens and London: University of Georgia Press, 1996), pp. xiv, 144, 194–7, 331–2.

30. George M. Fredrickson, *The Black Image in the White Mind: The Debate on Afro-American Character and Destiny, 1817–1914* (New York: Harper and Row, 1971); Matthew Pratt Guterl, *The Color of Race in America, 1900–1940* (Cambridge, MA: Harvard University Press, 2001).

31. George Brown Tindall, *The Emergence of the New South, 1913–1945* (Baton Rouge: Louisiana State University Press/The Littlefield Fund for Southern History of the University of Texas, 1967), p. 159.

32. Sitkoff, *Struggle for Black Equality*, p. 6.

33. Charles Reagan Wilson and William Ferris (eds), *Encyclopedia of Southern Culture* (Chapel Hill and London: University of North Carolina Press, 1989), p. 177.

34. Sitkoff, *Struggle for Black Equality*, p. 8; Nancy J. Weiss, 'From Black Separatism to Interracial Organization: The Origins of Organized Efforts for Racial Advancement, 1890–1920', in Barton J. Bernstein and Allen J. Matusow (eds), *Twentieth-Century America: Recent Interpretations*, 2nd edn (New York: Harcourt Brace Jovanovich, 1972), p. 55.

35. Weiss, 'From Black Separatism to Interracial Organization', p. 55; Tindall, *Emergence of the New South*, p. 541.

36. Raymond Wolters, *Negroes and the Great Depression: The Problem of Economic Recovery* (Westport, CT: Greenwood, 1970), p. ix.

37. Harvard Sitkoff, 'The Impact of the New Deal on Black Southerners', in James C. Cobb and Michael Namorato (eds), *The New Deal and the South* (Jackson: University Press of Mississippi, 1984), pp. 120–1; Harvard Sitkoff, *A New Deal for Blacks: The Emergence of Civil Rights as a National Issue – Volume I: The Depression Decade* (New York: Oxford University Press, 1978), pp. 54–5.

38. Sitkoff, 'Impact of the New Deal', pp. 121–2; Sitkoff, *A New Deal for Blacks*, pp. 53–4; Harvard Sitkoff, 'The New Deal and Race Relations', in Harvard Sitkoff (ed.), *Fifty Years Later: The New Deal Evaluated* (New York: Alfred A. Knopf, 1985), p. 95.

39. Sitkoff, *A New Deal for Blacks*, pp. 50–1.

40. Sitkoff, 'New Deal and Race Relations', pp. 95–6.

41. Patricia Sullivan, *Days of Hope: Race and Democracy in the New Deal Era* (Chapel Hill and London: University of North Carolina Press, 1996), p. 49; Sitkoff, 'New Deal and Race Relations', p. 98; Tindall, *Emergence of the New South*, pp. 545, 548–9.

42. Sitkoff, 'Impact of the New Deal', pp. 122–3; Tindall, *Emergence of the New South*, pp. 545–6.

43. Sullivan, *Days of Hope*, pp. 25, 54–5, 121; Sitkoff, 'New Deal and Race Relations', pp. 99–100; John B. Kirby, 'The Roosevelt Administration and Blacks: An Ambivalent Legacy', in Bernstein and Matusow (eds), *Twentieth-Century America*, p. 276.

44. Sitkoff, 'Impact of the New Deal', pp. 125–6; Sitkoff, 'New Deal and Race Relations', p. 100.

45. Sitkoff, 'New Deal and Race Relations', p. 98; Sitkoff, 'Impact of the New Deal', pp. 126–7.

46. Lester M. Salamon, 'The Time Dimension in Policy Evaluation: The Case of the New Deal Land-Reform Experiments', *Public Policy* 27 (Spring 1979), pp. 129–32, 182–3.

47. Sitkoff, 'New Deal and Race Relations', p. 110.
48. Ibid. p. 102.
49. Sitkoff, 'New Deal and Race Relations', pp. 102–3; Meier and Bracey, 'NAACP as a Reform Movement', p. 16.
50. Sitkoff, 'New Deal and Race Relations', p. 106; Sullivan, *Days of Hope*, pp. 99–100.
51. Sitkoff, 'New Deal and Race Relations', p. 107–9; Tindall, *Emergence of the New South*, p. 712; Nancy J. Weiss, *Farewell to the Party of Lincoln: Black Politics in the Age of FDR* (Princeton: Princeton University Press, 1983), pp. 272–3.
52. Anthony J. Badger, *The New Deal: The Depression Years, 1933–1940* (Basingstoke: Macmillan, 1989), pp. 252–3; Barton J. Bernstein, 'The New Deal: The Conservative Achievements of Liberal Reform', in Barton J. Bernstein (ed.), *Toward a New Past: Dissenting Essays in American History* (New York: Pantheon, 1968), pp. 260–1; John B. Kirby, *Black Americans in the Roosevelt Era: Liberalism and Race* (Knoxville: University of Tennessee Press, 1980), pp. 222–5; Sitkoff, *A New Deal for Blacks*, pp. 328–9; Sitkoff, 'The New Deal and Race Relations', pp. 110–11; Weiss, *Farewell to the Party of Lincoln*, pp. xiii–xvi, 296–9; Wolters, *Negroes and the Great Depression*, pp. xi–xiii.
53. Badger, *The New Deal*, pp. 253–4; Sitkoff, *A New Deal for Blacks*, pp. 330–2; Sitkoff, 'New Deal and Race Relations', p. 93.
54. Kirby, *Black Americans in the Roosevelt Era*, pp. 227, 229–34.
55. Sullivan, *Days of Hope*, pp. 41–101.
56. Bernstein, 'New Deal,' pp. 260–1, 263.
57. Sitkoff, *A New Deal for Blacks*, pp. 96–7, 331; Sitkoff, 'New Deal and Race Relations', pp. 93, 110–11.
58. Weiss, *Farewell to the Party of Lincoln*, p. xiv.
59. Sitkoff, *A New Deal for Blacks*, p. 329; Sitkoff, 'New Deal and Race Relations', p. 94; Weiss, *Farewell to the Party of Lincoln*, pp. 34–40, 298–9.
60. Meier and Rudwick, 'Origins of Nonviolent Direct Action in Afro-American Protest', p. 386; Weiss, *Farewell to the Party of Lincoln*, p. 297; Susan Campbell, '"Black Bolsheviks" and Recognition of African-America's Right to Self Determination by the Communist Party USA', *Science and Society* 58 (Winter 1994–5), pp. 451, 461. African Americans comprised 7,000 of the Communist Party's 85,000 membership in 1939. Adam Fairclough, *Better Day Coming: Blacks and Equality 1890–2000* (2001; New York: Penguin, 2002), p. 145.
61. Charles D. Lowery and John F. Marszalek (eds), *Encyclopedia of African-American Civil Rights: From Emancipation to the Present* (New York, Westport, CT, and London: Greenwood Press, 1992), pp. 240–1.
62. Linda Reed, *Simple Decency and Common Sense: The Southern Conference Movement, 1938–1963* (1991; Bloomington and Indianapolis: Indiana University Press, 1994), p. 32.
63. Sitkoff, *A New Deal for Blacks*, p. 251.
64. Tindall, *Emergence of the New South*, p. 554. Like contemporaries, historians disagree on lynching statistics. Sitkoff, for example, claims that there were two lynchings in 1939. Sitkoff, *A New Deal for Blacks*, p. 295; Christopher Waldrep, 'War of Words: The Controversy over the Definition of Lynching, 1899–1940', *Journal of Southern History* 66 (February 2000), pp. 75–100.
65. Meier and Bracey, 'NAACP as a Reform Movement', pp. 17–19; Paula F. Pfeffer, *A.*

Philip Randolph, Pioneer of the Civil Rights Movement (1990; Baton Rouge and London: Louisiana State University Press, 1996), pp. 32, 34–40.

66. Meier and Rudwick, 'Origins of Nonviolent Direct Action in Afro-American Protest', pp. 314, 379.
67. Ibid. pp. 312–44.
68. Ibid. p. 387.

CHAPTER 2

The Emergence of the Movement, 1941–59

The 1940s and 1950s saw the acceleration of pre-war trends and new developments that made the civil rights successes of the 1960s possible. The NAACP's membership multiplied significantly, particularly in the South, and it achieved a series of court victories against racial discrimination that culminated in the *Brown* v. *Board of Education of Topeka, Kansas* school desegregation decision in 1954. The federal government, particularly the presidency and the Supreme Court, became more responsive to civil rights demands as continued black rural to urban migration increased the black electorate, created further bases of support for the movement, and made civil rights a national, rather than a sectional, issue. Sensitivity to Nazi racism and then during the Cold War to foreign propaganda highlighting America's mistreatment of its racial minorities, also exerted a largely, but not exclusively, positive influence on the federal government to act against discrimination.

However, southern segregationists red-baited the civil rights movement by accusing it of communist influence, hamstrung the NAACP's southern chapters using legislation, intimidation and violence, and, by evasion and outright opposition, severely limited school desegregation and black enfranchisement. The Congress of Racial Equality (CORE) pioneered interracial direct action in the 1940s, but, by the early 1950s, the organisation had been greatly weakened by red-baiting. Relatively muted during the 1940s after A. Philip Randolph's threatened mass March on Washington in 1941 led the Roosevelt administration to act against discrimination in the defence industry, direct action re-emerged in the late 1940s and again during the second half of the 1950s. The Montgomery bus boycott in Alabama made Martin Luther King, Jr, a national and international figure. King and other ministers created new local civil rights organisations, outside the embattled southern NAACP, which they affiliated under the umbrella of the Southern Christian Leadership Conference (SCLC) in 1957. A few NAACP youth and

CORE chapters staged sit-ins in border and southern states in the late 1950s. But by then, the civil rights movement had stalled, having secured legislative and court victories that had had little impact on altering the conditions of African-American life, while at the same time raising black expectations for change.

The Impact of the Second World War

The Second World War had significant effects on the lives of African Americans. The rapid growth of defence industries and hastily constructed military bases, many of them in the South, reignited African-American migration from the rural South to higher-paid jobs in the urban South, North and West, while, at the same time, increasing mechanisation pushed southern blacks from the land. As a result, the South's black rural population decreased by 30 per cent between 1940 and 1945, and the percentage of America's black population living in the South fell from 77 to 68 per cent during this time.[1] In some southern cities, African Americans could vote, as they could in the North. Consequently, politicians paid greater attention to black voters in northern and presidential elections during the 1940s, and in a few southern city elections towards the end of the decade.

During the war, one million African Americans joined the workforce, including 600,000 women.[2] Over one million blacks also served in the military.[3] Although the war gradually opened up some opportunities for African Americans in industry and the armed forces, initially they faced exclusion, or segregation and confinement to the most unattractive jobs. Aircraft and ship industries routinely excluded blacks. In 1940, the army only accepted African Americans for its four black army units, and the navy for its black messman's branch. The NAACP lobbied congressmen, and pressured federal agencies and the president to tackle racial discrimination. Rebuffed, the NAACP sponsored protest meetings in January 1941, but only twenty-five branches responded. In the same month, Randolph announced that he would organise a March on Washington to protest against discrimination in defence industries and the military. Exasperated by President Roosevelt's inaction, the NAACP agreed to participate in the march, which Randolph declared would be 10,000 strong. Encouraged by a positive black response, Randolph raised the figure to 50,000 and then 100,000.

Wary of domestic disruption while America aided the western powers and prepared for war, in June 1941 Roosevelt responded to the threatened march by issuing Executive Order 8802, which established a wartime Committee on Fair Employment Practice (FEPC) to promote nondiscriminatory policies in defence industries. Although the FEPC lacked enforcement powers and Roosevelt took no action regarding the military, Randolph and the NAACP called off the march, having secured the first presidential order supporting civil rights since 1875. In the event, labour shortages boosted black employment more than the FEPC, which nevertheless had some impact on employers' practices. But discrimination remained rife, leaving blacks confined mostly to lower-paid jobs. As the last hired and the first fired, African-American women suffered even more than black men from discrimination, and they were even more likely to lose their jobs when America reconverted to a peacetime economy after the war. Nevertheless, average black wages rose during the war from $457 annually to $1,976, compared to an increase in white average pay from $1,064 to $2,600, and black union membership more than doubled to 1,250,000.[4]

The Japanese attack on Pearl Harbor brought America into the war in December 1941. Military necessity and continued pressure from the NAACP, Randolph and the African-American press gradually opened up opportunities for blacks in the armed forces. Even before Pearl Harbor, the army began training African-American pilots at Tuskegee, and in 1942 the navy and the marines accepted blacks for general service within segregated units, while the army increasingly accepted black volunteers and draftees. A German offensive in the Ardennes in December 1944, forced the army to abandon segregation temporarily and fight in integrated units to defeat the attack.

To maintain pressure for change, Randolph created a mass membership organisation, the March on Washington Movement (MOWM), in December 1941. Although the movement's ultimate goal was racial equality and desegregation, it excluded whites in order to deter communist infiltration, build black esteem, and attract lower-class blacks by appealing to race pride as Marcus Garvey had done in the 1920s. Fearing the development of a rival organisation, the NAACP kept aloof from the MOWM, which held well-attended rallies in New York, Chicago and St Louis during 1942. Thereafter the movement lost momentum and direction as it failed to develop a specific programme under Randolph's autocratic leadership, or to organise its promised mass protests.

Randolph's increasing advocacy of nonviolent direct-action techniques also alienated many MOWM supporters. Inspired by union sit-down strikes in the 1930s and by Mohandas K. Gandhi's policy of mass civil disobedience against British colonial rule in India during the 1920s and 1930s, Randolph envisaged not only large-scale civil disobedience campaigns, but also a programme of small, interracial nonviolent sit-ins in public accommodations that discriminated against blacks. Many blacks (and whites) found the idea of Gandhian nonviolence alien and its precepts and requirements difficult to understand or follow. A poll by the *Pittsburgh Courier* found that 70.6 per cent of African Americans opposed Randolph's call for a week of civil disobedience against segregated schools and transport in 1943.[5] Consequently, the protests were cancelled. Whatever its failings, the MOWM influenced a later generation of civil rights leaders, among them Bayard Rustin, James Forman and E. D. Nixon, by making them aware of racial issues and, in some cases, providing them with training. However, it was a small interracial group of contemporary northerners who first applied Gandhian nonviolence techniques to American race relations.

In April 1942, fifty members of the Fellowship of Reconciliation (FOR), a predominantly white Christian pacifist organisation, formed the Committee (later Congress) of Racial Equality in Chicago, with the intention of applying modified Gandhian methods against racial discrimination. James Farmer, one of CORE's founders and its first national chairman, had grown up in Mississippi and Texas. A black Methodist, he had earned a divinity degree at Howard University, where he had been deeply influenced by the Christian pacifism and Gandhianism of his teacher Howard W. Thurman, the vice-chairman of FOR. In May 1942, CORE organised its first protest, an interracial sit-in at a Chicago restaurant that denied African Americans service. Further protests against discrimination in public accommodations followed in Chicago and in the few other northern cities in which CORE chapters developed. However, CORE remained a small, primarily white, group, largely ignored by the black and white press. The organisation proved unable to achieve its ambition of developing into a mass movement.

There were also other nonviolent protests in the early 1940s. In 1941, Adam Clayton Powell, Jr, pastor of Harlem's Abyssinian Baptist Church, organised a successful bus boycott that increased black employment in two local bus companies. Students at Howard University held sit-ins during 1943 and 1944 against stores in Washington DC that refused them service at lunch counters. African Americans also sat-in at

St Louis. But, such protests were rare, local, and not part of a coordinated regional or national campaign.

Although few blacks became involved in organised direct action, historian Robin D. G. Kelley contends that working-class African Americans engaged in various forms of day-to-day resistance to oppression, which he labels 'infrapolitics'.[6] Kelley also argues that black working people created an alternative culture that affirmed their dignity, self-respect and, in some cases, resistance to white norms. Even if they simply replicated white mainstream norms by dressing in their finest clothes on Friday and Saturday nights out on the town, blacks challenged white notions of their subordinate place. Some young men, Kelley notes, wore zootsuits, illegal because of their generous use of rationed cloth, and adopted assertive and distinctive language in an open challenge to white authority.[7] Although Kelley distinguishes between alternative and oppositional culture, his work sometimes implies that almost every aspect of black working-class culture somehow expressed opposition. Furthermore, the black press and community spokespeople widely condemned zoot-suiters for their strutting behaviour. Rather than opposing 'racist oppression through public displays of masculinity' as Kelley maintains, the zoot-suiters may simply have been revelling in excess after the scarcities of the Depression.[8]

More concretely, African-American resistance also took the form of migration to urban America. The manpower needs of the defence industries brought large-scale black and white migration to cities such as Detroit, Los Angeles, Mobile, Alabama, Beaumont, Texas, Norfolk, Virginia and Charleston, South Carolina. Unable to cope with the sudden influx, towns and cities quickly became overcrowded and their housing and transportation systems severely strained. Interracial tensions soon developed, particularly on crowded buses, in recreation areas and at places of employment.

African Americans in the segregated South resented being humiliated and insulted by white bus drivers. However crowded the black section became, drivers determined the amount of space available to black customers to ensure the seating and comfort of whites. Buses sometimes departed after blacks had paid at the front door and disembarked, as segregation required, with the intention of reboarding through the centre door to reach the rear section. In overcrowded wartime conditions, spontaneous individual acts of African-American resistance to unfair treatment rose significantly, particularly among women since they depended on buses more than men, and, if they worked as domestics for white employers, could assert their right to sit in a white section when travelling with their employers' children. Incidents of resistance to discrimination on buses occurred routinely in southern cities, such as Beaumont, Birmingham, Mobile and Norfolk.

Although white support for segregation was greatest in the South, which had the nation's largest share of the African-American population, many northern whites also did not favour integration. In 1942, the proportion of southern whites who supported integration of schools, public transportation and housing stood at 2 per cent, 4 per cent and 12 per cent respectively, compared with 40 per cent, 57 per cent, and 42 per cent of northern whites.[9] Wartime conditions of urban overcrowding and increased contact between the races led to riots in every region of America.

Racial violence first broke out at military bases, many of them in the South, where over 80 per cent of African-American soldiers, including thousands from the North, underwent training.[10] For the most part, conflict resulted from white violence against individual blacks, either by fellow soldiers, or by police and civilians in nearby towns and cities who feared armed African Americans and objected when black northerners failed to respect Jim Crow. African Americans often retaliated against their white attackers, and, occasionally, they took up arms in response to their treatment. In 1941, brutality by military police resulted in a gun battle with black troops in Fayetteville, North Carolina. Other armed conflicts between black and white soldiers broke out in Fort Bragg, Camps Davis, Gibbon, and Jackson Barracks during 1941, followed by increased racial violence at southern, northern and western bases a year later, notably in Alexandria, Louisiana, where thirteen blacks were shot.

Violence also affected many cities that had undergone significant black and white migration, but, in almost all cases, whites instigated the outbreaks. Interracial violence peaked in 1943, with an estimated 242 outbreaks in forty-seven cities across America.[11] When the Alabama Dry Dock and Shipbuilding Company in Mobile finally responded to FEPC pressure and gave twelve African Americans welding jobs in May, white workers, particularly the young and women, attacked as many black workers as they could find, fearing that blacks would replace them in skilled jobs. Eventually, the FEPC acquiesced in an agreement to allow skilled blacks to work in a segregated yard under white foremen. A rumour that an African-American man had raped a white woman, and fears that the FEPC would give their shipyard jobs to blacks, led over three thousand whites to rampage through the black section of Beaumont in June, resulting in two deaths.

Outside the South, whites, most of them servicemen, stripped black and Chicano zoot-suiters in Los Angeles and other cities for wearing supposedly unpatriotic clothes and failing to enlist. In June 1943, a race riot erupted in Detroit after interracial clashes at an amusement park led blacks to attack whites and their property in the ghetto, and white mobs to assault blacks found in white neighbourhoods. Thirty-four people died before federal troops quelled the riot. Within two months, African Americans rioted in Harlem, New York, and destroyed white-owned property, following a rumour that a white policeman had killed a black soldier. Five African Americans died in the conflagration. In both ghettoes, the riots were a response to *de facto* segregation, discrimination, unemployment, poor white-owned housing, police brutality and ill-treatment of black servicemen. However, African-American leaders were quick to distance themselves from black violence. In the *Crisis*, the NAACP likened the Harlem rioters to a southern white lynch mob, and Adam Clayton Powell, Jr, condemned their 'wanton violence'.[12] A survey found that less than a third of Harlem's population endorsed the riot.[13]

In the 1970s, Harvard Sitkoff contended that the Second World War witnessed a new militancy in the African-American community which led to the interracial violence of 1943, after which black 'leaders then retreated, eschewing mass movements and direct action in favor of aid from white liberals for their congressional and court battles'.[14] Lee Finkle notes that the black press adopted militant rhetoric during the war, most notably the *Pittsburgh Courier*'s call in February 1942 for a 'Double V' campaign of victory abroad and advancement of equality at home.[15] However, Finkle maintains that the press avoided 'a direct assault on segregation' and relied, instead, on 'traditional methods of protest such as lobbying committees, letter writing campaigns, and appeals to the courts and the executive branch'.[16]

Revising his views, Sitkoff now argues that both the black press and the large majority of African Americans gave priority to winning the war, with the result that militancy and support for the fledgling MOWM declined after Pearl Harbor. What distinguished wartime black America from the 1930s was a comparative lack of direct action.[17] Furthermore, Sitkoff notes, opinion polls conducted in mid-1943 found northern

African Americans far more dissatisfied with conditions than southern blacks, which also implies that the war did not mark a watershed for the civil rights movement in the South. Thirty-two per cent of northern blacks expressed discontent with job opportunities compared with 13 per cent of those in the South. Mistreatment of African Americans in the military brought complaints from 19 per cent of blacks in the North and 10 per cent in the South, while social discrimination upset 14 per cent of black northerners but only 3 per cent of southern African Americans.[18]

The NAACP's membership grew from 50,556 in 1940 to over half a million by 1946, with three-quarters of its new branches in the South. However, Sitkoff maintains that the southern branches did not pursue 'confrontations, direct action, or extralegal tactics'. Instead, as in the 1930s, they concentrated on lobbying and litigation 'against the poll tax, the white primary, and lynching, and requested a more equitable share of educational facilities and funds'.[19] Rather than returning to challenge racial discrimination, most of the southern black veterans who had been alerted to their own potential and sensitised to the nature of southern racial oppression by military service, either migrated north in search of opportunity, or re-enlisted. In sum, there was no direct line or simple continuity between wartime civil rights activities and the mass direct action, southern civil rights movement of the 1960s.[20] Sitkoff's interpretation neglects the fact that the wartime growth of the NAACP's southern chapters created bases of support for the later movement, and that voter registration formed an important part of civil rights activity from the 1940s onward.

Sitkoff also argues that elite black leaders relied on white liberals in the struggle for equality. These whites weakened the struggle by advocating gradualism and progress within continued segregation. In October 1942, a group of prominent southern black professionals met in Durham, North Carolina, in the hope of alleviating racial tension and violence. Accordingly, they excluded more militant northern African Americans and tried to ensure southern black support by appearing assertive, without alienating southern white liberals with whom they hoped to work. The Durham group declared its opposition to compulsory segregation, but focused its demands on improvements within Jim Crow, elimination of the poll tax and the white primary, and a federal anti-lynching law. In June 1943, southern white liberals met with the Durham group in Richmond. The two groups issued a joint statement that sidestepped the issue of Jim Crow and endorsed equal opportunity.

The next year, members of both groups established the Southern Regional Council (SRC), in succession to the CIC. The SRC advocated equal facilities and opportunities, and equality under the law, but, until 1949, it did not reject Jim Crow.[21]

The SCHW, a pre-war liberal group, also did not denounce segregation during the war. Instead, it campaigned against the poll tax, which disfranchised more whites than blacks. In 1941, the Conference organised the National Committee to Abolish the Poll Tax, a coalition of civil rights groups, which included the NAACP, CIO labour unions and liberal sympathisers. Although federal anti-poll-tax bills twice passed the House of Representatives, President Roosevelt kept silent and southern-organised filibusters kept the bills from coming to a vote in the Senate. Some southern states later exempted veterans from the poll tax, but white officials generally excluded African-American veterans from voting.

Historian Neil McMillen's interviews with black Mississippi veterans demonstrated that they, like many other southern blacks in the 1940s, resented exclusion and disfranchisement, but, for the most part, veterans did not return with an expectation that discrimination would change, or with the intention of making such change happen. McMillen's evidence corroborates Sitkoff's point that only a minority of black soldiers connected the war for democracy overseas with its denial at home.[22]

The war, then, for the most part, did not bring about a new direction in black aspirations, or a change in the means of attaining them. However, the wartime southern expansion of the NAACP testifies to the emergence of a southern civil rights movement. A good deal of credit for the NAACP's expansion belongs to Ella Baker, who became an assistant field secretary in 1940 and later national director of branches. Born in Virginia and reared in North Carolina, Baker, a graduate of Raleigh's Shaw University, was a fervent believer in grass-roots organising and developing local leadership. She regarded many NAACP branches as little more than social clubs for the black middle-class elite of professionals, businessmen and ministers. However, state and local studies demonstrate than some chapters were vigorous in their activism and that in some urban areas a fruitful partnership developed between NAACP branches and trades unions that had a significant black membership.

Growing wartime cooperation between an expanding NAACP chapter in Mobile and black union members brought greater efforts, though limited success, in registering African Americans, increasing black job opportunities in war industries, and improving white bus drivers' behaviour. Although the NAACP had become moribund in Georgia by 1940, during the war it began to revive in Savannah under the leadership of Baptist minister Ralph Mark Gilbert. The Savannah NAACP, which impressed Ella Baker, organised meetings and marches, and used youth volunteers in a successful voter registration campaign. Gilbert became president of the Georgia NAACP and helped establish fifty chapters in the state.[23] Organised in 1943, the North Carolina State Conference of NAACP Branches had fifty affiliates two years later.[24] During the same period, the Texas NAACP increased from 36 chapters to 104, with 23,000 members, more than any other southern state.[25] By 1945, the NAACP had expanded from its stronghold in New Orleans to become a statewide organisation in Louisiana that filed teacher salary equalisation suits and helped blacks to register to vote. Formed in 1945, the Arkansas State Conference of NAACP Branches built on the CNO's work.

There were also numerous local organisations that emerged during the war, sometimes independently of the NAACP and sometimes with the help of its members. The Tuskegee Civic Association, an independent group organised in 1941 by Charles G. Gomillion of the Tuskegee Institute, and the Mississippi Progressive Voters' League, formed three years later under the leadership of Jackson NAACP secretary T. B. Wilson, both fought for voting rights.

Many local groups and NAACP branches focused primarily on voter registration, especially after the NAACP persuaded the Supreme Court in April 1944 to outlaw the white primary in *Smith* v. *Allwright*. In Texas, where the case originated, 70,000 African Americans registered to vote between 1940 and 1947, and during this period the proportion of eligible southern African Americans registered rose from 3 to 12 per cent. Limited mostly to urban areas, the increase was not simply confined to the peripheral South.[26] By 1947, black registration had reached 10,000 in Louisiana, 37,155 in Arkansas, 50,000 in South Carolina and, helped also by the state's abolition of the poll tax in 1945, 125,000 in Georgia.[27] Nevertheless, segregationists retained political power, and although moderate segregationist governors, such as Ellis Arnall of Georgia, sometimes allowed black voter participation, they did so merely to boost their support. However, some blacks tried to break the segregationist stranglehold. Working with the NAACP, African-American activists in South Carolina formed the Progressive Democratic Party (PDP) in May

1944, which, in a bold but unsuccessful move, tried to unseat the state's regular Democrats at the Democratic Party's national convention.

The PDP failed at the convention because the national Democratic Party was unwilling to alienate white voters in the South, who formed an important segment of President Roosevelt's support. In an effort to attract black voters, the Republicans adopted a stronger civil rights plank in their party platform than the Democrats, including abolition of poll taxes and anti-lynching legislation. To shore up black support, Roosevelt urged that the wartime FEPC be made permanent and called for equal voting rights. African-American votes helped ensure his re-election in 1944, but his administration did nothing to prosecute violators of the *Smith* ruling.

In *An American Dilemma: The Negro Problem and Modern Democracy* published in 1944, Swedish sociologist Gunnar Myrdal optimistically suggested that white Americans would gradually overcome the chasm between the nation's professions of equality and democracy, and their simultaneous denial to African Americans. Wartime Japanese propaganda appeals emphasising American racism troubled some federal officials, such as Assistant Attorney General Wendell Berge, and Nazi anti-Semitism increasingly sensitised northern liberals to the problem of white racism in America, but they did not bring about a widespread examination by white Americans of their own racial attitudes. However, with the development of the Cold War in the second half of the 1940s, foreign policy considerations began to influence federal civil rights policy.

Jim Crow under Attack

Although most African-American soldiers who returned home to the South after the war did not challenge discrimination, veterans were prominent in many early postwar attempts by blacks to vote. One hundred veterans marched to the registrar's office in Birmingham, Alabama, and ex-soldier Medgar Evers led a similar veterans' group in Decatur County, Mississippi. When intimidation and discrimination severely limited black voting in Mississippi's Democratic senatorial primary in 1946, the Progressive Voters' League challenged the re-election of outspoken racist Theodore Bilbo. African Americans, many of them veterans, testified in the hearings which followed, but Bilbo died in August 1947 before the Senate had decided whether he should be seated.

Progressive groups including NAACP branches, local voters leagues, churches, the CIO's Political Action Committee and the SCHW worked with some success, mostly in southern cities, to boost black voter registration. The CIO launched Operation Dixie in May 1946 and claimed to have increased black and white membership of its southern unions by 400,000 within eighteen months, although the project soon failed.[28] In Winston-Salem, the FTA, a biracial CIO union with communist influences, led the challenge against discrimination and made the local NAACP branch a mass organisation with 1,991 members. Between them, the FTA and the NAACP increased black voter registration in the city tenfold between 1944 and 1947. African-American votes ensured the election of Kenneth Williams to the Board of Aldermen in 1947, the first black person to defeat a white opponent in a southern-city election in the twentieth century.[29] In the late 1940s, nearly a dozen African Americans followed Williams into local municipal office in the South, and wherever blacks could vote in significant numbers improvements followed, such as the hiring of black policemen, and paved streets and street lighting in black neighbourhoods.

While the NAACP's southern branches focused primarily on voter registration, in the North NAACP chapters worked to outlaw employment and housing discrimination. Between 1945 and 1950, ten states established fair employment practice commissions. African Americans enjoyed a symbolic victory over employment discrimination, when Jackie Robinson joined the Brooklyn Dodgers in 1947 and desegregated major-league baseball. CORE chapters, some NAACP branches and local groups adopted direct action against discriminatory public accommodations in the North. As the practice of segregated facilities receded in the North, border state cities, such as Baltimore, Washington DC and Kansas City, became the focus of direct action in the late 1940s. There were also a few pickets of public accommodations in peripheral southern cities, such as Norfolk, and Austin, Texas.

CORE first ventured south in 1947 by organising the Journey of Reconciliation. Eight blacks, including Bayard Rustin, and eight whites rode interstate buses and trains in three peripheral southern states and Kentucky to test compliance with *Morgan* v. *Virginia* (1946), in which the Supreme Court had outlawed segregation in interstate transport. Argued by the NAACP, the suit arose from the wartime arrest of Irene Morgan for defying segregation, indicative of the importance of women in the struggle against discrimination. The Journey of Reconciliation brought twelve arrests, road-gang sentences for Rustin and three others, no desegregation and little press attention. CORE made no significant efforts in the South again for a decade.

The bus protesters had narrowly escaped violence in Chapel Hill, North Carolina, and violence remained a real danger to southern African Americans whom whites perceived as threatening their supremacy. Since the end of the war, there had been brutal attacks on returning black soldiers and several lynchings. Most of the violence occurred in the Black Belt, an area of heavily black-populated plantation counties that arced through the South.[30] In February 1946, the Batesburg, South Carolina, police chief beat returning soldier Isaac Woodward blind, after arresting him following a dispute between Woodward and his bus driver. Less than two weeks later, white and black communities in Columbia, Tennessee, took up arms against each other after a confrontation between a black veteran and a white store clerk. In the summer, whites murdered two African-American men and their wives near Monroe, Georgia, beat Battle of the Bulge veteran John C. Jones to death in Minden, Louisiana, and killed another black veteran, Macio Snipes, in Taylor County, Georgia.

Alarmed by escalating racial violence, civil rights, labour and religious groups and veterans formed the National Emergency Committee Against Mob Violence in the summer of 1946 and called for federal action. Motivated by the Democratic Party's need for black votes and personal revulsion at the violence, Harry Truman of Missouri, Roosevelt's successor, appointed the President's Committee on Civil Rights in December 1946. Comprised of moderates and civil rights sympathisers, the committee issued a far-reaching report, *To Secure These Rights*, in October 1947. The report called for federal legislation against lynching, abolition of the poll tax, the establishment of a Civil Rights Division in the US Justice Department, a permanent FEPC, and desegregation of federal employment, interstate transportation and the military. The committee opposed discrimination as morally wrong, economically damaging, and a threat to America's foreign policy since 'Throughout the Pacific, Latin America, Africa, the Near, Middle, and Far East, the treatment which our Negroes receive is taken as a reflection of our attitudes toward all dark-skinned peoples.'[31]

Civil rights groups were quick to exploit the issue of America's international reputation. In 1946, the communist-dominated NNC petitioned the United Nations (UN) to 'end the oppression of the American Negro', but the UN refused to review the petition without proof of discrimination and claimed that, in any case, it had no authority to intervene.[32] The NAACP took up the idea a year later by submitting a detailed petition. With the Soviet Union and America now firmly at odds in the Cold War, the Soviets championed the NAACP's petition. However, the US blocked its presentation to the UN, and the NAACP accepted the outcome for fear of being branded a communist front at a time when anti-communism had begun to dominate domestic American politics.

In recent years, civil rights historiography has called attention to the significance of foreign policy anxieties, alongside the civil rights movement and domestic political concerns, in motivating federal civil rights action. The desire to counter Soviet propaganda about American racism during the Cold War as both the Soviet Union and the US competed for the allegiance of newly independent countries in Africa and Asia, in part, motivated successive presidential administrations from Truman to Lyndon Johnson to support civil rights reform.[33] However, the Cold War and the domestic anti-communism that accompanied it also, as historian Mary L. Dudziak explains, 'left a very narrow space for criticism of the status quo' and 'led to a narrowing of acceptable civil rights discourse'.[34]

The early Cold War years witnessed the repression of leftist advocates of racial equality, together with growing attention to civil rights by both national political parties. Truman addressed a joint session of Congress in February 1948 and asked the legislature to implement many of the recommendations of To Secure These Rights. However, he made no subsequent effort to secure legislation. Aware that Congress would not act, Truman hoped to win black votes by making his gesture for civil rights, without alienating either congressional southern Democrats whose support he needed in foreign affairs, or southern white voters in the forthcoming presidential election. At the Democratic Party's national convention, liberals and northern political bosses forced through the adoption of a stronger civil rights platform than Truman wanted. The platform incorporated many of the recommendations of To Secure These Rights. Some disgruntled southern Democrats bolted the party and formed the States' Rights Party, or Dixiecrats, to run governors Strom Thurmond of South Carolina and Fielding L. Wright of Mississippi for the White House, with the intention of wringing concessions for the South by throwing the election into the House of Representatives. Truman also received a challenge from the left, when

Henry Wallace ran as the candidate of the Progressive Party, which called for cooperation rather than confrontation with the Soviet Union, and for racial equality.

Since late 1947, Truman had been under pressure from A. Philip Randolph to desegregate the armed forces. Frustrated that Truman would not use his executive authority, Randolph and black New York Republican Grant Reynolds threatened to organise a campaign of non-violent civil disobedience against military segregation. A poll by the NAACP's Youth Division found that 71 per cent of black draft-age college students supported the idea.[35] Furthermore, unlike Truman, Republican Thomas E. Dewey of New York headed a ticket committed to ending Jim Crow in the military.

The failure of the Dixiecrat revolt to incite widespread defections from the Democratic Party, a desire to attract black votes and the need to assuage Randolph led Truman to issue Executive Orders 9980 and 9981 in July 1948. The orders barred discrimination in federal government employment, and established a committee to ensure equal opportunity in the armed services, with the ultimate intention, Truman soon indicated, of abolishing Jim Crow. The president also recalled Congress and requested civil rights legislation, which southern Democrats obstructed as he had expected. Truman red-baited the Progressive Party, which had a visible communist presence. He became the first president to campaign in Harlem and lambasted the Republican-controlled Congress for failing to enact his civil rights proposals. Truman won the election, with black votes crucial in securing his victories in California, Illinois and Ohio. The Dixiecrats won only in the four states, Alabama, Louisiana, Mississippi and South Carolina, in which they had been able to run under the banner of the regular Democratic Party.

Returned to office with a Democratic Congress, Truman reintroduced his civil rights proposals to Congress in 1949, but they failed once more. The president continued to give priority to the Cold War, and he remained unwilling to work assiduously for civil rights legislation against entrenched and powerful southern Democratic opposition. Ironically, American involvement in the Korean War, which broke out in June 1950, created a manpower shortage that gave a reluctant military the impetus to desegregate, while, at the same time, the war diverted Truman's attention away from civil rights.

The Cold War and domestic anti-communism also constrained the civil rights movement by destroying its radical leftist wing and restricting opportunities for social criticism, since dissent quickly became equated with disloyalty and subversion. Over Truman's veto, Congress passed the Taft-Hartley Act in 1947, which obliged union officials to sign non-communist affidavits in order to secure recognition as bargaining agents by the National Labor Relations Board. Between 1949 and 1950, the CIO expelled eleven unions it viewed as communist dominated, including the International Union of Mine, Mill and Smelter Workers of America, and the FTA. Historians Robert Korstad and Nelson Lichtenstein found that in Winston-Salem, the R. J. Reynolds Tobacco Company used anti-communism to undermine and destroy the black-led FTA local. They argue that the postwar attack on radicalism stifled the opportunity for 'a very different sort of civil rights movement' with an economic agenda rooted in the working class, and for an alliance between the movement and the CIO.[36] Historian Manning Marable castigates Walter White and the NAACP, and A. Philip Randolph, for their outspoken anti-communism. 'By serving as the "left wing of McCarthyism"', writes Marable, 'Randolph, White and other Negro leaders retarded the black movement for a decade or more.'[37] The scope for permissable dissent became limited to issues of inequality under the law.

Southern whites and other conservatives used anti-communism as a means to discredit black and white civil rights activists by accusing them of serving communism. The SCHW disbanded in 1948, a victim of red-baiting by the House Un-American Activities Committee and problems regarding finance, leadership and direction. Its offshoot the Southern Conference Educational Fund (SCEF), founded in 1946, endured investigation by the Senate Committee on Internal Security under Mississippian James O. Eastland in 1954. The hearing isolated the SCEF from anti-communist liberals and initially weakened its financial support. Although CORE adopted an anti-communist stance in 1948, by the mid-1950s conservative red-baiting had weakened the organisation's reputation and membership, leaving it near collapse. Communist-dominated groups, such as the Civil Rights Congress, fell apart. The federal government withheld the passport of black actor and singer Paul Robeson, one of the Congress' most outspoken members, for eight years.

The NAACP distanced itself from the SCEF and leftist groups and prohibited communist membership. Its leaders affirmed their anti-communism, which was sincere and not simply a tactic to court favour with the Truman administration, or to destroy rival organisations. Even so, white southerners red-baited the NAACP, and, in the second half of the 1950s, they hamstrung much of its southern operations using obstructive legislation. Had the NAACP not been anti-communist, the organisation might not have survived to continue and support an attenuated civil rights struggle, while other groups wilted under the anti-communist assault.

Some southern whites resorted to violence against the movement. In December 1951, Harry T. Moore, until recently executive director of the Florida NAACP, became the first civil rights leader to be murdered, when his home was bombed, probably by members of the Ku Klux Klan.[38]

Although the expulsion of leftist unions by the CIO weakened the prospects for a civil rights movement attentive to labour issues, the potential for an effective civil rights–CIO alliance focused on the needs of the black working class should not be romanticised or overestimated. In the South and the nation, left-led unions and state and national CIO union leaders tended to oppose racial discrimination, but the vast majority of southern and northern white union members did not. They often derived economic benefits from the subordination of black workers which preserved the better-paid and more desirable jobs for themselves.[39] The CIO continued to oppose racism and worked with the NAACP in the Leadership Conference on Civil Rights, established in 1950, but it was much less able to eliminate discrimination in the workplace, despite some successes.

Notwithstanding the constraining effects of domestic anti-communism, the Cold War also afforded some support for the civil rights movement when the NAACP took cases to the Supreme Court in the late 1940s and early 1950s. Truman's Justice Department filed several supportive *amicus curiae* briefs, which were often rooted in concerns about the adverse affects of domestic racial discrimination on US foreign policy. The Supreme Court found racial covenants unenforceable in *Shelley* v. *Kraemer* (1948). Two years later, in *Henderson* v. *United States*, the Supreme Court determined that segregation in railway dining cars violated the Interstate Commerce Act. On the same day, the court ruled in *McLaurin* v. *Oklahoma State Regents for Higher Education* and in *Sweatt* v. *Painter* that separate but equal facilities in graduate education did not guarantee equal educational quality, thereby laying the way open for a constitutional challenge against segregation.

Between 1946 and 1953, school boycotts, usually with NAACP support, occurred in seventeen cities, including for the first time border and southern as well as northern states. The boycotts sought either to improve segregated education, as in Lafayette, Louisiana, in 1953, or to abolish it altogether, as in Long Branch, New Jersey, in 1947.[40] In 1948, the NAACP resolved not to take on cases that perpetuated segregation. The organisation reaffirmed that decision two years later in regard to education.[41] The Association made its intentions known through the media and in addresses to community groups, but it did not solicit clients and only responded to requests for aid by local communities. NAACP lawyers were usually part of the fabric of the African-American community from which cases arose, and they worked with and through community institutions. Consequently, NAACP cases enjoyed a broad spectrum of support from the communities in which they originated.

On 17 May 1954, the Supreme Court ruled on a group of NAACP school desegregation cases from South Carolina, Virginia, Delaware, Kansas, and Washington DC, consolidated as *Brown* v. *Board of Education of Topeka, Kansas*. Acutely aware of the strength of southern white support for Jim Crow, Chief Justice Earl Warren, appointed only months before by Republican President Dwight D. Eisenhower, worked hard to secure unanimity for the *Brown* decision, which declared segregation of state schools unconstitutional. In reaching its decision, the Court argued that the plaintiffs had been deprived of equal protection of the laws under the Fourteenth Amendment and that racially-segregated education harmed black children psychologically by implying their inferiority. In the last months of the Truman administration, the US Justice Department had submitted an *amicus curiae* brief in the *Brown* case which argued that 'Racial discrimination furnishes grist for the Communist propaganda mills ...'[42] The Voice of America, a United States government radio station, transmitted news of *Brown* to Eastern Europe less than an hour after the ruling. However, the Supreme Court would take another year before deciding how its decision should be enforced.

Massive Resistance

At the time of the *Brown* ruling, seventeen southern and border states, and the District of Columbia had school segregation laws, while four other states had allowed Jim Crow education without legislation. The border states, and western states with local option on segregation, soon desegregated their schools or announced their intention to comply with *Brown*. There were some demonstrations and disturbances in Delaware and West Virginia, but no violent resistance. At President Eisenhower's instruction, the District of Columbia desegregated its classrooms.

The response of the white South to *Brown* was generally calm and guarded, largely because it was not yet clear what the impact of the Supreme Court's ruling would be. However, some white southerners were prepared to accept change. The Southern Baptist Convention, by far the largest white denomination in the region, accepted *Brown* as constitutional and Christian, while the Southern Presbyterians' General Assembly supported the ruling and condemned segregation. Within and outside the white church, whites in the Deep South and in the Black Belt militantly opposed *Brown*. But whites who lived away from plantation areas in the urban and peripheral South were mostly stoical about desegregation.

No southern governor advocated compliance with *Brown*, but governors in the peripheral South generally urged calm and some, such as Frank G. Clement of Tennessee, recognised the ruling as 'the law of the land'.[43] Two school districts in Arkansas began desegregation in the fall of 1954. Alabama's populist governor Jim Folsom accepted the court's action as the law and sought to defuse tension, but other Deep South governors declared their intention of finding means to maintain segregated education, despite *Brown*, and many of them expressed their disquiet about the ruling. Opposition to *Brown* ensured the election of Marvin Griffin and George Bell Timmerman, Jr, as governors of Georgia and South Carolina respectively in 1954. There were no other major contests in the Deep South that year, and defiance of the Supreme Court had little impact on other southern elections.

The most hostile reaction to *Brown* came from the Black Belt. Sunflower County plantation owner and Mississippi US Senator James Eastland declared that the Supreme Court had been 'indoctrinated and brainwashed by Left-wing pressure groups'.[44] In July 1954, middle-class whites in Indianola, Sunflower County, formed the first Citizens' Council. Dedicated to the preservation of Jim Crow, the Council movement spread rapidly in Mississippi during the next few months.

White Mississippians exhibited the most virulent opposition to African-American aspirations, particularly after NAACP chapters and other black groups organised voter registration campaigns across the state in late 1954 and 1955. Under pressure from the Citizens' Council, Gus Courts relinquished the presidency of the Belzoni chapter of the NAACP in the Delta. Belzoni NAACP activist the Reverend George

W. Lee was murdered in May 1955, and Courts later left the state after being shot in his grocery store. In mid-August, Lamar Smith, a farmer, was slain in the southwest town of Brookhaven after urging African Americans to vote. Even more shockingly, in late August two Delta whites brutalised and killed fourteen-year-old Emmett Till from Chicago for supposedly whistling at or asking a white woman for a date. Outrage at the Till murder and the acquittal of his killers, who subsequently admitted their guilt, had a profound impact on the African-American community beyond simply Mississippi. It encouraged many blacks to become active in the civil rights movement, particularly those of Till's generation who joined SNCC and CORE in the 1960s.[45]

Brown II, the Supreme Court's implementation ruling, also sparked further black mobilisation and southern white reaction. Issued in May 1955, the ruling ordered that school desegregation occur 'with all deliberate speed' but at a pace determined by federal district courts.[46] The court did not call for immediate desegregation because southern political leaders had warned the justices that the Deep South would not comply, and President Eisenhower had refused to support the original decision beyond recognising its legality and his duty to uphold the law. Although Eisenhower had desegregated Washington DC and completed the desegregation of the military, he had a limited view of federal authority, sympathised with southern white fears about social equality, and favoured noncoercive gradualism for fear that rapid school desegregation would produce southern defiance.[47]

The NAACP urged its branches to petition school boards to implement desegregation, as some had done after the first *Brown* decision. During the summer of 1955, African Americans organised sixty petitions, many of them in the Deep South.[48] Their action stimulated the spread of the Citizens' Councils, particularly in the Deep South, which drew their greatest support from the Black Belt. By the end of the year, the Councils and other prosegregationist groups claimed to have 208,000 members in 568 chapters across the South.[49] Ostensibly committed to legal methods to preserve segregation, the Councils threatened black petitioners with dismissal from work, boycotts of their businesses and violence. Consequently, many blacks removed their names from school desegregation petitions.

In the wake of *Brown I*, several southern states had appointed committees to recommend ways of preserving segregation. Mississippi and then Alabama, Florida, Louisiana and North Carolina soon passed pupil placement laws, which allowed school boards to preserve segregation by assigning pupils using criteria that did not overtly refer to race, and established labyrinthine appeals procedures. Other southern states later adopted pupil placement, and, across the South, legislators sanctioned tuition grants for students to attend private schools, and measures to permit governors to close schools subject to desegregation.

Senator Harry F. Byrd, Sr, of Virginia called for 'massive resistance' by the white South to defend segregation.[50] The Byrd organisation had controlled Virginia politics since the 1920s from its stronghold in the Southside, southeast Virginia's tobacco country, where African Americans formed more than 40 per cent of the population.[51] The malapportioned state legislature gave the Southside, with fewer than 15 per cent of Virginia's population, great influence in the General Assembly.[52] Between them the Byrd machine, James J. Kilpatrick, editor of the *Richmond News Leader*, and the Defenders of State Sovereignty and Individual Liberty, a group allied with the Citizens' Council, shifted Virginia from an initial policy choice of local option on school desegregation to outright defiance. Byrd correctly feared that many white Virginians, beyond the Southside, were resigned to desegregation. In 1956, the Byrd organisation and Southside legislators pushed a package of massive resistance laws through the General Assembly in close votes. An interposition resolution declared that Virginia would resist the Supreme Court's 'illegal encroachment upon our sovereign powers', and the state mandated the closing of any school that desegregated under court order, and denied state funds to those that desegregated voluntarily.[53]

Byrd was instrumental in persuading southern congressmen to adopt the Southern Manifesto, proposed by Senator Strom Thurmond of South Carolina. Signed in March 1956 by 101 of the 128 senators and representatives from the states of the old Confederacy, the Manifesto condemned 'the unwarranted decision of the Supreme Court' and commended states determined 'to resist forced integration by any lawful means'.[54] Southern white leaders thereby legitimised resistance and helped rally many southern whites behind it by persuading them that segregation could be preserved.

Shortly before the Manifesto appeared, a poll by the American Institute of Public Opinion had found that 80 per cent of southern whites disapproved of *Brown* and only 16 per cent approved of the ruling. However, opinion was not uniform across the South. In the five Deep South states, 90 per cent of whites opposed *Brown* and one out of seventeen favoured it, but in Arkansas, Florida, North Carolina and Virginia about 20 per cent of whites approved of the ruling and nearly 25 per cent did so in Tennessee and Texas.[55] Even within segregationist ranks, whites divided between hard-line segregationists resolutely committed to maintaining Jim Crow, and moderate segregationists, whose support for Jim Crow was conditional on the maintenance of law and order, economic well-being and public education. The Southern Manifesto sought to ensure southern whites that Jim Crow could be maintained without chaos ensuing, and to deter the federal government and courts from enforcing change.

However, much depended on whether African Americans could be rendered quiescent. Voter registration campaigns by NAACP branches and local groups boosted black registration by 21 per cent between 1952 and 1956 to 1.2 million in the eleven southern states.[56] But by the early 1950s, direct action had virtually disappeared from both sections of the country. Public accommodations had desegregated in the North, *Brown* had initially made school boycotts for desegregation or improved education in Jim Crow states seem unnecessary, and the domestic Red Scare had weakened CORE and other radical groups that were committed to direct action.

One example of direct action stands out. In June 1953, the Reverend T. J. Jemison led a bus boycott in Baton Rouge, Louisiana. Only a week-long, the boycott achieved its goal of having seating allocated on a first-come, first-served basis. Blacks filled the bus from the back and whites from the front within a continued system of bus segregation. The arrangement spared African Americans from having to give up their seats to whites and from being forced to remain standing while seats reserved for whites remained empty. Short in duration, the boycott was not widely reported, and it did not stimulate similar efforts elsewhere.

Unaware of the earlier boycott in Baton Rouge, African Americans began a bus boycott in Montgomery, Alabama's capital city, in December 1955, which initially shared the demands of the earlier protest in Louisiana. Sparked by the arrest of Rosa Parks for refusing to give up her seat to a white man on a crowded bus, the boycott was forged, at first, by established local activists. Parks, a seamstress born in 1913, had joined the Montgomery NAACP in 1943 and registered to vote in 1945. She went on to serve as secretary of the Alabama State Conference of NAACP branches and to advise the local NAACP Youth Council. In 1955, Parks had attended the Highlander Folk School, which held workshops on desegregation for African-American and white community leaders from across the South, including many of those who were to become important in the civil rights movement. On several occasions since the 1940s, she had refused to give up her bus seat to whites.

NAACP activist E. D. Nixon paid Parks's bond, accompanied by a local white couple Virginia and Clifford Durr, who had been active in the SCHW and the SCEF and had recommended that Parks attend Highlander. President of the Montgomery NAACP between 1946 and 1950, and the state NAACP from 1947 to 1949, Nixon had worked with Parks for many years. A Pullman porter and long-time admirer of Randolph, he had been president of the Montgomery branch of the BSCP since 1938, worked with Myles Horton and the Highlander Folk School in the 1930s organising cucumber pickers in Alabama, and had travelled throughout the state in 1944 organising a black voter registration drive.

The idea for a bus boycott originated with Nixon and the Women's Political Council (WPC), headed by Jo Ann Robinson, a professor of English at all-black Alabama State College. Comprising 300 middle-class African-American women, the WPC, formed in 1949, had promoted voter registration and pressured Montgomery to hire black policemen and its merchants to desegregate public drinking fountains. The Council and Nixon had considered a boycott on several occasions after incidents involving black female bus passengers. Following Parks's arrest, Nixon suggested a bus boycott to prominent local blacks, while the WPC began organising a boycott for the day of Parks's trial. Robinson publicised the protest by producing 40,000 mimeographed handbills, which the WPC and her students distributed, and Nixon solicited the support of local black clergy. The two activists considered clerical endorsement essential to ensure widespread and disciplined community involvement in the boycott, since ministers enjoyed respect and authority across all classes. Economically independent from whites, clergymen also had greater freedom of manoeuvre than most African Americans.

Under pressure from Montgomery's black secular leaders and faced with a *fait accompli*, the majority of the city's initially reluctant African-American clergy endorsed and then helped to publicise the boycott. Parks was convicted and fined, while over 90 per cent of black customers observed the boycott. Buoyed by such strong community support, secular and particularly church leaders created the Montgomery Improvement Association (MIA) to continue the boycott, until its demands for employment of black bus drivers for black neighbourhoods, more courteous treatment, and first-come, first-served seating were met. The MIA chose Martin Luther King, Jr, the twenty-six-year-old pastor of Dexter Avenue Baptist Church, as its president. Unlike Nixon, the Atlanta-reared King was well educated, a charismatic orator and, resident only since 1954, not embroiled in Montgomery's factional black leadership struggles. Should the boycott fail, the burden, the MIA realised, would rest with King, who could more easily move on to new employment than established community leaders.

King's powerful speeches energised the MIA's regular church-based mass meetings and appealed to the Christian faith and culture of the African-American community. The church organised a car pool to transport people to work, and provided the boycott with moral sanction, a communications network, fund-raising mechanisms and meeting facilities. Women played a prominent role in the struggle, since they formed a large majority of the churches' congregations and participants at mass meetings, and many of those who ordinarily would have used the buses. Although some whites sympathised with the boycott and some aided it, consciously or otherwise, by driving their maids to work, the City Commission adopted an intransigent policy. Both the mayor and police commissioner, like increasing numbers of white Alabamians, joined the Citizens' Council. The police harassed King by arresting him on a spurious charge of speeding, and extremists dynamited his house at the end of January 1956. The bombing and the city's intractability led the MIA to abandon its reformist demand for improvements within segregation and, in February, to file suit against the constitutionality of segregation itself.

Two days later, the University of Alabama desegregated, when it admitted Autherine Lucy under federal court order. The national NAACP, which had declined to support the MIA's original gradualist approach, had argued Lucy's case. Within days, state police withdrew Lucy from campus, rather than subdue a white mob. The university later expelled her. Despite the disorder, flouting of federal law and adverse international publicity, the Eisenhower administration did nothing. What Mary L. Dudziak calls 'the Cold War imperative' for federal government action on civil rights was clearly less effective in an election year when Eisenhower sought southern white votes.[57] Inaction also characterised the administration in September, when Texas Governor Alan Shivers deployed state troopers to prevent federal court-ordered desegregation, opposed by white mobs at Texarkana Junior College and Mansfield High School. Unwilling to offend Shivers, a political ally, and hoping to maximise southern support, Eisenhower claimed that he had no reason to intervene as Texas had maintained order and desegregation was a matter for the courts to enforce.

Events in Alabama, and Eisenhower's failure to uphold federal court orders, encouraged southern whites, urged on by most of their political representatives, to believe that they could maintain segregation. Membership in the Citizens' Councils and similar groups boomed in Alabama and other southern states, reaching a peak of approximately 250,000 in the first few months of 1956.[58] Southern state governments began a widespread attack on the NAACP in 1956, which lasted throughout the decade. Five states required the NAACP to reveal its membership list, or donors, or both, while six states made it an offence to stir up litigation. Some states fired state employees for NAACP membership, and many launched investigations and hearings, claiming that the Association was either a communist front, or otherwise subversive. Alabama, Louisiana and Texas banned the NAACP from operating. By 1958, 246 of the NAACP's southern chapters had folded.[59]

Despite the segregationist onslaught, the Montgomery bus boycott demonstrated that African Americans could sustain a lengthy, mass protest. The boycott attracted national and international publicity, much of it centred on King's charismatic personality. Raised in comfortable middle-class surroundings and educated in prestigious southern and northern institutions, King was also the son of a prominent Atlanta minister who advocated equal rights and had participated in a postwar voter registration drive. Literature professor Keith Miller argues that King's primary influences were his father's example, black religious culture and popular sermons by African-American and white preachers.[60] More convincingly, Richard Lischer contends that King's study of philosophers and theologians in seminary and graduate school played an equally important role in the development of the civil rights leader's thought.[61]

When the boycott started, King was aware of but, by no means, fully conversant with Gandhi's philosophy of nonviolent civil disobedience. Although he advocated nonviolence in his speeches, pragmatically King responded to the bombing of his house by trying to get a gun permit and allowing his home to be guarded by church members. With A. Philip Randolph's approval, pacifist Bayard Rustin of the War Resisters League spent a week with King in February 1956 and helped educate him in Gandhian techniques of passive resistance, while Glenn E. Smiley, a white FOR official, also deepened King's understanding and appreciation of Gandhi. Although King began to fuse Gandhian precepts with Christian ideas in his speeches, both his and the MIA's commitment to nonviolent protest had been made earlier. This commitment flowed from Christian conviction and a realistic appreciation that black violence would only beget greater white violence. While depressed about the burden of leadership and the boycott's prospects, King underwent a profound religious experience that convinced him that God was with him and would be always. He also gained strength by linking the campaign in Montgomery with a larger struggle by oppressed peoples in Asia and Africa to throw off white exploitation and achieve freedom.

Despite harassment arrests by white authorities, the boycott continued, while, with NAACP assistance, the MIA sought to overturn segregation through the federal courts. In *Browder* v. *Gayle*, the Supreme Court invalidated bus segregation in Montgomery and the rest of Alabama. When the ruling went into effect in December 1956, the MIA lifted the bus boycott after 381 days of struggle. The NAACP had secured the victory that the boycott could not achieve, and, ironically, the relative conservatism of Montgomery blacks had originally dissuaded them from working through the NAACP because it opposed segregation outright and aroused the ire of whites.

Laypeople in Tallahassee, Florida, began a bus boycott in May 1956 that the church organised through a new group, the Inter-Civic Council, headed by the Reverend C. K. Steele, the president of the local NAACP. Although the protestors were well aware of the Montgomery boycott, they acted in response to local conditions. The obstructionist, and sometimes subtle, tactics of the Tallahassee city authorities delayed bus desegregation until May 1958. A boycott also occurred in Rock Hill, South Carolina, which resulted in the bus company's closure, and in Birmingham, Alabama, under the Alabama Christian Movement for Human Rights (ACMHR), which the Reverend Fred L. Shuttlesworth founded after Alabama suppressed the NAACP. The Birmingham effort failed, but in a few other southern cities short boycotts brought compliance with federal court-ordered bus desegregation.

The Montgomery bus boycott had demonstrated the potential for nonviolent mass protest in the South, but it did not spark a mass movement. Anxious not to let the opportunity pass, Rustin, Ella Baker and Stanley D. Levison, a leftist Jewish lawyer from New York, urged activist southern clergymen to create a black-led, southern-based civil rights organisation that would generate widespread indigenous direct-action protests. The result was the SCLC, formed in early 1957 from a nucleus of the MIA, the Inter-Civic Council and the ACMHR. However, the SCLC struggled in its early years to make an impact, and the civil rights movement failed to make significant headway in the South. The movement's limited progress in the late 1950s derived from its internal weaknesses, insufficient support from the federal government and courts, and the success of massive resistance.

The Movement Stalled

Sociologist Aldon D. Morris argues that the 1950s, beginning with the Baton Rouge bus boycott, marked 'the origins of the civil rights movement', which came to fruition in widespread direct-action protests in the South during the first half of the 1960s.[62] He contends that groups such as FOR, the Highlander Folk School and the SCEF acted as 'halfway houses' in training activists, linking them together, and providing networks of support.[63] At the same time, the SCLC developed much of the civil rights movement's infrastructure, its 'movement centres', by coordinating local church-based movements that sprouted in several southern cities.[64] Movement centres organised some sit-ins in the late 1950s, and provided crucial support for the mass student sit-in movement of 1960, by which time the centres were sufficiently numerous to foster widespread protest.

Although Morris rightly directs attention to the importance of halfway houses, local organisations and communities working across generational lines, most historians, barring exceptions such as Glenn T. Eskew, would not limit the movement's origins to the 1950s or define it primarily in terms of direct-action protest.[65] Focused on selected cities, Morris also misses the movement organising in towns and some rural areas, such as parts of the Mississippi Delta. Whereas Morris regards the SCLC as an effective force that began developing a mass movement though its affiliates in the late 1950s, historian Adam Fairclough argues, more convincingly, that during its first five years the SCLC was little more than a paper organisation.[66]

Anxious not to weaken the civil rights movement by competing with the NAACP, to which many of its founders and the leaders of its affiliates also belonged, the SCLC was not a mass membership organisation, but rather 'an umbrella organization' for a loose collection of urban groups, mainly church based and led by ministers.[67] King's status as the spokesman of the Montgomery bus boycott ensured his selection as the SCLC's president, but the Conference struggled to make an impact. Independent bodies, its affiliates did not mobilise collectively or coordinate their activities. Their small dues limited the SCLC's staff, based in Atlanta, to Ella Baker as executive director and two secretaries. SCLC affiliates were also restricted to several major cities in a few states, with the organisation's main area of strength in Alabama.

In his speeches and writings, King sought to popularise Gandhian nonviolent direct action and the notion of loving and converting one's oppressor, but many African Americans found these concepts alien, unattractive, or simply unrealistic. In rural areas, local NAACP leaders, such as Medgar Evers and Amzie Moore in Mississippi, and Robert Williams in Monroe, North Carolina, considered it essential to carry weapons for self-defence. Many rural African Americans agreed with them in a culture in which both blacks and whites often owned guns for hunting and protection. Although most African Americans bristled at discrimination, many rejected civil disobedience, which entailed the risk of physical or economic harm in a cause with uncertain prospects of success given massive resistance, and limited and inconsistent federal support.

King and the SCLC turned to voter registration, a path for African-American advancement supported by the national NAACP, and by President Eisenhower, who regarded the franchise as constitutionally guaranteed and a means by which African Americans could gradually end discrimination in the South without major disruption. Anxious to attract black votes without alienating southern whites by moving too fast, members of both political parties fashioned a civil rights bill from proposals made by the Eisenhower administration. Alongside Roy Wilkins, Walter White's successor at the NAACP, and A. Philip Randolph, Martin Luther King presided over a demonstration on *Brown*'s third anniversary of approximately 25,000 people in Washington DC to support the bill.[68] In addition to creating a federal Civil Rights Commission to investigate discrimination and propose remedies, the 1957 act established a Civil Rights Division in the US Justice Department which could initiate voting rights suits. Notable as the first civil rights legislation since Reconstruction, the act had only a slight effect in extending the franchise because suits could only be filed on a case-by-case basis, and they became subject to lengthy argument before generally unsympathetic southern federal judges.

The SCLC hoped to capitalise on the act. In 1958, Ella Baker organised the SCLC's Crusade for Citizenship, which sought to register three million African Americans within two years through the organisation's affiliates. Notwithstanding Baker's dedicated work, the campaign had little impact since the SCLC lacked sufficient funds and organisation at the local level. A separate NAACP campaign, indicative of a growing rivalry between the two groups, also had disappointing results. Between 1958 and 1960, southern black voter registration increased by only 160,000.[69]

Little noticed at the time, the Highlander Folk School began sponsoring a programme of citizenship schools in 1957 on the South Carolina Sea Islands. Organised by Septima Clark, a black Charleston teacher dismissed a year earlier for her NAACP work, Highlander connections and interracial activities, the schools eventually spread under SCLC auspices to other parts of the rural South in the early 1960s. Nearly 900 schools were created between 1957 and 1970.[70] They provided hundreds, then thousands, of African Americans with the literacy skills and confidence they needed to register to vote.

Influenced by the Montgomery bus boycott, the Tuskegee Civic Association organised a highly effective and lengthy African-American boycott of white merchants after the Alabama legislature redrew the city's boundaries in 1957 to exclude most of its 400 black voters. However, it required a lawsuit before the Supreme Court overturned the gerrymander three years later in *Gomillion* v. *Lightfoot*.

Stymied in voter registration and political representation in the late 1950s, the civil rights movement had also seen the promise of *Brown* unfulfilled in the South. By 1957, token school desegregation had occurred in a few areas of the peripheral South, including five Arkansas districts, Oak Ridge, Tennessee, Charlotte, Greensboro, and Winston-Salem in North Carolina, and the western part of Texas. However, Jim Crow education remained intact in the Deep South.

In a departure from his usual practice, President Eisenhower intervened to enforce school desegregation in Little Rock, Arkansas, in the autumn of 1957. After the NAACP Legal Defense and Educational Fund (which became autonomous in 1957) had won a federal court order to desegregate Central High School, Daisy Bates, president of the state NAACP, led nine black children to attend the school. On Governor

Orval Faubus's instruction, the Arkansas National Guard turned the children away, ostensibly to prevent disorder from occurring. Following discussions with Faubus, who was not one of his political supporters, Eisenhower believed that he had persuaded the governor to obey federal law and permit desegregation. However, Faubus, a former moderate who had seen an opportunity to secure re-election by defending segregation, simply withdrew the National Guard. His oft-repeated assertion that desegregation would create disorder proved to be self-fulfilling when over 500 angry whites converged on the school. To enforce the court order, Eisenhower dispatched paratroopers and federalised the National Guard, citing the need to uphold federal law, maintain order and counteract the adverse international publicity generated by the crisis.

Central High desegregated, but Faubus easily won re-election in July 1958. He closed all of Little Rock's high schools in September to preserve segregation. Unwilling to see their children's education damaged, moderate segregationists organised opposition and voted militant segregationists off the city school board. With outside investors deterred by adverse publicity, the Little Rock Chamber of Commerce professed its preference for segregation, but, pragmatically, called for desegregated schools, citing the need for lawful obedience and public education. In August 1959, Little Rock's white public high schools reopened, but with only four African-American students because of the effects of a pupil placement law.

In Virginia, Governor J. Lindsay Almond, like Faubus, also followed massive resistance to its conclusion. In September 1958, Almond closed nine schools in Warren County, Charlottesville and Norfolk, rather than desegregate them under federal court order. As in Little Rock, the decision divided segregationists, and led moderate parents and businessmen to advocate public education with desegregation. In January 1959, both state and federal courts of appeal ruled Almond's school closures unconstitutional. Virginia abandoned massive resistance as state policy, peacefully reopened the affected schools, and accepted token school desegregation under a local option policy.

Massive resistance as state policy had ended in the Upper South to be replaced by tokenism, but Jim Crow education remained intact in the Deep South. For all the promise of *Brown*, even the Supreme Court had tacitly accepted tokenism in 1958 by ruling in *Shuttlesworth* v. *Birmingham Board of Education* that pupil placement laws were constitutional. The court did not intervene to further school desegregation, apart from a few individual cases, for another ten years. Youth Marches for Integrated Schools, proposed by A. Philip Randolph with support from the NAACP and the SCLC, attracted 9,500 marchers to Washington DC in 1958 and 22,500 the next year, but they had no impact on Jim Crow.[71]

Law professor Michael J. Klarman has advanced a provocative 'backlash thesis' regarding *Brown*'s significance. Klarman argues that *Brown* 'was a relatively unimportant motivating factor for the civil rights movement'.[72] Instead, its real significance lay in driving southern politics to the right on racial issues and bringing to power segregationist hard-liners. Their brutality against direct-action protestors in the 1960s outraged northern whites, who then pressured the Kennedy and Johnson administrations to enact civil rights legislation. Political scientist David J. Garrow, Klarman's severest critic, contends that *Brown* directly influenced the Montgomery bus boycott's leaders, and that although southern politics shifted to the right, it did not do so until 1956 in response to 'the interactive manner in which *Brown and* the newly intensified black activism of 1956 *combined* to begin evoking [a] heightened segregationist response ...'[73]

Klarman argues in reply that his detractors fail to provide convincing evidence that *Brown* significantly influenced the further development of African-American protest, beyond having symbolic significance.[74] Although studies of the civil rights movement in Georgia and Louisiana lend weight to Klarman's claim that *Brown* did not stimulate much civil rights activity, Klarman overstates his case by underestimating the ruling's importance for the movement and, as Garrow points out, he presents a truncated explanation for the development of massive resistance.[75] Numerous African-American leaders and movement participants have testified to *Brown*'s impact in encouraging, and sometimes causing, their activism in both the short- and long-term. The cases that formed *Brown* arose from local communities working in partnership with the NAACP. *Brown I* and *II* led scores of communities to petition or file suit for school desegregation, albeit with disappointing results, and, citing *Brown*, the Supreme Court issued *per curiam* (by the court) orders supporting lower court decisions against segregated municipal facilities, such as public golf courses, parks, beaches and buses.

Aside from bus boycotts, direct action took the form of sit-ins and pickets, particularly towards the end of the 1950s. However, the protests were mostly confined to cities in border and Upper South states, where white opinion was more malleable.

Although NAACP branches were generally sceptical and even hostile towards direct action at this time, some of their Youth Councils adopted it with enthusiasm. NAACP Youth Council sit-ins desegregated lunch counters in Wichita, Kansas and in Oklahoma City in 1958, but failed to overturn Jim Crow in Louisville, Kentucky, a year later. In St Louis, NAACP youths allied with a weak CORE chapter used direct action successfully to desegregate and open up jobs to blacks in some public accommodations in the late 1950s. African-American clubwomen secured ministerial involvement and pressured a reluctant NAACP chapter to support a successful picket in Kansas City, Missouri, between 1958 and 1959 that desegregated lunch counters in department stores.

A biracial group of students from Duke University, conducted sit-ins in Durham, North Carolina, in the late 1950s. In 1959, members of CORE sat in in Lexington, Kentucky, and Miami, Florida. In the late 1950s, CORE also organised affiliates in South Carolina, which focused primarily on voter registration work but also conducted sit-ins. The Reverend James Lawson began holding workshops in nonviolence for the Nashville Christian Leadership Council (NCLC), an SCLC affiliate, in 1958, which attracted students from the city's many black higher education institutions. A year later, workshop members staged sit-ins at department stores. SCLC-affiliated movement centres also developed in the late 1950s in Petersburg, Virginia, and Shreveport, Louisiana.

Nevertheless, direct action penetrated very few areas of the South in the late 1950s. The civil rights movement remained stalled in the region, with the NAACP fighting for its organisational survival, the SCLC a shoe-string operation despite its affiliates, and CORE barely a presence. Although cracks in massive resistance to African-American civil rights had appeared, with token school desegregation in peripheral southern states and forced retreats from defiance in Arkansas and Virginia, Jim Crow education remained unchallenged in the Deep South by either the Eisenhower administration or the federal courts. Hopes that African Americans might gain political leverage were dashed by the weak provisions of the 1957 Civil Rights Act, the failure of SCLC and NAACP voter registration campaigns, and, above all, by the opposition of many southern whites and their representatives to black enfranchisement. From the perspective of the late 1950s, it would have seemed inconceivable that by 1965, the civil rights movement would have overturned *de jure* segregation and legal barriers to voting.

Notes

1. Morton Sosna, 'Introduction', in Neil R. McMillen (ed.), *Remaking Dixie: The Impact of World War II on the American South* (Jackson: University Press of Mississippi, 1997), p. xv.
2. Karen Tucker Anderson, 'Last Hired, First Fired: Black Women Workers during World War II', *Journal of American History* 69 (June 1982), p. 82.
3. Neil A. Wynn, *The Afro-American and the Second World War*, rev. edn (New York and London: Holmes and Meier, 1993), p. 134.
4. Martin Folly, *The United States and World War II: The Awakening Giant* (Edinburgh: Edinburgh University Press, 2002), p. 60; Wynn, *The Afro-American and the Second World War*, p. 58.
5. Steven F. Lawson, *Running for Freedom: Civil Rights and Black Politics in America Since 1941*, 2nd edn (New York: McGraw-Hill, 1997), p. 10; Harvard Sitkoff, *The Struggle for Black Equality, 1954–1992*, rev. edn (New York: Hill and Wang, 1993), pp. 12–13; Harvard Sitkoff, 'African American Militancy in the World War II South: Another Perspective', in McMillen (ed.), *Remaking Dixie*, p. 75.
6. Robin D. G. Kelley, '"We Are Not What We Seem": Rethinking Black Working-Class Opposition in the Jim Crow South', *Journal of American History* 80 (June 1993), pp. 77–8.
7. Ibid. pp. 77–112.
8. Kelley, 'We Are Not What We Seem', p. 87; Eric Arnesen, 'Up From Exclusion: Black and White Workers, Race, and the State of Labor History', *Reviews in American History* 26 (March 1998), p. 160; Sitkoff, 'African American Militancy', p. 86.
9. Herbert H. Hyman and Paul B. Sheatsley, 'Attitudes toward Desegregation', *Scientific American* 195 (December 1956), pp. 36–7.
10. David R. Goldfield, *Black, White, and Southern: Race Relations and Southern Culture 1940 to the Present* (1990; Baton Rouge and London: Louisiana State University Press, 1991), p. 36.
11. Harvard Sitkoff, 'Racial Militancy and Interracial Violence in the Second World War', *Journal of American History* 58 (December 1971), p. 671.
12. Sitkoff, 'African American Militancy', p. 86.
13. Ibid. p. 85.
14. Sitkoff, 'Racial Militancy and Interracial Violence', p. 661.
15. Lee Finkle, 'The Conservative Aims of Militant Rhetoric: Black Protest during World War II', *Journal of American History* 60 (December 1973), pp. 693, 704–5.
16. Ibid. p. 693.
17. Sitkoff, 'African American Militancy', pp. 71–6, 86–8.
18. Ibid. p. 78.
19. Ibid. p. 77.
20. Ibid. p. 92.
21. Ibid. pp. 79–81.
22. Neil R. McMillen, 'Fighting for What We Didn't Have: How Mississippi's Black Veterans Remember World War II', in McMillen (ed.), *Remaking Dixie*, pp. 108–9.
23. Stephen G. N. Tuck, *Beyond Atlanta: The Struggle for Racial Equality in Georgia, 1940–1980* (Athens and London: University of Georgia Press, 2001), pp. 50–1, 74.
24. Raymond Gavins, 'The NAACP in North Carolina during the Age of Segregation', in Armstead L. Robinson and Patricia Sullivan (eds), *New Directions in Civil Rights*

Studies (Charlottesville and London: University Press of Virginia, 1991), pp. 109, 110.

25. Michael L. Gillette, 'The Rise of the NAACP in Texas', *Southwestern Historical Quarterly* 81 (April 1978), p. 409; Adam Fairclough, *Better Day Coming: Blacks and Equality 1890–2000* (2001; New York: Penguin, 2002), p. 184.

26. Lawson, *Running for Freedom*, p. 16.

27. Steven F. Lawson, *Black Ballots: Voting Rights in the South, 1944–1969* (New York: Columbia University Press, 1976), p. 134.

28. Michael Honey, 'Operation Dixie: Labor and Civil Rights in the Postwar South', *Mississippi Quarterly* 45 (Fall 1992), pp. 443–4. By the end of 1946, the CIO halved Operation Dixie's staff, and by 1949, the CIO's southern membership was little different, at about 400,000, than before the project's launch. Historian Barbara S. Griffith attributes the recruitment drive's failure chiefly to repressive measures by southern white employers that cowed their workers, white workers' hostility to biracial unionism, red-baiting of unions, competition from the AFL, Operation Dixie's misdirected focus on the textile industry, and CIO in-fighting. Circumstances, argues Griffith, doomed Operation Dixie to defeat. (Barbara S. Griffith, *The Crisis of American Labor: Operation Dixie and the Defeat of the CIO* (Philadelphia: Temple University Press, 1988.) By contrast, Michael Honey, contends, somewhat optimistically, that had the project concentrated on racially mixed industries, such as tobacco and meatpacking, and 'helped to advance the cause of black civil rights as well as unionization, it might have produced a significantly different result'. (Michael Honey, '"Operation Dixie": Two Points of View', *Labor History* 31 (Summer 1990), pp. 373–8.)

29. Robert Korstad and Nelson Lichtenstein, 'Opportunities Found and Lost: Labor, Radicals, and the Early Civil Rights Movement', *Journal of American History* 75 (December 1988), pp. 791–3.

30. Numan V. Bartley, *The New South 1945–1980* (Baton Rouge: Louisiana State University Press/The Littlefield Fund for Southern History of the University of Texas, 1995), p. 76.

31. 'To Secure These Rights: The Report of the President's Committee on Civil Rights (1947)', in Steven F. Lawson and Charles Payne, *Debating the Civil Rights Movement, 1945–1968* (Lanham, Boulder, New York and Oxford: Rowman and Littlefield, 1998), p. 52.

32. Quoted in Carol Anderson, 'From Hope to Disillusion: African Americans, the United Nations, and the Struggle for Human Rights, 1944–1947', *Diplomatic History* 20 (Fall 1996), p. 545.

33. Mary L. Dudziak, *Cold War Civil Rights: Race and the Image of American Democracy* (Princeton and Oxford: Princeton University Press, 2000); Azza Salama Layton, *International Politics and Civil Rights Policies in the United States, 1941–1960* (Cambridge: Cambridge University Press, 2000).

34. Dudziak, *Cold War Civil Rights*, p. 13.

35. Paula A. Pfeffer, *A. Philip Randolph, Pioneer of the Civil Rights Movement* (1990; Baton Rouge and London: Louisiana State University Press, 1996), p. 141.

36. Korstad and Lichtenstein, 'Opportunities Found and Lost', p. 811 (quotation); Robert Rodgers Korstad, *Civil Rights Unionism: Tobacco Workers and the Struggle for Democracy in the Mid-Twentieth-Century South* (Chapel Hill and London: University of North Carolina Press, 2003), pp. 9–12, 415–16.

37. Manning Marable, *Race, Reform, and Rebellion: The Second Reconstruction in Black America, 1945–1990*, 2nd edn (Basingstoke: Macmillan, 1991), p. 32.
38. James C. Clark, 'Civil Rights Leader Harry T. Moore and the Ku Klux Klan in Florida', *Florida Historical Quarterly* 72 (October 1994), pp. 166–83; Ben Green, *The Untold Story of Harry T. Moore, America's First Civil Rights Martyr* (New York: Free Press, 1999).
39. Alan Draper, *Conflict of Interests: Organized Labor and the Civil Rights Movement in the South, 1954–1968* (Ithaca, NY: ILR Press, 1994), pp. 3–16, 168–9; Bruce Nelson, 'Organized Labor and the Struggle for Black Equality in Mobile during World War II', *Journal of American History* 80 (December 1993), pp. 954–5, 987–8; Tuck, *Beyond Atlanta*, pp. 33–4.
40. August Meier and Elliott Rudwick, 'The Origins of Nonviolent Direct Action in Afro-American Protest: A Note on Historical Discontinuities', in August Meier and Elliott Rudwick, *Along the Color Line: Explorations in the Black Experience* (Urbana, Chicago and London: University of Illinois Press, 1976), pp. 360–1.
41. Mark V. Tushnet, *The NAACP's Legal Strategy against Segregated Education, 1925–1950* (Chapel Hill and London: University of North Carolina Press, 1987), pp. 115, 136.
42. Mary L. Dudziak, 'Desegregation as a Cold War Imperative', *Stanford Law Review* 41 (November 1988), p. 111.
43. Reed Sarratt, *The Ordeal of Desegregation: The First Decade* (New York and London: Harper and Row, 1966), p. 4.
44. Numan V. Bartley, *The Rise of Massive Resistance: Race and Politics in the South During the 1950's* (1969; Baton Rouge: Louisiana State University Press, 1999), p. 67.
45. Stephen J. Whitfield, *A Death in the Delta: The Story of Emmett Till* (1988; Baltimore and London: Johns Hopkins University Press, 1991), pp. 89–100; Clenora Hudson-Weems, 'Resurrecting Emmett Till: The Catalyst of the Modern Civil Rights Movement', *Journal of Black Studies* 29 (November 1998), pp. 179–98; Clenora Hudson-Weems, *Emmett Till: The Sacrificial Lamb of the Civil Rights Movement*, 3rd edn (Troy, MI: Bedford, 2000), pp. xv, 4, 5–6, 19–24, 77, 83–101, 104–7, 136–49, 252–4, 287–324; John Dittmer, *Local People: The Struggle for Civil Rights in Mississippi* (Urbana and Chicago: University of Illinois Press, 1994), pp. 57–8; Charles M. Payne, *I've Got the Light of Freedom: The Organizing Tradition and the Mississippi Freedom Struggle* (Berkeley, Los Angeles and London: University of California Press, 1995), pp. 54, 144.
46. Peter B. Levy (ed.), *Let Freedom Ring: A Documentary History of the Modern Civil Rights Movement* (New York, Westport, CT, and London: Praeger, 1992), p. 41.
47. Michael S. Mayer, 'With Much Deliberation and Some Speed: Eisenhower and the *Brown* Decision', *Journal of Southern History* 52 (February 1986), pp. 44–6, 49, 59–62, 69, 73–6.
48. Bartley, *Rise of Massive Resistance*, pp. 82–3.
49. John Bartlow Martin, *The Deep South Says 'Never'* (London: Victor Gollancz, 1958), p. 37.
50. James W. Ely, Jr, *The Crisis of Conservative Virginia: The Byrd Organization and the Politics of Massive Resistance* (Knoxville: University of Tennessee Press, 1976), p. 43.
51. Ibid. p. 12.

52. Benjamin Muse, *Virginia's Massive Resistance* (Bloomington: Indiana University Press, 1961), p. 2.
53. Ely, *Crisis of Conservative Virginia*, p. 40.
54. Bartley, *Rise of Massive Resistance*, p. 116.
55. Ibid. pp. 13–14.
56. Lawson, *Black Ballots*, p. 134.
57. Dudziak, *Cold War Civil Rights*, p. 151.
58. Bartley, *Rise of Massive Resistance*, p. 84.
59. Sitkoff, *Struggle for Black Equality*, p. 27.
60. Keith D. Miller, *Voice of Deliverance: The Language of Martin Luther King, Jr., and Its Sources* (New York: Free Press, 1992), pp. 7–8, 11, 17, 58, 59, 60, 63, 65, 99, 189. For a critique of Miller see Richard King, 'The Role of Intellectual History in the Histories of the Civil Rights Movement', in Melvyn Stokes and Rick Halpern (eds), *Race and Class in the American South Since 1890* (Oxford, Eng., and Providence, RI: Berg, 1992), pp. 159–60, 172–9.
61. Richard Lischer, *The Preacher King: Martin Luther King, Jr., and the Word that Moved America* (New York and Oxford: Oxford University Press, 1995), pp. 5–7, 33–7, 43–4, 51–5, 57–62, 64–6, 94–108.
62. Aldon D. Morris, *The Origins of the Civil Rights Movement: Black Communities Organizing for Change* (New York: Free Press, 1984), pp. vi, ix–x.
63. Ibid. pp. xiii, 139–73.
64. Ibid. p. 76.
65. Glenn T. Eskew, *But for Birmingham: The Local and National Movements in the Civil Rights Struggle* (Chapel Hill and London: University of North Carolina Press, 1997), pp. 14–15.
66. Morris, *Origins of the Civil Rights Movement*, pp. 86–99; Adam Fairclough, *To Redeem the Soul of America: The Southern Christian Leadership Conference and Martin Luther King, Jr.* (Athens and London: University of Georgia Press, 1987), pp. 35, 47–48, 53–55, 58.
67. Fairclough, *To Redeem the Soul of America*, p. 33.
68. Ibid. p. 40.
69. Lawson, *Running for Freedom*, p. 68.
70. Richard H. King, *Civil Rights and the Idea of Freedom* (1992; Athens and London: University of Georgia Press, 1996), p. 43.
71. Pfeffer, *A. Philip Randolph*, pp. 181, 183.
72. Michael J. Klarman, '*Brown*, Racial Change, and the Civil Rights Movement', *Virginia Law Review* 80 (February 1994), pp. 82 n. 353, 85.
73. David J. Garrow, 'Hopelessly Hollow History: Revisionist Devaluing of *Brown* v. *Board of Education*', *Virginia Law Review* 80 (February 1994), p. 160.
74. Michael J. Klarman, '*Brown* v. *Board of Education*: Facts and Political Correctness', *Virginia Law Review* 80 (February 1994), pp. 186–91.
75. Tuck, *Beyond Atlanta*, 100; Adam Fairclough, *Race and Democracy: The Civil Rights Struggle in Louisiana, 1915–1972* (Athens and London: University of Georgia Press, 1995), pp. 188–9; Garrow, 'Hopelessly Hollow History', pp. 158–60.

CHAPTER 3

The End of Jim Crow in the South, 1960–5

Direct action came to the fore of the African-American struggle between 1960 and 1965 and played a crucial role in securing the Civil Rights Act of 1964 and the Voting Rights Act in 1965. African-American youth created SNCC out of the sit-ins of 1960. Both SNCC and CORE undertook direct action despite violent assaults on their members by white segregationists, and the two groups also conducted voter registration campaigns in parts of the rural Deep South, the South's most repressive region. The SCLC gradually developed a staff base and assisted some of its affiliates and other local organisations in direct-action campaigns. Typically, SCLC campaigns produced mixed results and even some failures at the local level, but those in Birmingham and Selma, Alabama, played a direct role in securing federal legislation against discrimination. By placing black demands within the context of America's Judaeo-Christian tradition and the US Constitution, Martin Luther King and the SCLC were uniquely placed within the movement to articulate African-Americans concerns and aspirations sympathetically to a white audience.

While the national NAACP remained sceptical about direct action, at least until 1963, it often provided the bail money, lawyers and litigation that helped make direct action successful. Furthermore, local NAACP Youth Councils and some chapters participated in direct action, and local branches also helped negotiate settlements with white authorities that regarded the NAACP as more responsible and conservative than either SNCC, CORE, or the SCLC. While sometimes disruptive and destructive, for the most part rivalry and competition between the major civil rights groups drove the civil rights movement forward in pursuit of common goals. Although each group engaged to some extent in direct action, voter registration and lobbying the federal government, each organisation's particular emphasis generally, although not always, complemented, rather than undercut, those of the other groups.

The Sit-ins

Four African-American students from the North Carolina Agricultural and Technical College unwittingly began the mass student sit-in movement of 1960, when they sat down at a lunch counter in a Woolworth store in Greensboro on 1 February, and refused to leave after being denied service. Segregation dictated that while blacks could buy goods at department stores, they could not use the restaurants. The four students, Ezell Blair, Jr, Franklin McCain, Joseph McNeil and David Richmond, returned the next day, joined by more than twenty other students. By the end of the week, several hundred students, including some whites, had sat in at downtown stores. Sit-ins soon spread to nearby cities, and then to urban areas in other parts of the Upper South, the border South, and even the Deep South, except Mississippi. By April, seventy-eight southern and border state cities had experienced sit-ins that involved perhaps as many as 50,000 protesters and brought 2,000 arrests.[1]

Historians Clayborne Carson and William H. Chafe regard the student sit-ins as essentially spontaneous with little involvement by existing civil rights organisations.[2] However, sociologist Aldon Morris argues that, unprecedented in their scale, the sit-ins were nevertheless but part of a chain of such protests that had begun in the late 1950s. Rather than being spontaneous, Morris contends, the sit-ins spread rapidly from Greensboro because they were planned, coordinated and sustained by a pre-existing network of local movement centres based on African-American churches, colleges and civil rights groups.[3]

Morris notes that the four students who began the Greensboro protest had all been members of the local NAACP Youth Council headed by lawyer Floyd McKissick, and they knew about earlier sit-ins in Durham, North Carolina, and other cities in the late 1950s.[4] Although the four students acted alone, they soon turned to Dr George Simkins, head of the local NAACP chapter, for support. Unable to persuade the national office of the NAACP to aid the protest, Simkins asked CORE's headquarters in New York for help, while McKissick served as counsel for the four students.

McKissick and other local people who had, like him, organised sit-ins in the state during the late 1950s, now sought to spread the Greensboro protest across North Carolina. They were assisted in their plans by Gordon Carey and James McCain, two white field secretaries sent by CORE in response to Simkins's request. Together, local activists and the CORE workers urged urban movement centres in North Carolina,

South Carolina and Virginia to train students for sit-ins, and they visited many of them to offer help. Morris argues that churches pastored by clergymen and church leaders active in SCLC affiliates played a crucial role in training many of the students who staged sit-in protests in the South during 1960. He credits the SCLC, aided by CORE and NAACP Youth Councils, with either directly organising the protests or urging movement centres to initiate them.[5]

With justice, Carson argues that Morris made 'insufficient use of primary sources' and that, at least in some cases, he drew the wrong conclusions from interviews, his main source.[6] Interviewing some of the same people as Morris, Carson found that they sometimes 'placed greater emphasis on the restraining influence on black activism of preexisting organizations'.[7] He argues that members of civil rights groups often took an active role in the sit-ins despite, rather than because of, the organisations to which they belonged and that 'these voluntary actions served as catalysts for mobilizing existing institutions into action'.[8]

Morris also pushes his argument too far when he contends that the sit-ins demonstrated the strength and initiative of the SCLC.[9] Historian Adam Fairclough notes that 'the sit-ins caught SCLC by surprise', as they did the other major civil rights organisations.[10] Although King encouraged the sit-ins once they had begun, 'with little money and no field staff, SCLC's role in the sit-ins depended for the most part upon initiatives from its local affiliates'.[11] While many SCLC affiliates gave the protests useful support, particularly in Birmingham, Montgomery and Tallahassee, the student protesters acted independently. In Nashville, the NCLC provided bail money for the students, organised an economic boycott of downtown merchants, and had, through James Lawson's workshops, trained many of the leaders of the city's sit-in protesters. Nevertheless, in Nashville as in other cities with active SCLC affiliates, 'the focus of black protest' passed from the affiliates to the students.[12] For the most part, SCLC affiliates assisted, rather than initiated, sit-ins. Ella Baker commented that 'None of the great leadership had anything to do with the sit-ins starting ... [They] spread, to a large extent, because of ... the young enthusiasm and the need for action.'[13]

The national NAACP did not prevent its chapters from contributing to the protests, but Roy Wilkins remained sceptical about the efficacy of direct action, and he feared that much of the NAACP's southern middle-class constituency would be unwilling to participate in civil disobedience. Herbert Wright, the NAACP National Youth Director, toured North

Carolina in February 1960, conferring with the heads of local chapters and their Youth Councils, student leaders, CORE and the SCLC. Wright asked Wilkins for permission to organise a conference in Washington DC to coordinate a national NAACP sit-in campaign against discrimination in public facilities. The cautious Wilkins declined. Nevertheless, the national NAACP publicly endorsed the sit-ins in March, and it provided the protesters with essential legal support and bail funds.

Although established local black leaders and the anxious parents of the protesters sometimes privately opposed the sit-ins, they tended to rally behind them, especially when the protesters were arrested or attacked by white hoodlums.[14] Raised in an era of rising but thwarted expectations after the *Brown* decision, the Montgomery bus boycott and the Civil Rights Act of 1957, and influenced by Gandhi and African independence movements, the students adopted direct action in frustration at the lack of progress in eradicating discrimination but also in the hope and expectation that they could effect change.[15] Without the responsibilities of career, home and family, and therefore with less to lose than adult blacks, the students were able and willing to adopt direct action against oppression.[16] The very act of protesting gave the students a sense of their own worth and efficacy, while the volume of protests exposed the myth perpetuated by many southern whites that African Americans were content with their lot unless incited by outside agitators.[17] When they sat in, the students practised nonviolence, dressed in their best clothes and studied books.[18] Their demeanour helped rally black community support, including boycotts of downtown stores, and earned the protesters the respect and even admiration of some whites.[19] Even some supporters of segregation, such as James J. Kilpatrick, editor of the *Richmond News Leader*, commented on the contrast between the disciplined behaviour of the students and the brutality and vulgarity of white youths who attacked the protesters.[20]

By 1961, over 70,000 African Americans and whites had joined the protests, but, for the most part, the sit-ins and accompanying boycotts enjoyed success only in the peripheral and border South states, where almost 200 cities had started to desegregate at least some of their public accommodations.[21] In the Deep South, whites refused to desegregate, and the protesters faced unyielding resistance from white authorities. Thousands of students suffered expulsion from state-funded black colleges for their participation in sit-ins.

Despite the risks, the example of the southern sit-in movement led

NAACP chapters in the Delta and Gulf Coast of Mississippi to pressure the state NAACP to act. Consequently, Medgar Evers, field secretary of the Mississippi NAACP, organised a partially successful Easter boycott of downtown Jackson stores in 1960, with the demand that the merchants treat African-American customers with courtesy and employ black clerks. Adult NAACP members on the Gulf Coast initiated direct action in the state with a wade-in in April at beaches in Biloxi that excluded African Americans. Police stood by while whites attacked the protesters with chains, baseball bats and iron pipes. Although unsuccessful, the wade-ins persuaded Charles R. Darden, the conservative president of the Mississippi NAACP, to step down in favour of the more militant Aaron Henry from the Delta town of Clarksdale.

Nine students from the NAACP Youth Council at Tougaloo College, a private institution near Jackson, conducted a sit-in at the Jackson Public Library in March 1961. Their jailing brought 700 students from Jackson State College to attend a prayer meeting in support and hundreds of black adults to demonstrate in sympathy with those arrested. Thereafter, with the endorsement of the Mississippi NAACP, black youths across the state engaged in a variety of protests against segregated public accommodations, which failed, like the Tougaloo protest, to overturn Jim Crow, but left no doubt as to the dissatisfaction of most black Mississippians with Jim Crow.

By contrast in Louisiana, the NAACP, struggling to recover from four years of persecution by the state, played little part in the sit-ins. In March 1960, students at Southern University, a black institution, conducted sit-ins in Baton Rouge, after seeking advice from CORE's New York office. However, divisions within the African-American community and poor organisation undermined the protest. CORE field secretary James McCain moved on to New Orleans and helped found a CORE chapter in the city. In September, local CORE members sat in at a segregated Woolworth store and were arrested. Their arrest, together with more arrests at another CORE sit-in, rallied the black community in support. The city's intransigence served only to bolster protest and enabled the New Orleans CORE chapter to thrive. The chapter's lack of hierarchy and activism attracted the young, while the city's NAACP Youth Council, anxious to engage in direct action, chafed at the adult NAACP branch's caution. CORE gained an important foothold in Louisiana. The sit-ins invigorated the Louisiana civil rights struggle and rescued it from NAACP leaders who had become old and largely ineffective, presiding over a membership base devastated by years of state harassment. Beyond Louisiana, the southern sit-ins contributed to the gradual revival of CORE, which had already begun to develop chapters in a few southern cities during the late 1950s.

The sit-ins also spawned SNCC. Ella Baker organised an SCLC-funded meeting in April 1960 of over 120 black and a dozen white students from across the South at Shaw University in Raleigh, North Carolina. Martin Luther King, the keynote speaker, urged the students to establish a permanent organisation that would take the struggle for equality into every southern community, and to adopt a strategy of filling the jails by refusing to pay bail when imprisoned. The students, instead, created SNCC as a temporary organisation without affiliation to any existing civil rights organisation. At a meeting held in Atlanta, SNCC voted in October to become a permanent group.

Baker subsequently claimed that she influenced the students in Raleigh to reject an attempt by the SCLC to coopt them.[22] Baker disliked King's caution and domination of the SCLC, which sat uneasily with her belief that the civil rights movement should seek to enable local communities to develop their own leaders and resources. She urged the students to form their own organisation with group-centred leadership, rather than be leader-oriented. In fact, King did not use his considerable influence to persuade the students to link up with the SCLC, although he hoped that they would make that choice.

The emphasis that the students placed on nonviolence accorded with King's beliefs, but it was James Lawson who had exerted greater influence on the gathering in Raleigh. Although little known outside Nashville, Lawson at thirty-one, the same age as King, made a convincing plea on behalf of the philosophy of nonviolent direct action, while at the same time criticising the NAACP for pursuing litigation. Raised in the North, Lawson had refused to serve in the Korean War in the early 1950s and had been imprisoned for his objection. On his release, he spent three years in India as a Methodist missionary, where he studied the techniques of Gandhi. Lawson later became FOR's first southern field secretary, in which capacity he organised nonviolent workshops in Nashville and then continued them after enroling in theology at Vanderbilt University. Lawson trainees, such as Marion Barry, James Bevel, John Lewis and Diane Nash, played an important role in the Nashville sit-in movement, attended SNCC's organising meeting in Raleigh, and contributed to the civil rights movement's subsequent development. Despite some opposition from students who were more interested in action than reflection, SNCC adopted a statement of purpose written by Lawson. The statement declared:

> We affirm the philosophical or religious ideal of nonviolence as the foundation of our purpose, the pre-supposition of our faith, and the manner of our action. Nonviolence as it grows from Judaic-Christian traditions seeks a social order of justice permeated by love. Integration of human endeavor represents the crucial first step towards such a society.[23]

Despite his influence in its formation and early direction, Lawson did not become a member of SNCC. Expelled from Vanderbilt because of his civil rights protests, he enrolled in the spring of 1960 at Boston University, where he completed his theology degree.

Devoid of funds and dependent on the SCLC's Atlanta headquarters for office space and mailing privileges, SNCC initially had little influence on the direction of the civil rights movement. Nevertheless, it was during these early months that, influenced by Baker, SNCC affirmed the principles that would guide its early years. SNCC rejected hierarchical authority, determined that action required approval by two-thirds of the membership, and decided that it would assist rather than direct local protest organisations in the belief that local communities should determine their goals and thereby ensure sustained activism.

While SNCC developed its operating philosophy, both the Republican and Democratic parties became increasingly attentive to civil rights, aware that northern black votes would help decide the forthcoming presidential election. Anxious to appeal to the Democratic Party's centre as he sought the party's nomination, Senate Majority leader Lyndon B. Johnson proposed a mild civil rights bill in January 1960. While liberals considered Johnson's proposals too weak, the Eisenhower administration followed a middle course. Passed in April, the Civil Rights Act made it a federal crime to obstruct court-ordered school desegregation and to escape prosecution for bombing buildings by crossing state lines. In an effort to correct some of the weaknesses of the 1957 Civil Rights Act, federal judges could appoint referees to investigate denial of voting rights. A bipartisan compromise, the act had little impact on black disfranchisement since the US Justice Department had to act on a case-by-case basis and provide proof of racial discrimination before a court would appoint a referee.

The Republican Party platform claimed credit for the 1957 and 1960 acts and advocated vigorous use of federal authority on behalf of civil rights. Richard M. Nixon, the party's presidential nominee, seemed well placed to secure African-American votes since as vice president he had enjoyed a good relationship with civil rights leaders, such as King and Wilkins. By contrast, Democratic nominee Senator John F. Kennedy of Massachusetts had voted to weaken the 1957 Civil Rights Act, shown little interest in civil rights, and had chosen Lyndon Johnson, a native Texan, as his running mate to attract the white South. Nevertheless, Kennedy ran on a Democratic Party platform, shaped by liberals, which promised vigorous enforcement of voting rights legislation and social-welfare programmes for the poor. He promised new civil rights legis-lation to implement the platform and executive action at the 'stroke of a presidential pen' to end racial discrimination in federally-subsidised housing and in businesses with federal contracts.[24] While both party platforms averred support for peaceful sit-ins, civil rights initially played little part in a campaign dominated by foreign policy and economic issues, and both candidates were as anxious to court the white South as they were African-American voters.

In October, SNCC protesters in Atlanta persuaded a reluctant Martin Luther King, now relocated to the city as co-pastor of his father's church, to join them in a sit-in at a downtown lunch counter. SNCC hoped that King's arrest would generate national publicity and lead the presidential candidates to speak out forcefully on civil rights. Soon arrested, King received a four-month hard labour sentence for violating an earlier probation order. John Kennedy's liberal advisers persuaded their candi-date to telephone King's pregnant wife Coretta to express his concern at her husband's imprisonment, and Kennedy's brother Robert contacted the judge and helped persuade him to release King on bail. However, Nixon remained silent, anxious not to alienate southern white voters. The Kennedy camp was quick to publicise the Kennedys' intervention to black voters, and, influenced perhaps in part by the action, African Americans contributed to Kennedy's narrow electoral victory.

Within days of the election, four African-American girls entered two formerly white elementary schools under federal court order in a working-class district of New Orleans. The result of ten years of effort by African-American parents supported by the city's NAACP under A. P. Tureaud, Louisiana's first incidence of school desegregation passed off peacefully. But two days later, white high students rampaged through the city centre attacking African Americans, while a growing white boycott of the desegregated schools became almost uniformly observed. The state legislature, which had passed bill after bill in a vain effort to frustrate desegregation, commended the boycott, which the local Citizens' Council helped maintain by intimidating white parents. Unwilling to prepare the city for desegregation and themselves racist, New Orleans' white businessmen and professionals had stepped aside and allowed militant segregationists to dominate. A year later, appreciative of the economic damage done to the city, white businessmen worked with city authorities and the police to ensure the peaceful extension of token desegregation to other schools.

Tragically, the desegregation of the University of Georgia, under federal court order, by two African-American students in January 1961 led to a campus riot. Under Georgia's massive resistance laws, the university faced withdrawal of state funds as an integrated institution. Elected on a promise to maintain segregated education, Governor Ernest Vandiver manoeuvred the legislature to allow local option on desegregation, which also paved the way for peaceful token desegregation of Atlanta schools under federal court order in the fall.

The Kennedy administration, then, faced a civil rights movement that combined widening direct action with litigation, voter registration and lobbying, and increasingly challenged Jim Crow in the Deep South, the heartland of southern white resistance. In the early 1960s, the NAACP, the SCLC, CORE and SNCC placed unprecedented pressure on the federal government to intervene against racial discrimination.

The Kennedy Administration and Civil Rights

Elected by a margin of eighty-four electoral college votes and with less than a 1 per cent advantage in the popular vote, Kennedy lacked a mandate for change when he took office in January 1961. He also faced a powerful coalition of southern Democrats and conservative Republicans in Congress that could stall his legislative programme if the new president pushed for civil rights legislation. By virtue of their seniority, southern Democrats controlled powerful congressional committees, which, Kennedy believed, gave the southerners the potential to frustrate his administration. Southern senators could also use a filibuster against legislation they disapproved of.

Primarily concerned, in any case, with foreign policy and reviving the American economy, Kennedy chose not to propose civil rights legislation.

Instead, he sought, at first, to conciliate African Americans by using his executive powers in their interest and easing the path of black voter registration, while at the same time, seeking to avoid steps that might alienate southern whites.[25] In his first two years in office, Kennedy regarded the civil rights movement as a difficulty to manage, contain and keep off the streets. The president hoped to avoid civil rights incidents that might divide his party and be exploited by communist propaganda as the superpowers competed for the allegiance of the newly independent countries of the developing world.[26]

Kennedy appointed African Americans to some high-level government positions and federal judgeships. He made Robert C. Weaver Administrator of the Housing and Home Finance Agency, and appointed Thurgood Marshall to the Second Court of Appeals in New York. Kennedy significantly increased the number of blacks in the civil service, particularly at its highest grades. His Executive Order 10925 directed federal agencies and departments to cease racial discrimination in hiring, and created the President's Committee on Equal Employment Opportunity, which, under vice president Johnson, pressed corporations and unions engaged in government contracted work to adhere to anti-discrimination policies. However, the administration avoided the emotive issue of school and housing desegregation. It delayed the promised executive order on housing until after the mid-term congressional elections and issued a weak order. Although the US Justice Department, under Attorney General Robert F. Kennedy, filed far more voter registration suits than the previous administration had, their impact was undermined by the segregationist federal judges that the Kennedy administration initially appointed in the South, with excessive deference to Senator James Eastland of Mississippi, the chairman of the Judiciary Committee.

Although the major civil rights organisations sought to work with the administration, they also recognised the need to exert pressure upon it. In February 1961, James Farmer, a believer in Gandhian nonviolent direct action, rejoined CORE as national director, after two frustrating years as the NAACP's programme director. Responding to a staff suggestion that recalled CORE's Journey of Reconciliation in 1947, Farmer appealed for volunteers for a biracial Freedom Ride from Washington DC to New Orleans that would test implementation of the 1960 *Boynton* v. *Virginia* ruling, in which the Supreme Court had outlawed segregation in interstate transportation terminals. Anticipating arrest and even attack in the South, the Riders hoped to prod the US

Justice Department to enforce *Boynton*. However, the Kennedy administration did not reply to letters from CORE outlining the Freedom Ride, which began with thirteen volunteers, including seven African Americans, on board a Greyhound bus and a Trailways bus in May.

John Lewis, a veteran of the Nashville movement and a SNCC member, and some other Riders were attacked by white youths in Rock Hill, South Carolina, but otherwise the Freedom Riders proceeded peacefully until the Greyhound bus pulled into Anniston, Alabama. A white mob attacked the bus, which departed pursued by whites in cars. When the bus's slashed tyres brought it a halt, the mob attacked once more and tossed an incendiary bomb through a broken window. An armed Alabama state investigator held the mob at bay, as the Riders abandoned the bus, which subsequently exploded. Fred Shuttlesworth of the ACMHR led an armed group of cars from Birmingham to rescue the wounded.

Within an hour, a white mob boarded and beat Riders on the the Trailways bus when it arrived in Anniston, leaving retired professor Walter Bergman with brain damage. The bus continued on to Birmingham, where T. Eugene 'Bull' Connor, the city's Commissioner of Public Safety, allowed a mob to attack the Riders. Freedom Rider James Peck, rendered unconscious by a lead pipe, required fifty-three stitches to his head. Choosing to continue on a single bus, the Riders were unable to find a driver willing to take them. Consequently, most of the Riders decided to fly to New Orleans.

With Diane Nash playing a coordinating role in Nashville, SNCC volunteers, including John Lewis, continued the Freedom Ride from Birmingham to Montgomery, after sitting in at the bus station until they got a ride. Robert Kennedy pressed Alabama Governor John Patterson to provide security, but the police cars and helicopters which accompanied the bus disappeared outside Montgomery. When the Riders disembarked in an eerily silent bus terminal, they were viciously attacked by a white mob encouraged by a crowd that grew to over 1,000. John Lewis suffered concussion, and James Zwerg, a white student, was hospitalised with an injured spinal cord, having also had his teeth knocked out. John Siegenthaler, President Kennedy's emissary to Governor Patterson, was beaten unconscious when he tried to help two fleeing Riders. Concerned by Siegenthaler's treatment and motivated by stinging national and international publicity, the Kennedy administration announced it would send US marshals to Montgomery. They arrived after a white mob had begun attacking a church, pastored by Martin Luther King's chief aide Ralph D. Abernathy, where King had organised a reception for the Freedom Riders. Governor Patterson sent in the National Guard to help the beleaguered marshals disperse the mob.

When the protesters announced their intention to continue the Freedom Ride to Jackson, Mississippi, Robert Kennedy negotiated an agreement with Senator Eastland, whereby Mississippi Governor Ross Barnett agreed to protect the Riders in exchange for being permitted to arrest them for violating segregation laws. Although the agreement held, it did not end the Freedom Rides as the Kennedy administration had hoped. Worried that the protest undermined American foreign policy, Robert Kennedy urged the Freedom Riders to observe a 'cooling-off period'.[27] However, CORE, SNCC, the NCLC, the SCLC and the National Student Association established a Freedom Ride Coordinating Committee that sent more riders to Mississippi and elsewhere in the South. By summer's end, Jackson authorities had arrested 328 of the more than 360 riders apprehended. Three-quarters of those arrested were male and a little over half were African American. The NAACP Legal Defense and Educational Fund provided many of those arrested with essential bail money and legal representation.[28] The Freedom Rides significantly increased CORE's profile, membership and donations, making it a major civil rights organisation, and forced the Kennedy administration to act.

With support from Secretary of State Dean Rusk, who regarded the change as necessary for American foreign policy, Robert Kennedy successfully urged the Interstate Commerce Commission (ICC) to mandate desegregated interstate terminals. Implemented on 1 November, the ICC order was widely observed, except in parts of the Deep South's Black Belt. By the end of 1962, the civil rights movement had forced the end of Jim Crow in most of intra- and interstate transportation.

The Kennedy administration remained anxious to keep civil rights activity away from direct action. In the summer of 1961, Robert Kennedy and Justice Department officials met with CORE, SNCC, the SCLC and the National Student Association. Kennedy and federal officials offered the movement financial support from northern philanthropic foundations for a voter registration campaign and, so the civil rights activists believed, federal protection for activists and voter applicants. The offer divided SNCC between those who favoured direct action and regarded the administration's motives as self-serving, and others who argued that whatever the Kennedys' reasons, the vote would enable African Americans eventually to reshape Congress and improve the everyday lives of blacks. At Ella Baker's suggestion, SNCC agreed to operate both voter registration and direct-action wings. After considerable debate, CORE adopted a similar position. Consequently, SNCC and CORE participated along with the NAACP, the SCLC and the NUL in a $870,000 Voter Education Project (VEP), funded by the Stern Family Fund and the Taconic and Field Foundations. Administered by the SRC, the VEP began in April 1962 for a two and a half year period, with SNCC and CORE opting to focus their energies on the rural Deep South, where African Americans experienced the greatest level of repression and had been largely untouched by the movement.

SNCC had made its first foray into rural organising a few months earlier under Bob Moses in southwest Mississippi. A black teacher of mathematics in his native New York City, Moses held a master's degree from Harvard University. Committed to social activism, he had assisted Bayard Rustin during the second Youth March for Integrated Schools in 1959, and he had joined a sit-in while visiting his uncle in Newport News, Virginia, in the spring of 1960. At Rustin's urging, Moses joined the SCLC office in Atlanta in the summer. He contacted Amzie Moore in Cleveland, Mississippi, while touring the Deep South on the SCLC's behalf. A long-time activist in the NAACP, Moore urged Moses to assist in developing a voter registration project.

When Moses returned a year later, he found conditions unpromising in Cleveland, and instead responded to an invitation from C. C. Bryant, head of the Pike County NAACP, to launch a voter registration drive in McComb, southwest Mississippi. Moses, by now a SNCC member, began in August, and soon African Americans in neighbouring counties requested voter registration classes, which Moses and the other SNCC workers that he invited organised. Moses and his co-workers suffered beatings and police harassment, and Herbert Lee, an Amite County farmer who had helped Moses, was murdered with impunity in September by Mississippi State Representative E. H. Hurst. Consequently, attendance at voter registration classes and visits to county registration offices plummeted.

Other SNCC activists in McComb had conducted workshops to train black youth in direct action since August, but youths faced expulsion from school and, in some cases, jail for participation in sit-ins and marches. In November, five CORE Freedom Riders were beaten for testing desegregation at McComb bus station. After serving time in jail for demonstrating, Moses and the remaining SNCC workers left town in December, having increased black voter registration by less than a handful. Ready to learn from its mistakes, SNCC returned to Mississippi in 1962 to open up a new voter registration project in the Delta.

By then, SNCC had also launched a project in Georgia's Black Belt. In October 1961, two SNCC field secretaries, Charles Sherrod and Cordell Reagon, opened up an office in Albany, a city of 60,000 people in southwest Georgia. Sherrod, a Baptist preacher from Richmond, Virginia, and Reagon, who had been part of the Nashville movement, sought to unite the community in a challenge against discrimination. They organised workshops in nonviolent resistance that attracted black youths and led in November to a student sit-in at the bus station, which refused to obey the ICC's desegregation order. Dissatisfied with conservative local NAACP leadership, African-American community groups worked with SNCC and formed the Albany movement, under osteopath William G. Anderson. The subsequent arrest of five black youths for attempting to breach segregation at the bus station led to a mass meeting and protest march, followed by a boycott of white merchants who had condemned the demonstration. The arrest of an integrated group of SNCC workers from Atlanta on 10 December for sitting in at the train station led to a week of mass protests and over 500 arrests. City authorities agreed to set up a biracial committee in response to the Albany movement's call for desegregated terminals and the release of jailed protesters.

Anderson asked Martin Luther King to address a mass meeting in Albany in the belief that King's presence would generate national publicity and force the city to capitulate to the movement's demands. However, SNCC staff maintained that reliance on prominent outsiders would undermine the strength of the local movement and its prospects for achieving a lasting settlement. King and Ralph Abernathy addressed two rallies in Albany churches, and, after negotiations had stalled, they led a march, in which they and over 250 others were arrested. King announced his intention to stay in jail.

Concerned about adverse publicity, Kennedy administration officials pressured city officials to reach a settlement with the Albany movement. In return for the cessation of protests, the city agreed that it would finally establish a biracial committee to address black grievances. Consequently, King and Abernathy left Albany on bail.

Their departure led the city to break its agreement. Although the Albany movement instituted an economic boycott and SNCC activists restarted direct action, the renewed protest garnered little media coverage. The return of King and Abernathy for sentencing in July 1962 and their decision to serve a jail term, rather than pay a fine, returned the spotlight to Albany and revived mass protest in the city. However, Police Chief Laurie Pritchett realised that if his forces treated the protesters non-violently in public, ensured ample jail room for them across the county, and prevented segregationist violence, he could exhaust the Albany movement's supply of demonstrators, and starve King and the movement of the publicity they needed to stimulate local business or federal government pressure on city authorities to negotiate. The strategy worked. Pritchett even arranged for King and Abernathy to have their fines paid, leading Abernathy to comment that it was the first time that he had ever been thrown out of jail.

Frustration at lack of progress twice led some black youths to throw bricks and bottles at the police, which enabled Pritchett to depict the movement as ill-disciplined and violent in contrast to his own forces. By the time President Kennedy publicly appealed for the city government to negotiate with the protesters, the movement had run out of steam. King and Abernathy left Albany in August. Although SNCC continued to work in the city and the Albany movement functioned until the late 1960s, the momentum of its early days was never regained.

Albany convinced SNCC of the efficacy of its evolving policy of patient community organising in support of local leaders and the dangers of relying on charismatic figures. SNCC workers became increasingly resentful of King and the SCLC, which they claimed had undermined a burgeoning local movement by taking over the protest. Some SNCC workers mocked King's religiosity, dubbing him 'De Lawd', and, with justification, SNCC felt that the SCLC had received publicity for work that SNCC had undertaken. King and the SCLC, which had come to the city at first merely to offer the Albany movement support but had then felt morally compelled by events to return, learnt that they would need to be thoroughly prepared before becoming involved in a local campaign and that they would also need to possess stronger ties with the local community. The SCLC had lacked an affiliate in Albany to work with. The Albany campaign, like the Freedom Rides, also confirmed that while the civil rights movement needed federal assistance to succeed, such assistance was unlikely to come unless incidents occurred that generated adverse national and international publicity, and local authorities proved themselves to be either unable or unwilling to maintain order.

The desegregation crisis at the University of Mississippi in September 1962 also demonstrated the reluctance of the Kennedy administration to act publicly in support of civil rights. With support from the NAACP Legal Defense and Educational Fund, James Meredith, an air force veteran, secured a federal court order for admission to his home state's leading university, in Oxford. In public, Governor Ross Barnett fiercely asserted his determination to maintain segregation at Ole Miss and urged Mississippians to join him. Privately, Barnett strung the Kennedys along in protracted negotiations. Accepting Barnett's word that he would maintain order and permit Meredith to register, the Kennedys dispatched a small group of federal marshals to accompany Meredith to the university. Meredith's arrival sparked a riot on campus. The 375 people injured included 160 marshals, 28 of whom had been shot. Two people died: a reporter and a local man. Belatedly, the Kennedys, who had naïvely trusted Barnett and feared alienating southern white voters, sent in the army, which they had left on standby in Memphis, some seventy miles away. The army arrived just as the marshals' supply of tear gas ran out and subdued the crowd. Largely ostracised by his fellow students and given armed protection, Meredith graduated in the summer and left Mississippi.[29]

The Kennedy administration had once more shown itself unwilling to intervene directly in a civil rights crisis unless state and local authorities failed to maintain order. Like Eisenhower in Little Rock, the Kennedys intervened to ensure implementation of a federal court and in response to adverse international publicity.

While the Ole Miss crisis did not bring any reorientation in the administration's civil rights policy, the Leadership Conference on Civil Rights, comprising civil rights, labour and church groups, lobbied congressmen to support civil rights legislation. In a partisan move designed to discomfort the Democrats, the Republican leadership in the House sponsored civil rights bills in February 1963. President Kennedy countered by proposing weak voter rights legislation in a special message to Congress. Although he explained that racial discrimination damaged America's foreign policy, Kennedy made no subsequent effort to win support for his proposal, which died of neglect.

However, the SCLC's Birmingham campaign in April and May 1963 forced civil rights on to the Kennedy administration's agenda and increased the organisation's status. During its early years, the SCLC had led a weak voter registration campaign and failed in Albany. Although King advocated nonviolent direct action, the SCLC had supported, rather than initiated, the sit-ins and Freedom Rides. Until May 1960, the SCLC had only three full-time staff, but thereafter it recruited a core of veteran activist ministers, whose tactical and organisational abilities made the group effective, at key moments, in working with local leaders and influencing the federal government. The new recruits included James Lawson, C. T. Vivian and James Bevel from the Nashville movement, Wyatt T. Walker of the Petersburg Improvement Association in Virginia, and Hosea Williams, whose Chatham County Crusade for Voters, along with its NAACP rival, mounted an effective voter registration and desegregation campaign in Savannah, Georgia. The Reverend Andrew J. Young from Louisiana joined the SCLC in 1961 and proved to be a skilled strategist and negotiator. The SCLC deliberately promoted King as the personification of the African-American struggle in order to win support from the black masses and to help its fund-raising activities. In practice, the SCLC's strong-willed staff forged policy together, after often fierce debate.[30]

As the SCLC created an effective staff base, Fred Shuttlesworth asked the organisation to assist the ACMHR's long-standing campaign against racial discrimination in Birmingham, Alabama. Led by Shuttlesworth since its formation in 1956, the ACMHR had agitated against Jim Crow for seven years. Its 600 activists, more than half of them female, constituted the SCLC's strongest affiliate.[31] A man of immense physical courage and unbending determination, Shuttlesworth had braved white mobs and suffered violence in his efforts to overturn segregation. Shuttlesworth and the ACMHR represented lower-class blacks, who rejected the conservative leadership of the middle-class NAACP which sought improvements within segregation, rather than Jim Crow's abolition. Local white authorities consistently refused to negotiate or even meet with Shuttlesworth and the ACMHR, preferring instead to work with traditional black leadership.

Shuttlesworth invited King and the SCLC to Birmingham in the belief that their participation in a sustained campaign would focus national attention on the city and force Birmingham to concede the ACMHR's goal of complete desegregation and the employment and promotion of African Americans in downtown stores. Although

Birmingham was reputedly the most segregated and racially repressive city in America, dubbed 'Bombingham' because of dynamite attacks on civil rights activists' homes and churches, it also offered an opportunity for progress since the white community was not monolithically aligned behind militant segregationists. Birmingham's white business elite and lawyers feared that Bull Connor's vigorous defence of segregation and the city's violent response to the Freedom Rides in 1961 deterred potential investors. Consequently, the SCLC hoped to exploit white divisions.

Leading King scholars Fairclough and David Garrow argue that King, Walker and the SCLC planned an economic boycott of downtown stores and mass demonstrations that were designed to exert pressure on white merchants and force the Kennedy administration on to the movement's side. The SCLC relied primarily on the expectation that Connor would order police violence against the protesters that would be public and reported by the media. The developing crisis would, the SCLC intended, force the Kennedy administration to intervene in order to placate outraged northern white opinion. Consequently, Birmingham's white officials would concede the movement's demands.[32]

Before the campaign had begun, white reformers successfully sponsored the replacement of the commission system of governing Birmingham with an elected mayor and council in order to curb Connor's power. When moderate segregationist Albert Boutwell defeated Connor for the mayoralty in a run-off election, black business leaders and conservatives urged the SCLC to call off its planned campaign in the belief that they could work with the new city administration. However, King and Shuttlesworth insisted that the campaign, begun the day after Boutwell's victory, go on as without it the new administration would have no incentive to relinquish segregation.

Although the economic boycott was effective, and inadvertently helped by whites who, fearing disorder, decided not to shop downtown, the SCLC experienced difficulty in recruiting sufficient volunteers to go to jail by sitting in at segregated lunch counters or marching. Few blacks wanted to risk the certainty of arrest in a cause that seemed unlikely to succeed. Many blacks also wanted to give the Boutwell administration a chance. At first, Connor exercised restraint, which deprived the campaign of an incident around which to rally the local black population and elicit federal intervention.

Placed under a state injunction that barred them from public protest activities, King, Abernathy and Shuttlesworth broke the injunction and entered jail. King hoped that his incarceration would stimulate greater local support, attract national media coverage, and lead the federal government to pressure Birmingham's merchants to negotiate. The Kennedys had earlier urged SCLC to postpone its campaign, and they resented the protests as an effort to force their involvement. Beyond telephoning Coretta King to express their concerns about her husband's safety, the Kennedys declined to intervene since local forces maintained order. From his cell, King wrote a 'Letter from Birmingham Jail'. Published too late to influence events in Birmingham, the letter castigated white moderates for being concerned with order rather than justice, set out King's rationale for civil disobedience in answer to his critics, and helped rally white liberals across America behind the civil rights struggle.

King and Abernathy left jail on bond. Subsequently given a five-day sentence but freed pending an appeal, King left Birmingham for an SCLC Board meeting in Memphis. With King and the top SCLC leaders absent, Bevel began organising a children's march. Although not without misgivings, King accepted the idea on his return. Over several days, thousands of children marched, filled the jails and saved the campaign from collapse. On 3 May, Connor allowed fire hoses and police dogs to be used against the demonstrators and a crowd of African-American onlookers. Shocked by scenes reported around the world and fearful that blacks outside the movement might retaliate, Robert Kennedy dispatched Burke Marshall, the chief of the Justice Department's Civil Rights Division, to Birmingham. Marshall pressured the merchants, who were seeking a way out of the crisis, to reach a settlement with the SCLC.

In return for an immediate end to the protests and the economic boycott, the merchants committed themselves to the formation of a biracial committee, gradual employment of black clerks and lunch counter desegregation within ninety days. Although far short of the SCLC's original demands, Fairclough argues that the agreement was the most that the SCLC could have realistically achieved with the businessmen and that the organisation wisely settled as it was beginning to lose control over the situation.[33] Shortly after the agreement, militant segregationists resorted to bombing the accommodation of leading activists, the city jailed King and Abernathy, and, in response to growing segregationist and police violence, the black ghetto erupted in a night of rioting. White merchants subsequently reneged on hiring blacks and delayed the biracial committee, but lunch counters began to desegregate in July.

Scholars disagree about the nature and outcome of the Birmingham campaign. Garrow argues that the campaign was a 'qualified success' produced by a change in King's approach that reflected lessons learned at Albany.[34] According to Garrow, King concluded after Albany that the strategy of nonviolent persuasion that he had consistently advocated since the late 1950s, 'focused on changing the hearts and minds of ... opponents was unrealistic and ineffective'. Consequently, he switched at Birmingham to a policy of 'coercive nonviolence', designed to elicit violent resistance, attract extensive media coverage, generate northern white sympathy for the movement and force the federal government to intervene to effect change in the South.[35] More convincingly, Fairclough contends that King had always recognised that nonviolent protest entailed mass organised resistance against oppression. Indeed at Montgomery, he had presided over a year-long economic boycott of the segregated bus system, and King had tried at Albany to pressure local whites through direct action and economic boycotts, and to generate a crisis that would bring federal intervention.[36]

Garrow also argues that the Birmingham demonstrations did not motivate President Kennedy to propose a civil rights bill on 11 June 1963 outlawing segregated public accommodations.[37] However, most historians, including Fairclough, argue justifiably that events in Birmingham, combined with a fear of further campaigns, retaliatory black violence and the possibility that frustrated African Americans might turn to extreme nationalist groups, convinced Robert Kennedy that legislation was necessary. Consequently, he prevailed on his brother to introduce the civil rights bill.[38]

Historian Glenn T. Eskew agrees with Fairclough that the Birmingham campaign led to the civil rights bill, but, using strong evidence, he rejects the standard interpretation of King's role within it.[39] According to Eskew, King and the SCLC favoured economic sanctions against white merchants, and 'contained demonstrations' focused on the limited goals of 'desegregation of store facilities, equal employment opportunities, and the creation of viable biracial discussions with the white officials'.[40] King and the SCLC 'did not set out to provoke brutality in Birmingham'.[41] Instead, they envisaged 'nonviolent sanctions with limited direct action that focused attention on the boycott and avoided violent confrontations with municipal authorities'.[42] King and the SCLC did not expect to enlist the support of the Kennedy administration, which 'had proven itself hostile to the movement'.[43] Walker and the SCLC did not devise a detailed plan for escalating direct action prior to the campaign, rather in response to press indifference to the economic boycott, 'the ACMHR-SCLC leaders altered their campaign strategy to include marches and other forms of direct action'.[44] As the campaign developed, King became focused on securing federal commitment to the civil rights movement, and, consequently, he was willing to settle for considerably less than Shuttlesworth and the ACMHR wanted.[45]

In response to Eskew, Fairclough argues that the SCLC chose Birmingham because of its violent reputation and that 'Connor or no Connor, they were virtually guaranteed a rough reception'.[46] Although the organisation engaged in some advance planning, it improvised 'when its plans came unstuck'. The SCLC hoped that its demonstrations would elicit a media-reported 'visually dramatic confrontation' and thereby 'evoke sympathy for the protesters', but not 'serious bloodshed and fatalities' that would harm its supporters, bring violent black retaliation and lead whites to condemn the group for irresponsible provocation.[47] Shuttlesworth's biographer Andrew M. Manis argues that Eskew 'overstates the distinction between national and local goals in the Birmingham movement', and he 'overplays the degree to which Shuttlesworth was willing to turn over the decisions to King'.[48] Manis also offers a more critical perspective on Shuttlesworth.

Although the Birmingham campaign failed to bring significant change to the city in the short term and Shuttlesworth did not displace conservative local black leadership, the campaign helped inspire a summer of direct action in many urban areas. According to the SRC, during 1963 930 demonstrations occurred in at least 115 cities in the eleven southern states. Over 20,000 people were arrested, compared with 3,600 in nonviolent protests before the autumn of 1961.[49] Many areas experienced civil rights protests for the first time, with local groups aided by one of the major civil rights organisations.

Birmingham led a hitherto reluctant national NAACP to support a boycott by the Jackson movement in Mississippi, which in consequence grew from a movement of largely African-American youth to one that also incorporated the traditionally more conservative elements of the black community. Medgar Evers, who had long supported the boycott, welcomed the beginning of mass marches in the city. Roy Wilkins even joined Evers in being arrested on a downtown picket line. Tragically,

Evers was murdered on 12 June, one of ten people to die as a result of
their civil rights activities in the South during 1963. Even before Evers's
death, the national NAACP had broken the momentum of the Jackson
movement by ending mass marches. The Kennedy administration then
successfully pressed the city to make a few token concessions in June,
which prevented a resumption of direct action. Nevertheless, swept
along by the new wave of direct action in the South, in July 1963, the
NAACP's annual convention called on its local chapters to picket,
engage in mass protest and adopt economic boycotts. In South Carolina,
the NAACP State Conference of Branches vigorously pursued direct
action during 1963 and 1964. Elsewhere, NAACP branches varied from
noninvolvement to active participation in direct action.

The Civil Rights Act of 1964

The onset of mass southern protests was ironic in that the Kennedy
administration had intended in part for its civil rights bill to remove the
need for demonstrations and so keep African Americans off the streets.
Wedded to order, the administration, learned from its earlier mistake at
the University of Mississippi, and federalised the Alabama National
Guard to ensure the peaceful desegregation of the University of Alabama
on 11 June 1963 over the objections of the state's outspoken segregationist governor, George C. Wallace. Only hours later, Kennedy
delivered a televised national address on behalf of the civil rights bill, in
which he argued that the issue was a moral one. Although the administration had previously positioned itself almost as a referee between the
civil rights movement and its segregationist opponents, John Kennedy
now worked assiduously for the bill's passage. Encouraged by Roy
Wilkins and the Leadership Conference on Civil Rights, liberals later
added a section to create an equal employment opportunity commission
and bar discrimination in employment.

Kennedy at first opposed a march on Washington which the the major
civil rights groups proposed in support of the bill. But he endorsed the
protest after accepting its organisers' assurances that the march would be
peaceful and orderly, and its list of sponsors expanded to include the
National Council of Churches (NCC), the National Catholic Conference for Interracial Justice, the American Jewish Congress and the
UAW. Conceived initially by A. Philip Randolph as a March for Jobs
and Freedom, the demonstration added passage of the civil rights bill to
its demands for immediate school desegregation, an end to police

brutality, a large-scale federal public works programme and the elimination of racial discrimination in employment.

Organised by Bayard Rustin and held in August 1963, the march attracted at least 250,000 people, including approximately 40,000 whites.[50] Despite internal tensions between the civil rights groups, the march successfully presented a united front that was capped by Martin Luther King's stirring 'I Have a Dream' speech. King presented his vision of a harmonious, integrated society in which people would 'not be judged by the color of their skin but by the content of their character'.[51] King's use of religious phraseology, his appeal to the nation's democratic traditions and his emphasis on nonviolence and racial reconciliation typified his approach of communicating in a way that blacks and whites could understand, while also seeking to reassure whites.

Although Kennedy received the march's leaders in the White House, the march had little influence on Congress, where there was considerable opposition to the civil rights bill, which extended beyond simply southern preferences for segregation to wider concerns that the bill unconstitutionally threatened property rights. Public opinion polls consistently found that a majority of northern and southern whites opposed actions taken by African Americans in the first half of the 1960s to obtain civil rights, including 59 per cent and 78 per cent respectively in December 1963.[52]

However, by the closing months of 1963 a large northern white and a small southern white majority supported integrated transportation and residential integration, while large southern and northern white majorities endorsed voting rights for African Americans and equal employment opportunities.[53] In both the North and the South, white support for integration increased with education and decreased with age, and the growing trend in favour of integration was partly accounted for by acceptance of such integration as had already occurred and by a belief that it was inevitable.[54] But whites drew the line at intimate contact, with large majorities across the nation opposed to interracial dating and marriage.[55] Despite their support for residential integration in principle, 46 per cent of northern whites and 74 per cent of southern whites said they would object to having a black neighbour.[56] The regional divide widened regarding token school desegregation, to which 61 per cent of southern whites objected but only 10 per cent of northern whites.[57]

The civil rights bill remained stalled in Congress at the time of Kennedy's murder in November 1963, but opinion poll evidence suggests that although many whites objected to civil rights demonstrations, such protests, along with instances of and expectations of desegregation, drew their attention to, and helped move white opinion against segregation and discrimination.[58] Increasing numbers of whites also concluded that the damage done to social order and economic well-being by opposition to desegregation was too great to bear. Three months before Kennedy's death, 63 per cent of white Americans and 31 per cent of southern whites supported his civil rights bill.[59]

Kennedy's successor, Lyndon Johnson, committed himself to the bill, saying that it would be a fitting memorial to the slain president. To maintain pressure on Congress to act, King and the SCLC mounted a direct-action campaign in St Augustine, Florida, in the spring of 1964, following a request for assistance by Robert Hayling, a black dentist who headed the local civil rights movement. Hayling, who advised the city's NAACP Youth Council, had organised a series of demonstrations in the summer of 1963, supported mostly by local black college students. However, led by St Augustine's militant segregationist mayor and police chief, local whites refused to concede desegregation or agree to a biracial commission. St Augustine seemed an opportune target for the SCLC since the city depended heavily on tourism and was promoting its forthcoming quadricentennial celebration in 1965. The presence of the diehard segregationist Ancient City Gun Club, which harassed African-American leaders, also made violent white resistance likely and hence national publicity that might influence Congress to support the civil rights bill.

Demonstrations, sit-ins and pickets began in late March 1964, with little support from older African Americans, who feared violence and economic retaliation by whites. The protesters mostly comprised local black youths and students, concerned New England students, and white clergy and other white sympathisers from around the country, including Mrs Malcolm Peabody the seventy-two-year-old wife of an Episcopal bishop in Massachusetts and the mother of Massachusetts' governor, Endicott Peabody. The SCLC sought to fill the jails and harm the city's tourist trade during the Easter holiday. The arrest of Mrs Peabody ensured national press coverage, and her subsequent interview on the NBC *Today Show* brought the campaign further publicity. Daytime protests and evening marches maintained the pressure on city authorities, which nevertheless remained determined to hold firm. Whites repeatedly attacked the protesters, and gunfire raked King's accommodation.

By the end of June, a stalemate had left both sides anxious to find a way out. With SCLC resources depleted, older black residents unenthusiastic about the protests and US Senate approval for the civil rights bill rendered on 20 June, King was ready to end the campaign. Concerned by escalating white violence and under pressure from the Johnson administration to arrange a settlement, Governor Farris Bryant announced the formation of a biracial commission in St Augustine. Aware that a commission had not actually been created, King nevertheless ended the demonstrations and left town, satisfied with a national victory in the form of the Civil Rights Act.

Historian David R. Colburn argues that without King and the SCLC's intervention the local movement which had begun the protests in St Augustine 'would have probably collapsed'. Yet, King and the SCLC failed to 'develop or encourage a grass roots movement', leaving African Americans largely leaderless and without direction in the face of recurrent white violence and intimidation, which the city's white leaders encouraged by their continued intransigence. However, Colburn credits the St Augustine campaign with helping to ensure passage of the Civil Rights Act by influencing public opinion.[60] With justice, historian Robert Cook contends that there is no firm evidence to support Colburn's view regarding a link between the protest and enactment of legislation.[61]

In fact, it took months of congressional lobbying by Lyndon Johnson, the NAACP, the AFL–CIO and the NCC to help create a bipartisan coalition that defeated southern white opposition and passed the Civil Rights Act. Anxious to establish his legitimacy as president and genuinely committed to civil rights, Johnson used his legendary powers of persuasion and coercion to engineer cross-party support for the bill against opposition from his native South. The Leadership Conference on Civil Rights, and especially its legislative director and NAACP Washington Bureau director Clarence Mitchell, Jr, lobbied congresspeople relentlessly. The NCC, part of the Leadership Conference, proved particularly effective in mobilising its supporters to pressurise midwestern Republicans to vote for the bill.

Signed into law on 2 July, the Civil Rights Act outlawed segregation in public accommodations; set up an Equal Employment Opportunity Commission (EEOC) with job discrimination prohibited on the grounds of race, religion, sex, or national origin; established a Community Relations Service to foster voluntary compliance with the act's provisions; empowered the Attorney General to file suit against segregated school

districts; and barred federal funding of racially-discriminatory programmes and institutions including schools. Most of St Augustine's
businesses initially declared their intention to comply with the act, but
after the SCLC departed, they maintained segregation. Such defiance
was not uncommon and was most marked in the Black Belt and more
generally in the Deep South. Some businesses closed altogether rather
than desegregate, or they redesignated themselves as private clubs to
evade the Civil Rights Act, which the Supreme Court upheld under the
Commerce Clause since private businesses affected interstate commerce.
Nevertheless, segregated public accommodations began to disappear in
the South, and 199 southern colleges agreed to abide by the act. But ten
years after *Brown* I, only 34,110 (1.18 per cent) of the 2,900,000 African-
American school-age children living in the eleven southern states were
attending schools with whites.[62] Minuscule in the other Deep South
states, token school desegregation began in Mississippi only in September
1964. Despite the Civil Rights Act, school segregation remained largely
intact in the South as federal courts and officials permitted token
integration.

Selma and the Voting Rights Act of 1965

The Civil Rights Act contained only weak provisions regarding voting
rights, and it did not provide federal protection for civil rights workers.
These issues were of particular concern to SNCC and CORE since they
undertook voter registration work, assisted by VEP funds, in some of
the most repressive rural areas of the Deep South. Local Federal Bureau
of Investigation (FBI) agents failed to intervene to halt racist thuggery
and harassment. The US Justice Department claimed that federalism
denied it authority to act against violence and intimidation, but SNCC
and CORE workers believed that the federal government had promised
them and voter applicants protection.

Seven hundred thousand southern African Americans registered to
vote between 1962 and 1964 (287,000 of them aided by the VEP), raising
the per cent age of eligible blacks registered from 29.4 to 43.1.[63] The
increase came mainly in urban areas and in the peripheral South. In
Florida, Tennessee and Texas, a majority of eligible blacks had
registered by 1964, but in Alabama, Louisiana and Mississippi, less than
one-third had done so. In Mississippi, black registration stood at 6.7 per
cent in 1964, with harassment and intimidation so rife that the VEP had
withdrawn from the state in November 1963.[64]

SNCC and CORE increasingly began to doubt the civil rights movement's strategy of working with the federal government and white liberals. After objections by the Catholic Archbishop of Washington DC Patrick A. O'Boyle and Eugene Carson Blake of the NCC, John Lewis, chairman of SNCC, had to be persuaded by Bayard Rustin and other civil rights leaders to temper Lewis's criticisms of the Kennedy administration and the civil rights bill's shortcomings, when he addressed the March on Washington in 1963.

Rustin, Roy Wilkins and Whitney Young of the NUL remained strong advocates of working with the national Democratic Party. As Lyndon Johnson had advocated, Wilkins called for a moratorium on demonstrations during the 1964 presidential election, so as not to undercut support for Johnson's campaign against Barry Goldwater of Arizona, who opposed the Civil Rights Act as a violation of states' and property rights. Eager to keep the movement together and to maintain his ties with its two wings, King assented to a vague compromise agreement to reduce protests during the election. However, James Farmer and John Lewis refused to sign the statement and consequently found themselves excluded from the White House. Johnson won the election overwhelmingly, losing only Arizona and the Deep South to Goldwater. King remained committed to working with federal authorities, unaware that the Kennedy (and then the Johnson) administration had permitted the FBI to place him under electronic surveillance because of King's contacts with leftists, such as Stanley Levison.

King and the SCLC decided to launch a campaign in Selma, deep in Alabama's Black Belt, in January 1965 to dramatise the need for voter registration. Although SNCC had operated a project in Selma since 1963, two years later only 2 per cent of Dallas County's eligible African Americans were registered to vote. Concerned that King's presence might undermine their efforts to develop local leadership, SNCC activists nevertheless agreed not to hinder the SCLC's campaign, which focused on Selma in the expectation that County Sheriff Jim Clark would be unable to contain his habitual brutality.

After three months of demonstrations and arrests in Selma, and the killing of black Alabamian Jimmie Lee Jackson by state troopers in nearby Marion, the SCLC organised a march from Selma to Montgomery. State troopers tear-gassed and beat the marchers, led by Hosea Williams and John Lewis, as they began crossing the Edmund Pettus Bridge. King, who had been out of town, quickly scheduled a second march to

Montgomery. Forewarned by federal authorities of an impending federal court injunction against the march obtained by the state of Alabama and unwilling to defy federal law, King agreed to a compromise, arranged by LeRoy Collins of the Community Relations Service, whereby King would lead a march until halted peacefully and turned back in Selma by Clark and Public Safety Director Al Lingo. King kept to the agreement but state troopers parted in front of the march, leaving the road to Montgomery open as King led the bemused marchers back into town after a brief prayer. Unaware of the agreement, which King had kept to himself, SNCC was furious at what it saw as his deceptive charade.

Committed to the ballot as the means of effecting change, President Johnson had begun preparing voting rights legislation before the Selma campaign forced his hand. The attack on the bridge, followed days later by the murder of James Reeb, a white clergyman from Boston, led to calls for federal legislation from national religious leaders, many of the nation's newspapers and thousands of letter writers to the White House. Anxious to heed these calls and to avoid further bloodshed, Johnson proposed a voting rights bill to Congress and included in his address the words 'We shall overcome' from the civil rights movement's anthem. According to an opinion poll, southern whites supported the bill by a margin of 49 per cent to 37 per cent.[65] With the federal injunction against marching lifted following pressure from Johnson and protected by a federalised contingent of the Alabama National Guard, King led the postponed march from Selma to Montgomery six days after Johnson's congressional address. Ku Klux Klansmen murdered Viola Liuzzo, a white civil rights sympathiser from Detroit, on the march's last day.

The voting rights bill became law in August 1965 and replaced the slow litigation approach of earlier legislation. The act suspended literacy tests, required preclearance or prior federal approval of any changes in voting procedures under section five, and allowed the attorney general to dispatch federal registrars to enrol voters in states and areas that had a literacy test and in which neither a majority of the voting-age population had either registered or voted in the 1964 presidential election. While a constitutional amendment had outlawed poll taxes in federal elections in 1964, the Voting Rights Act ordered the US Justice Department to challenge poll taxes in state and local elections through the courts, which it did successfully in 1966. By the end of 1965, federal registrars had enrolled 79,593 voters, while fear of federal intervention induced many counties to allow black registration.[66]

The civil rights movement had succeeded in overturning *de jure* segregation and legal barriers to enfranchisement, yet the movement was already beginning to rupture as SNCC and CORE began to question and then reject many of the movement's hallmarks. At the same time, the movement faced new challenges from outside its ranks as whites across America became increasingly resistant to its demands and African Americans considered alternative forms of protest and development.

Notes

1. Harvard Sitkoff, *The Struggle for Black Equality, 1954–1992*, rev. edn (New York: Hill and Wang, 1993), p. 64; Clayborne Carson, *In Struggle: SNCC and the Black Awakening of the 1960s* (Cambridge, MA, and London: Harvard University Press, 1981), p. 11.
2. Carson, *In Struggle*, pp. 9–18; William H. Chafe, *Civilities and Civil Rights: Greensboro, North Carolina, and the Black Struggle for Freedom* (1980; Oxford and New York: Oxford University Press, 1981), p. 86.
3. Aldon D. Morris, *The Origins of the Civil Rights Movement: Black Communities Organizing for Change* (New York: Free Press, 1984), pp. 195–215.
4. Ibid. p. 198. According to Chafe, only two of the four original protesters had been members of the Greensboro NAACP Youth Council. Chafe, *Civilities and Civil Rights*, p. 81.
5. Morris, *Origins of the Civil Rights Movement*, pp. 200–3, 205.
6. Clayborne Carson, 'Civil Rights Reform and the Black Freedom Struggle', in Charles W. Eagles (ed.), *The Civil Rights Movement in America* (Jackson and London: University Press of Mississippi, 1986), p. 31. Whereas Morris emphasised the contribution of CORE, Franklin McCain told interviewer Howell Raines that he and the other three original sit-in protesters in Greensboro rejected CORE's attempt to take control of the protest. Howell Raines, *My Soul is Rested: Movement Days in the Deep South Remembered* (1977; Harmondsworth and New York: Penguin, 1983), p. 81.
7. Carson, 'Civil Rights Reform and the Black Freedom Struggle', p. 30.
8. Ibid.
9. Morris, *Origins of the Civil Rights Movement*, p. 203.
10. Adam Fairclough, *To Redeem the Soul of America: The Southern Christian Leadership Conference and Martin Luther King, Jr.* (Athens and London: University of Georgia Press, 1987), p. 58.
11. Ibid. p. 59.
12. Ibid. p. 62.
13. Ibid.
14. Raines, *My Soul is Rested*, pp. 85, 99; Chafe, *Civilities and Civil Rights*, pp. 94–7; Sitkoff, *Struggle for Black Equality*, pp. 78–9.
15. Raines, *My Soul is Rested*, pp. 79–80; Cleveland Sellers with Robert Terrell, *The River of No Return: The Autobiography of a Black Militant and the Life and Death of SNCC* (1973; Jackson and London: University Press of Mississippi, 1990), pp. 16–17; Chafe, *Civilities and Civil Rights*, pp. 80–3; Sitkoff, *Struggle for Black Equality*, pp. 73–6; Carson, *In Struggle*, p. 16.

16. Chafe, *Civilities and Civil Rights*, p. 94.
17. Raines, *My Soul is Rested*, p. 78; Sitkoff, *Struggle for Black Equality*, pp. 80–2.
18. Raines, *My Soul is Rested*, p. 99.
19. Raines, *My Soul is Rested*, p. 77; Chafe, *Civilities and Civil Rights*, pp. 94–7; Sitkoff, *Struggle for Black Equality*, pp. 79–80.
20. Raines, *My Soul is Rested*, p. 99.
21. Sitkoff, *Struggle for Black Equality*, pp. 64, 73.
22. Fairclough, *To Redeem the Soul of America*, p. 63.
23. 'Student Nonviolent Coordinating Committee Statement of Purpose', in Clayborne Carson, David J. Garrow, Gerald Gill, Vincent Harding and Darlene Clark Hine (eds), *The Eyes on the Prize Civil Rights Reader* (New York: Penguin, 1991), p. 119.
24. Mark Stern, *Calculating Visions: Kennedy, Johnson, and Civil Rights* (New Brunswick, NJ: Rutgers University Press, 1992), p. 32.
25. Carl M. Brauer, *John F. Kennedy and the Second Reconstruction* (New York: Columbia University Press, 1977), pp. 61–88; Robert E. Gilbert, 'John F. Kennedy and Civil Rights for Black Americans', *Presidential Studies* 12 (1982), pp. 391–3; Stern, *Calculating Visions*, pp. 43–4, 48–9, 53, 56, 63–4, 69–70.
26. Brauer, *John F. Kennedy and the Second Reconstruction*, pp. 87, 110, 112; Stern, *Calculating Visions*, pp. 58–9, 63–4, 69–70; Sitkoff, *Struggle for Black Equality*, pp. 96–101, 116.
27. Taylor Branch, *Parting the Waters: America in the King Years 1954–63* (New York: Simon and Schuster, 1988), p. 475.
28. August Meier and Elliott Rudwick, *CORE: A Study in the Civil Rights Movement* (1973; Urbana, Chicago and London: University of Illinois Press, 1975), pp. 140, 142–3.
29. John Dittmer, *Local People: The Struggle for Civil Rights in Mississippi* (Urbana and Chicago: University of Illinois Press, 1994), pp. 138–42; Sitkoff, *Struggle for Black Equality*, p. 114.
30. Adam Fairclough, 'The Preachers and the People: The Origins and Early Years of the Southern Christian Leadership Conference, 1955–1959', *Journal of Southern History* 52 (August 1986), pp. 433–40; Fairclough, *To Redeem the Soul of America*, pp. 60, 66–70, 91, 94–5, 165–9; Adam Fairclough, 'The Southern Christian Leadership Conference and the Second Reconstruction, 1957–1973', *South Atlantic Quarterly* 80 (Spring 1981), pp. 179–82.
31. Fairclough, *To Redeem the Soul of America*, p. 113. Glenn T. Eskew cites a 1959 sociological survey that estimated the ACMHR's membership at 1,000: 60 per cent women and 40 per cent men. Glenn T. Eskew, '"The Classes and the Masses": Fred Shuttlesworth's Movement and Birmingham's Black Middle Class', in Marjorie L. White and Andrew M. Manis (eds), *Birmingham Revolutionaries: The Reverend Fred Shuttlesworth and the Alabama Christian Movement for Human Rights* (Macon, GA: Mercer University Press, 2000), p. 38.
32. Fairclough, *To Redeem the Soul of America*, pp. 114–15, 137–8; Adam Fairclough, 'Martin Luther King, Jr., and the Quest for Nonviolent Social Change', *Phylon* 47 (Spring 1986), pp. 5, 6–7; David J. Garrow, *Protest at Selma: Martin Luther King, Jr., and the Voting Rights Act of 1965* (New Haven and London: Yale University Press, 1978), pp. 2–3, 221–2; David J. Garrow, *Bearing the Cross: Martin Luther King, Jr., and the Southern Christian Leadership Conference* (New York: William Morrow, 1986), pp. 226–9; Sitkoff, *Struggle for Black Equality*, p. 121.

33. Fairclough, *To Redeem the Soul of America*, pp. 127–31.
34. Garrow, *Protest at Selma*, p. 4.
35. Ibid. p. 221.
36. Adam Fairclough, 'Martin Luther King, Jr.', pp. 2–7; Fairclough, *To Redeem the Soul of America*, pp. 52–3.
37. Garrow, *Protest at Selma*, pp. 135–49.
38. Fairclough, *To Redeem the Soul of America*, pp. 133–6; Stern, *Calculating Visions*, pp. 81–91; Eskew, *But for Birmingham*, pp. 17, 299, 310–2, 338, 393 n. 27; Andrew M. Manis, *A Fire You Can't Put Out: The Civil Rights Life of Birmingham's Reverend Fred Shuttlesworth* (Tuscaloosa and London: University of Alabama Press, 1999), pp. ix, 5–6.
39. Eskew, *But for Birmingham*, pp. 336–8.
40. Ibid. p. 211.
41. Ibid. p. 212.
42. Ibid.
43. Ibid. p. 213.
44. Ibid. pp. 209–12, 225, 255 (quotation).
45. Ibid. pp. 296, 336–8. Like Eskew, Morris also emphasises the centrality of the economic boycott. Morris rejects as 'simplistic' the contention of Garrow and others that King chose Birmingham with the intention of provoking Connor to unleash white violence that would induce federal intervention and thereby enable the campaign to achieve its goals. However, unlike Eskew, Morris contends that King and the SCLC sought at the outset to 'force the federal government to take a firm stand against racial domination'. (Morris, *Origins of the Civil Rights Movement*, pp. 250–2 (first quotation on p. 252; second quotation on p. 251), 257–8, 321–2 n. 94.)
46. Adam Fairclough, *Better Day Coming: Blacks and Equality 1890–2000* (2001; New York: Penguin, 2002), pp. 277–8.
47. Ibid. p. 278.
48. Manis, *A Fire You Can't Put Out*, pp. 384, 489 n. 70 (first quotation), 496 n. 89 (second quotation).
49. Carson, *In Struggle*, p. 90.
50. Robert W. Spike, *Civil Rights Involvement: Model for Mission* (Detroit: Detroit Industrial Mission, 1965), p. 11.
51. Peter B. Levy (ed.), *Let Freedom Ring: A Documentary History of the Modern Civil Rights Movement* (New York, Westport, CT, and London: Praeger, 1992), p. 124.
52. Hazel Erskine, 'The Polls: Demonstrations and Race Riots', *Public Opinion Quarterly* 31 (Winter 1967–8), p. 656.
53. Hazel Erskine, 'The Polls: Negro Housing', *Public Opinion Quarterly* 31 (Fall 1967), pp. 486, 488; Herbert H. Hyman and Paul B. Sheatsley, 'Attitudes toward Desegregation', *Scientific American* 211 (July 1964), p. 19.
54. Hyman and Sheatsley, 'Attitudes toward Desegregation', pp. 20–2; Erskine, 'The Polls: Negro Housing', p. 490.
55. Hazel Erskine, 'The Polls: Interracial Socializing', *Public Opinion Quarterly* 37 (Summer 1973), pp. 288–9, 290.
56. Erskine, 'The Polls: Negro Housing', p. 485.
57. John Shelton Reed and Merle Black, 'Jim Crow, R.I.P.', in John Shelton Reed, *Surveying the South: Studies in Regional Sociology* (Columbia and London: University of Missouri Press, 1993), p. 98.

58. Erskine, 'The Polls: Demonstrations and Race Riots', p. 660; Paul B. Sheatsley, 'White Attitudes toward the Negro', *Daedalus* 95 (Winter 1966), pp. 220–5, 231–2, 235–7. More generally, see Paul Burstein, 'Public Opinion, Demonstrations, and the Passage of Antidiscrimination Legislation', *Public Opinion Quarterly* 43 (1979), pp. 158, 169–70.

59. 'How Whites Feel About Negroes: A Painful American Dilemma', *Newsweek* 62 (21 October 1963), pp. 45, 47.

60. David R. Colburn, *Racial Change and Community Crisis: St. Augustine Florida, 1877–1980* (1985; Gainesville: University of Florida Press, 1991), pp. xv, 208–16 (first quotation on p. 208; second quotation on p. 210).

61. Robert Cook, *Sweet Land of Liberty? The African-American Struggle for Civil Rights in the Twentieth Century* (London and New York: Longman, 1998), p. 142.

62. Reed Sarratt, *The Ordeal of Desegregation: The First Decade* (New York and London: Harper and Row, 1966), p. 350.

63. Steven F. Lawson and Charles Payne, *Debating the Civil Rights Movement, 1945–1968* (Lanham, Boulder, New York and Oxford: Rowman and Littlefield, 1998), p. 25; Steven F. Lawson, *Running for Freedom: Civil Rights and Black Politics in America Since 1941*, 2nd edn (New York: McGraw-Hill, 1997), p. 80.

64. Lawson and Payne, *Debating the Civil Rights Movement*, pp. 25–6; Dittmer, *Local People*, p. 212.

65. David Alan Horowitz, 'White Southerners' Alienation and Civil Rights: The Response to Corporate Liberalism, 1956–1965', *Journal of Southern History* 54 (May 1988), pp. 184–5.

66. Garrow, *Protest at Selma*, p. 185.

CHAPTER 4

The Disintegration of the National Civil Rights Coalition, 1964–8

The national civil rights coalition fractured in the mid-1960s. Their experiences in the Deep South and the failure of white liberals to support the Mississippi Freedom Democratic Party (MFDP) at the Democratic Party's national convention in 1964 led SNCC and CORE to reject integration, interracialism and nonviolence, and SNCC, the more radical of the two groups, to also lose all faith in working with the federal government. Influenced by the New York-based Black Muslim Malcolm X, who advocated black nationalism, SNCC and CORE called for Black Power. Just as the civil rights movement overturned legalised racial discrimination in the South, a series of urban riots in the North and West drew attention to the depth of racism and poverty across the nation, and propelled the SCLC to move north in a vain attempt to find solutions using nonviolent means. At first, Martin Luther King tried to hold the national civil rights coalition together, but he broke with the Johnson administration over its escalation of the war in Vietnam. President Johnson continued to work with the NAACP and the NUL, and to support federally-funded local anti-poverty programmes run by moderate whites and blacks. Still committed to nonviolence but privately supportive of democratic socialism, an increasingly radical King was murdered in 1968 shortly before the SCLC's last major protest, the failed Poor People's Campaign in Washington DC.

The Mississippi Summer Project

Committed to generating sustainable local activism and to working in the most repressive areas, SNCC and CORE had established voter registration projects in parts of the Deep South and a few other areas in the early 1960s. SNCC concentrated primarily on southwest Georgia, Mississippi, portions of Arkansas and Selma, Alabama. CORE focused on parts of South Carolina and Louisiana, northern Florida and the Fourth Congressional District in Mississippi, especially Madison County.

In Mississippi, SNCC, CORE, the Mississippi NAACP and the SCLC cooperated by reviving the Council of Federated Organizations (COFO) in February 1962, with Mississippi NAACP president Aaron Henry as COFO president, Bob Moses of SNCC as programme director, and Dave Dennis of CORE as assistant director. By virtue of having the largest number of field workers in Mississippi, SNCC dominated COFO, which acted as a channel for VEP funds and sought to defuse tensions and rivalry between member groups.

The SCLC had a minor role in COFO. However, the citizenship education programme, which the SCLC had taken over from the High-lander Folk School in 1961 and then expanded to Mississippi and other southern states, trained voter applicants and local activists, many of them women, in community-organising techniques. Run from a headquarters in Dorchester, Georgia, by Septima Clark and Dorothy Cotton, and largely ignored by the SCLC's leaders, the programme shared SNCC's distrust of hierarchy.

By spring 1963, SNCC had six offices in Mississippi, staffed by twenty black field secretaries, seventeen of whom were indigenes. SNCC worked with existing networks of prominent adults who usually had some degree of economic independence from the white community as businesspeople or farmers, and the group also enlisted black youths. In Hattiesburg, SNCC recruited local businesswoman Victoria Gray, who later helped run the SCLC's citizenship education programme in Mississippi, and in Canton, Madison County, CORE worked with local businesspeople C. O. Chinn and Annie Devine. Mileston in Holmes County had an unusually large group of independent black farmers because of a New Deal land resettlement programme, and, at the farmers' request, SNCC began a county project there in 1963. Frequently, mothers followed their teenage children into the movement, while older black women often participated and sheltered civil rights workers in their homes. Through church and family ties and traditions of community work, women helped sustained the movement in the rural Deep South. They circulated information, usually formed a majority at mass meetings, and called on reluctant black clergy to open their churches to the movement. They also urged African Americans to attend citizenship education classes and attempt to vote, often canvassing door to door.

Nonhierarchical and committed to local activism, SNCC gravitated to pre-existing female-based community networks, and the organisation itself was significantly influenced by women, such as Ella Baker and

Diane Nash. While executive secretary Ruby Doris Smith Robinson was the only woman to achieve high elective office in SNCC and some SNCC men exhibited chauvinism, the group's emphasis on decentralisation and equalitarianism enabled women to play a significant role within it.

SNCC also helped local female leaders to emerge. Although black church pastors were male, their congregations were predominantly female. Their religious faith helped sustain women's involvement in the movement, and their church participation made them at ease expressing themselves in mass meetings. In her early thirties, Unita Blackwell, a sharecropper from Mayersville, Mississippi, met civil rights activists when they came to her church. Blackwell was one of only eight people, who initially volunteered to attempt voter registration. She subsequently became a SNCC voter registration worker, and in 1977 mayor of Mayersville.

Fannie Lou Hamer, a forty-four-year-old timekeeper on a Sunflower County, Mississippi, plantation, attended a SNCC meeting at Williams Chapel Church and agreed to join a voter registration attempt at the end of August 1962. Swiftly evicted from her plantation, Hamer was repeatedly refused registration. In December 1962, Hamer became a SNCC field worker and a month later she finally registered to vote. She attended a training session at the SCLC's centre in Dorchester in April, and then another in Charleston, South Carolina, in May taught by Bernice Robinson, who had worked with Septima Clark on the Sea Islands. On their return to Mississippi, Hamer and the rest of her group, all but one of them female, were arrested and severely beaten in Winona jail for demanding equal treatment during the bus journey. Although Hamer and some other female activists, such as Winson Hudson in Harmony, Mississippi, later said that women could be more involved in the movement than men because segregationists would simply try to kill male activists, the violence at Winona showed that their femininity did not necessarily protect women from physical assault.

Violence and harassment dogged the movement in Mississippi, as it did a similar SNCC project in rural southwest Georgia overseen by Charles Sherrod. In October 1962, the Leflore County Board of Supervisors in the Mississippi Delta declared that the county would not participate in a federal surplus food programme that ordinarily sustained plantation workers through the winter months when the planters did not need their labour. However, SNCC responded to this retaliation against its voter registration campaign with its own aid programme, and continued an enfranchisement drive. SNCC intensified its canvassing efforts after Jimmy Travis, an indigenous black SNCC worker, survived being shot in February 1963. The group also organised demonstrations in Greenwood, the county seat, in an effort to induce federal intervention. Whites set fire to SNCC's Greenwood office and shot at its staff and their local supporters.

The US Justice Department filed for a temporary restraining order to prevent the city from obstructing the voter registration campaign and peaceful protest, and to force the release of eight SNCC workers who had been jailed for marching. However, the department dropped its request in exchange for the activists' release, and in response to heavy criticism from Mississippi's powerful US Senators James Eastland and John Stennis. The action increased SNCC's growing disillusionment with the Kennedy administration, which the group believed had repeatedly reneged on promises to protect civil rights activity, and preferred order and political pragmatism to justice. SNCC activists in southwest Georgia accused the administration of colluding with local segregationist officials.

Bob Moses, who had been active in the Greenwood protests, nevertheless remained convinced that national publicity could force federal government intervention on behalf of voter registration in Mississippi. Allard K. Lowenstein, a well-connected white activist who had come to Mississippi in July 1963, suggested a Freedom Vote to Moses. Blacks would demonstrate their desire to participate in the political process by holding an unofficial ballot. With the agreement of Moses and Charles Evers, who had succeeded his murdered brother as the NAACP's Mississippi field secretary, Lowenstein recruited over 100 white students, mostly from Yale and Stanford, to assist COFO in the organising campaign for the vote. Held in November 1963, the Freedom Vote paralleled the regular gubernatorial election. Over 83,000 blacks participated in the COFO ballot and supported Aaron Henry and Ed King, a white chaplain at Tougaloo College, for governor and lieutenant governor respectively.[1]

Anxious not to lose southern white support, the Kennedys ignored the campaign. Nevertheless, Moses and Lowenstein decided to repeat the experiment in the summer but this time with hundreds more white volunteers. The two men believed that a large-scale campaign would create a crisis that would force federal intervention, if only to protect white students from prestigious universities and well-connected families.

Press attention during the Freedom Vote, they knew, had primarily focused on the white student volunteers, rather than on the recurrent discrimination that African Americans experienced.

Tensions emerged when COFO discussed the proposal in November 1963. Several black SNCC workers complained that whites tended to take over leadership roles in civil rights projects, thereby denying African Americans the opportunity to develop their leadership skills and perpetuating racial subordination. Despite misgivings among some staff, SNCC and COFO agreed to back the plan. By then, VEP had withdrawn funds from COFO. Rejecting the official reason that white resistance had severely restricted black registration, COFO believed that the foundations which funded the VEP had balked at COFO's involvement in political organising through the Freedom Vote. Despite misgivings, the Summer Project indicated that SNCC was still prepared to look to the federal government and whites for assistance.

A similar debate emerged among CORE organisers in rural Louisiana, who faced the same conditions that hurt COFO's efforts in Mississippi: police harassment, obstructionism by voter registrars, FBI indifference to discrimination and violence, and local black fear of and deference to whites. Although CORE's organising helped fill the vacuum left by the repression of the NAACP in Louisiana, only 4,677 new voters registered in the state between 1962 and 1964.[2] As in Mississippi, most of CORE's field secretaries were indigenous African Americans, and they too had reservations about using white summer volunteers.

CORE and SNCC workers also began to realise, as local blacks had long known, that in the rural Deep South carrying weapons was necessary for those who challenged white dominance. After he had tried to register to vote in 1963, black farmer Hartman Turnbow's home in Holmes County, Mississippi, was attacked at night by two whites with Molotov cocktails. Turnbow drove the men off after an exchange of gunfire. SNCC and CORE field workers accepted the choice of local people involved in civil rights to defend themselves. By the summer of 1964, many field workers in Mississippi and Louisiana were themselves carrying guns.

COFO hoped that the Mississippi Summer Project would involve African Americans in the political process, reform the Democratic Party, and transform blacks' sense of their rights, history and capabilities after years of denigration and dominance by whites. In April 1964, COFO created the MFDP to challenge the right of the regular Mississippi

Democratic party, which excluded blacks, to represent the state at the national party's convention at Atlantic City, New Jersey, in August; and to run candidates in the June Democratic congressional primaries. The MFDP hoped to break the segregationist stranglehold on the Democratic Party in Mississippi, and to refashion it into a champion of political, economic and social justice. Begun in late June 1964, the Summer Project encompassed voter registration for both regular and parallel MFDP elections; freedom schools to offset the inferior, limited and limiting education available in black state schools; and community centres to help local people pursue their aims.

The NCC, which had recently taken over a voter registration project in Hattiesburg from the United Presbyterian Church, USA, sponsored two training sessions for Summer Project volunteers at Oxford, Ohio, in June. Approximately 650 students went to Mississippi during the course of the summer, about 10 per cent of them African American.[3] Women comprised a substantial minority of the volunteers, but they were restricted mostly to teaching and office work. Aside from the students, hundreds of other volunteers, most of them white, came to Mississippi for stays of up to two weeks. They included almost 150 lawyers and law students; 300 NCC clergymen who worked in local projects; and 100 medical staff.[4] Historian John Dittmer argues that the volunteers augmented a struggle that local people were already undertaking through statewide COFO projects. The volunteers' presence helped focus national attention on Mississippi and most of them made a positive contribution to the struggle.[5]

The large number of white volunteers exacerbated the anxieties of some black SNCC and CORE staff in Mississippi and Louisiana as they used white volunteers to assist summer voter registration drives in both states. Concerned African-American staff argued that whites not only tended to displace them from leadership and organisational positions but also that local blacks sometimes deferred to white volunteers, thereby perpetuating racial inequality. Some African-American staffers also questioned the volunteers' motives and their understanding of the cause. The increasing number of white SNCC personnel, many of whom had been volunteers, also produced concern. By mid-1964, 20 per cent of SNCC's approximately 150 field secretaries were white, compared with sixty mostly black staffers in late 1963.[6]

Although they should not be overplayed, there were also sexual tensions within the movement. Sexual relationships between white female volunteers and black male civil rights workers, whether they were the results of mutual attraction, white guilt, or black aggressiveness, alienated local blacks and black female workers alike.

However, in most cases, activists and volunteers worked cooperatively during the Mississippi Summer Project, and local blacks welcomed the white volunteers and the assistance they provided. With some exceptions, freedom schools proved to be a great success. Attended by 2,500 people of all ages in nearly fifty sites across Mississippi, the schools taught literacy, mathematics, citizenship, typing, languages, art, drama, and black history and culture.[7] They also encouraged their students to question existing structures of power and authority, and to conceptualise alternatives. Community centres, which sometimes housed freedom schools and roughly equalled them in number, offered various services, such as vocational and basic skills training, and libraries.

During the summer, 17,000 African Americans completed voter registration tests in Mississippi but only 1,600 succeeded in registering.[8] CORE's voter registration drive in Louisiana produced 1,070 black registrants and over 3,000 unsuccessful applications.[9] These disappointing results reflected continued obstructionism by white registrars, but also the deterrent affect of white violence and economic retaliation against black applicants. Support for the Ku Klux Klan rose in both Mississippi and Louisiana in 1963 and 1964, and the two states' Klans, which were closely linked, carried out a campaign of violence and intimidation.

By the time the Mississippi Summer Project terminated at the end of August 1964, four civil rights activists had been killed, four badly injured, and eighty beaten. There had been thirty-five firearms attacks, and sixty-five African-American churches and homes bombed or set ablaze. Determined to repel what they saw as invaders, Mississippi authorities had also arrested 1,000 civil rights workers.[10]

The fear and reality of violence led many, and probably most, SNCC and CORE field activists in Mississippi and north Louisiana to accept armed protection from local people and to carry guns themselves. In July, African Americans in Jonesboro, Louisiana, some of them war veterans, formed an armed organisation, the Deacons for Defense and Justice, to protect CORE. With three chapters, all in Louisiana, and probably less than 100 members, the Deacons offered essential but localised protection for CORE workers.

The Mississippi Summer Project failed to elicit large-scale federal intervention to protect civil rights workers and local blacks. However,

President Johnson acted after two CORE activists, Michael Schwerner, a Jewish New Yorker, and James Chaney, a black Mississippian, disappeared, along with white student volunteer Andrew Goodman, in Neshoba County in late June. Johnson ordered soldiers to search for the missing men, and he pressed the FBI to increase its presence in the state and to work assiduously on the case. After a tip-off by a paid informer, the FBI discovered the men's bodies in an earthen dam and later made nineteen arrests. Seven men, among them Neshoba County deputy sheriff Cecil Price and Sam Bowers, leader of the White Knights of the Ku Klux Klan of Mississippi, were eventually convicted in 1967 for 'violating the civil rights' of the three men, by which time FBI infiltration had severely weakened the Klan in Mississippi.[11] Many SNCC and CORE staff thought that the Johnson administration had acted quickly in the Neshoba case only because two whites had been murdered. This belief deepened the two groups' long-festering distrust of the federal government.

The MFDP's treatment at the Democratic Party's national convention provided further evidence for many SNCC and CORE workers that neither the federal government, nor the movement's white liberal allies could be trusted to place justice before expediency. To show black Mississippians that white dominance of the state Democratic Party could be challenged, the MFDP ran four candidates in the June 1964 Democratic congressional primaries. They lost heavily because of African-American disfranchisement, but their effort helped demystify politics. The MFDP also sought to participate in the regular party's precinct, county and state conventions that chose the regular state delegation to the national convention. Excluded from most of the regulars' meetings by a variety of subterfuges, the MFDP created a parallel, but nondiscriminatory, political structure to select its own delegation of sixty-four blacks and four whites to challenge the seating of the regulars in Atlantic City.

Chaired by Aaron Henry, with Fannie Lou Hamer as vice-chair, the MFDP delegation comprised sharecroppers, maids, mechanics, small independent farmers, businessmen and teachers. Women formed a third of its membership. The MFDP delegation asked to be seated in place of the regular state party delegation because, unlike the official Mississippi Democratic Party, the MFDP did not practise racial discrimination and pledged its loyalty to the national party. President Johnson feared that recognition of the MFDP delegation would lead to a walkout by delegates from the Deep South and might lose him southern white votes in the upcoming presidential election. Johnson's fears increased when Hamer made a powerful televised plea for MFDP recognition before the credentials committee that would decide the issue. The president held a hastily convened press conference in order to cut in to Hamer's live coverage. Nevertheless, Hamer's full testimony was later broadcast nationally. Hamer recounted her efforts to register to vote and the beating she had received in Winona jail, before concluding with the words, 'I question America, is this America, the land of the free and the home of the brave where we have to sleep with our telephones off the hooks because our lives be threatened daily because we want to live as decent human beings, in America?'[12]

Minority support on the credentials committee for the MFDP challenge raised the prospect that the issue might go to a convention vote. To avert the possibility of a divisive floor fight, the Johnson administration proposed a compromise whereby the MFDP would have two at-large seats at the convention, the regulars would be seated if they pledged loyalty to the national ticket, and the national party would eliminate racial discrimination by state delegations at subsequent conventions. Despite sustained pressure from Senator Hubert H. Humphrey, UAW leader Walter Reuther, the NCC, Roy Wilkins, and Whitney Young, the MFDP rejected the compromise as tokenism. Although Martin Luther King suggested that the MFDP should accept the deal, he also told the group that he would reject the compromise were he part of the MFDP delegation.

Despite its disappointment, the MFDP supported the Johnson ticket in the presidential election. The party also staged a challenge to Mississippi's congressmen by running a parallel freedom election, and then asking Congress to seat the MFDP's victorious candidates Annie Devine, Victoria Gray and Fannie Lou Hamer. The House of Representatives finally rejected the challenge by 228 votes to 143 in September 1965.

For many black SNCC and CORE field secretaries, the Atlantic City convention confirmed their experience that neither the national Democratic Party, nor white allies, could be relied upon. Bob Moses and other some veteran black civil rights workers began to reject integration and mainstream coalition politics as unrealistic and unappealing, and many field workers abandoned nonviolence for the same reasons. Inspired by the creation of the MFDP and freedom schools, many black SNCC veterans began to think in terms of creating independent black structures.

Northern Protests

Thwarted rising expectations, and frustration at the persistence of racism and inequality, stoked rising disaffection within SNCC and CORE. They also contributed in a different context to a series of urban ghetto riots, primarily in the North and West, between 1964 and 1968. During these years, 329 major riots occurred in 257 cities, leaving 220 people dead, 8,371 injured, and 52,629 under arrest.[13] The first of the riots broke out in New York City, two weeks after the signing of the 1964 Civil Rights Act. Sparked by the shooting of a black youth by an off-duty policeman, the week-long upheaval began in Harlem before spreading to Bedford-Stuyvesant. Riots followed soon after in Rochester, Philadelphia and some northeastern cities. Five days after the Voting Rights Act became law, a massive riot erupted in the Watts section of Los Angeles, resulting in 34 deaths, 1,000 people injured, and $200 million in property damage.[14] The National Guard was dispatched to Watts and also to riots that subsequently developed in Chicago and Springfield, Massachusetts. The summers of 1966 and 1967 witnessed riots in several major cities, including a colossal tumult in Detroit, which brought 43 deaths, 7,200 arrests and $50 million of property damage in 1967.[15] The last major series of riots occurred in 1968 and, like those a year before, broke out in halves of the country.

Frustrated African Americans rioted in response to police brutality, slum housing, high unemployment, inferior education and poverty, and to draw national attention to these conditions. In 1964, over 37 per cent of black families (and a little more than 15 per cent of white families) had incomes below the $3,000 federal poverty line.[16] The success of the civil rights movement in the South and President Johnson's declaration in 1964 of an 'unconditional war on poverty in America', which combined welfare benefits, education, health and local community action programmes, and job training, gave black ghetto dwellers hope that rioting might lead to positive change.[17] Although federal programmes and a strong economy reduced the number of poor Americans from 34.6 to 25.9 million between 1964 and 1967, Johnson's rhetoric also raised unrealistic expectations that could not be fulfilled.[18] The War on Poverty, part of Johnson's Great Society economic and social reform programme, was inadequately funded to meet its lofty goal, with the Office of Economic Opportunity (OEO), established by Johnson in 1964, receiving only $962.5 million in its first year, with half of the money derived from existing programmes.[19]

Johnson condemned the riots, but he also expressed concern about the socio-economic conditions that fostered them. Many white Americans were less understanding. The McCone Commission, appointed by California governor Pat Brown to investigate the Watts riot, conceded that blacks resented high unemployment, inferior education and hostile policing, but its report, nevertheless, argued that the rioters essentially comprised the underclass, leftists and black nationalist troublemakers whose actions the local population widely condemned. In reality, rioters and looters in Watts and elsewhere typically included a cross-section of the local population, enjoyed significant neighbourhood support or sympathy, and were motivated by a heightened but frustrated desire to be included in the political and economic mainstream.

The riots helped to focus the SCLC's attention on the North. Invited by the local Council of Churches, SCLC staff visited Rochester, New York, after the 1964 riot, but they found the antipathy of young blacks towards nonviolence so great that they withdrew after conducting a short programme. However, after its success in Selma, the SCLC decided, with King's enthusiastic support, that it would conduct a project in the North and considered various locales. The Watts riot subsequently brought a new urgency to the SCLC's deliberations. King wanted to show ghetto blacks that nonviolent protest could work in the North and so avert further riots, which only hurt the community. Consequently, the SCLC accepted an invitation from the Coordinating Council of Community Organizations (CCCO), a coalition of forty Chicago civil rights groups, to bolster the Council's unsuccessful two-year effort to end the city's *de facto* school segregation and improve schooling.

Determined to move north, the SCLC accepted the only clear request that it had received, confident that the CCCO formed a cohesive movement. Chicago's three million population included 700,000 African Americans, most of whom were confined to the ghettoes of the South and West Sides. The city's size posed significant organisational problems for the SCLC, which, in any case, was oriented towards dramatic protests, rather than the time-consuming and often unrewarding task of community organising. Moreover, Mayor Richard J. Daley was a deft operator, who headed a Democratic political machine based on white working-class and black support. Daley's hold over black voters, forged by dispensing a slice of municipal employment and services to them and by cultivating black political leaders, had enabled him to ignore the

CCCO. King erroneously believed that a combination of moral exhortation and calculated nonviolent protest could sway the wily Daley, and that the mayor controlled a power structure that could deliver the changes King wanted.

James Bevel undertook three months' preparatory work on Chicago's West Side in late 1965. Bevel formed tenant unions, which he hoped would give ghetto residents a sense of agency, break their allegiance to the Daley machine, and enable them to confront the discriminatory policies of the Chicago Real Estate Board (CREB) that perpetuated residential segregation and ensured that blacks paid high rents for dilapidated housing. However, the West Side was too big to organise effectively, and in Chicago clergymen and the church lacked the same authority and community outreach that the SCLC had depended on in the South. As in Rochester, African-American youths were often hostile to interracialism and nonviolence, and, even when some SCLC workers began emphasising racial pride, they had little success in bringing black Chicago's numerous teenage gangs onside.

While Bevel and an SCLC team worked on the West Side, Jesse Jackson enjoyed greater success in developing a job creation programme. Modelled on an SCLC project in Atlanta, Operation Breadbasket used economic boycotts to pressure white employers to hire blacks and later to ensure that white companies included black businesses among their contactors. Born in South Carolina, Jackson had participated in the 1963 Greensboro direct-action campaign while at the North Carolina Agricultural and Technical State University. After graduation, he had enrolled at the Chicago Baptist Theological Seminary. Jackson joined the SCLC's staff after participating in the Selma campaign.

Jackson met King at the airport in January 1966, when he arrived to head the SCLC's Chicago campaign. King proposed a series of direct-action protests that he hoped would be supported by an alliance of religious leaders, unions and white liberals. He intended the protests to pressure the city to end school and residential segregation, and Congress to pass an open housing bill that the Johnson administration had sponsored. However, Mayor Daley proved adept at blunting the attacks of the Chicago Freedom Movement (CFM), which the CCCO and the SCLC formed to coordinate their campaign. Although he conceded nothing in practice, Daley expressed sympathy with the movement's concerns, publicised the city's efforts to improve slums and promised to cooperate. Many blacks remained loyal to the Daley machine or simply apathetic as the CFM launched the direct-action phase of its campaign in July 1966, which focused on housing discrimination. Before the first marches began, a black riot broke out in which two people died and eighty suffered injuries. Daley falsely accused the SCLC of encouraging the riot, which ended after Governor Otto Kerner dispatched the National Guard to the city.

Despite the riot, the SCLC pressed ahead with planned marches into Chicago's white neighbourhoods. The SCLC expected that their lower-class inhabitants would respond with hostility and violence, and that in the ensuing crisis Daley would meet the CFM's demands. As anticipated, whites showered the marchers with bottles, bricks, rocks and abuse. The residents considered themselves to be defending their cohesive ethnic neighbourhoods from outside invasion, and they feared that should African Americans move in from adjoining ghettoes, rising crime and falling house prices would follow. While Daley felt compelled to provide the marchers with police protection, the demonstrations threatened to undermine the lower-class white and black electoral coalition which sustained his machine. Similarly, while supportive of the CFM's aims, John Cody, the Catholic Archbishop of Chicago, and the leadership of the UAW, worried that the campaign was splitting their respective memberships and appealed for an end to the protests.

Daley readily agreed to a summit meeting with the CFM, the CREB and other interested parties. To maintain pressure on Daley during the negotiations, the CFM scheduled further marches, but the mayor obtained an injunction limiting their size and frequency in the city. Consequently, the CFM held marches outside city limits, and King announced that he would lead a march into Cicero, a racist white suburb where fierce resistance seemed inevitable. The prospect helped produce a ten-point agreement on 26 August 1966 in return for a cessation of marches.

As Fairclough observes, 'the Summit Agreement amounted to little more than various pledges of nondiscrimination' by the city and its various departments, without a schedule for action, or an effective means of enforcement.[20] The city restated its commitment to a fair housing ordinance, adopted in 1963, and the Chicago Commission on Human Relations agreed to 'a significantly higher level of effective enforcement activity' regarding the neglected ordinance.[21] Relevant city departments would not racially discriminate in allocating public housing, which would henceforth be built in more dispersed parts of the city. The Chicago Conference on Race and Religion agreed to develop an educative programme for open housing. Although the CREB accepted the 'philosophy of open occupancy legislation at the state level', it refused to abandon a legal appeal against the city's own nondiscriminatory ordinance.[22]

King's acceptance of the agreement reflected a naïve faith that it would be honoured, his reluctance to expose his followers to extreme violence by marching into Cicero, and sensitivity to opposition to the marches from white religious and trade union leaders who otherwise supported the CCCO. After King left Chicago, the city ignored the agreement, Daley's biracial support secured his re-election in April 1967 and the CCCO disintegrated. Daley had succeeded in outmanoeuvreing and outlasting King, and in avoiding a politically damaging clash with powerful banking and real estate interests. Since Daley had managed the crisis and acted to protect the marchers and contain disorder, the federal government had not intervened as it had done earlier in Birmingham and Selma. Furthermore, Johnson regarded the Daley machine as a political ally and the president's relationship with King had deteriorated because of personality clashes and King's muted but growing opposition to American escalation in the Vietnam War.

Fairclough characterises the campaign in Chicago as a defeat for the SCLC, which failed to achieve its objective of open housing, although he notes that Operation Breadbasket became a successful programme.[23] Historian James R. Ralph, Jr, concedes these points, and notes that King, himself, subsequently, wondered whether the campaign should have had a more realistic objective, or marched into Cicero.[24] Nevertheless, Ralph maintains that the Chicago campaign demonstrated the SCLC's capacity to organise northern urban dwellers in a nonviolent direct-action protest that highlighted the neglected issue of *de facto* segregation. The SCLC generated 'national debate about housing discrimination just as Congress was considering legislation to promote equal housing opportunity'.[25]

Ralph notes that the campaign failed to generate northern white demands for Congress to pass the civil rights bill that President Johnson had proposed in April 1966, in response to long-standing pressure from the Leadership Conference on Civil Rights and liberals in both parties to strengthen Kennedy's 1962 Executive Order on housing.[26] Johnson included both sale and rental accommodation in his bill, and federal protection for civil rights workers. However, moderates in the House of Representatives weakened the measure by excluding home owners and sales agents. Southern senators filibustered the bill, which had little support, in September 1966. Although the bill's failure was in part a product of popular white and congressional reaction against black riots and recent calls by SNCC and CORE for Black Power, of greater importance was significant white opposition to housing desegregation and a belief that home owners had an inviolable right to dispose of their property as they chose without interference from government. The civil rights movement could no longer count on mobilising northern white support after switching from attacking *de jure* discrimination in the South to confronting *de facto* segregation in the North.

Even before the 1960s, white working-class and lower middle-class city dwellers had repeatedly responded with hostility and violence when African Americans attempted to move into white neighbourhoods. Pressure on limited city housing stock increased with the resumption of mass southern black migration to the urban North in the 1940s and postwar decades as African Americans sought industrial employment. Historian Thomas J. Sugrue found over 200 incidents against blacks, who relocated to white areas of Detroit, 'between the Second World War and the 1960s'. Such activity included 'harassment, mass demonstrations, picketing, effigy burning, window breaking, arson, vandalism, and physical attacks'.[27] Anxious to protect their communities from the perceived criminality and licentiousness of African Americans, whites formed neighbourhood associations and elected segregationists to replace racially liberal politicians. Arnold R. Hirsch records that Chicago also witnessed many attacks on blacks who moved into formerly white neighbourhoods during the 1940s and 1950s.[28] Hence, white resistance in both cities to open housing in the 1960s was part of a continuum dating back at least to the 1940s. Furthermore, Stephen Grant Meyer demonstrates that since the beginning of the Great Migration earlier in the century, white Americans across the US had generally opposed African-American attempts to move into white neighbourhoods.[29]

Signs of a growing white backlash against civil rights and a liberal interventionist federal government that supported them were apparent in 1964. George Wallace, the ambitious segregationist governor of Alabama, entered three Democratic presidential primaries. A foe of the civil rights bill, Wallace campaigned as a states' rights politician, who opposed a government that centralised power in Washington DC and interfered in local schools, private businesses and neighbourhoods. He won 34 per cent of the poll (some 264,000 votes) in the Wisconsin primary and 29.8 per cent in Indiana. Both states allowed cross-over voting, and Wallace drew support from Republican suburbs and white working-class areas.

He also chalked up 42.7 per cent of the vote in Maryland.[30] In the same year, California voters rejected open housing legislation, and two years later they elected conservative Republican Ronald Reagan governor.

According to a 1966 poll, 51 per cent of white Americans opposed and 49 per cent favoured an open housing law, reflecting a division not only about integration but also about the idea of government compulsion. Opposition to fair housing legislation among low-income whites stood at 69 per cent, compared with support from 61 per cent of upper-income earners.[31] Whites in the lower-income bracket felt themselves to be directly in competition with African Americans for housing, schooling and employment, and they knew that it was their neighbourhoods that would mostly likely be affected by fair housing legislation and school desegregation.

Many whites argued that their taxes paid for Great Society and welfare programmes that fostered dependency and benefited the undeserving poor, particularly African Americans, who formed a disproportionate number of the impoverished. In September 1965, a Gallup poll found that 88 per cent of whites believed that blacks should advance through self-improvement, education and hard work, rather than by government assistance.[32] Many whites also resented the fact that cities subject to rioting received the greatest proportion of federal anti-poverty monies. Rather than rewarding rioters, disgruntled whites argued that the federal government should secure law and order. Such antipathy helped bring Republican gains in the November 1966 congressional elections; the Democrats lost forty-seven seats in the House and three in the Senate.[33] Demands for Black Power, first popularised during the Meredith March in June 1966, also contributed to the backlash.

Black Power

The origins of the call for Black Power lay primarily in the experience of black SNCC and CORE workers in the rural South, the influence of Black Muslim preacher Malcolm X upon them and black youth more generally, and an influx of black nationalists into SNCC and CORE in the mid-1960s. In some ways a continuation of the civil rights movement's concerns and in others a departure from them, Black Power divided the national civil rights coalition, alienated white movement supporters, destroyed SNCC, decimated CORE, produced a range of competing visions, and fanned an already advanced white reaction against black demands for the substance of equality. Black Power was part of a new wave of black nationalism which boosted black pride, consciousness and identity, but enjoyed little success politically. Along with Black Power, the Vietnam War, escalated by President Johnson in 1965, also fractured the national civil rights coalition. The war became a consuming issue for Martin Luther King that set him against the Johnson administration, diverted federal money and effort from fighting poverty, and absorbed the energies of many of the civil rights movement's white supporters.

Following years of patient organising in extremely dangerous conditions for little practical change in the lives of the rural black poor, many black SNCC and some black CORE field workers in the South had begun by the end of 1964 to reject nonviolence and integration into mainstream America and its institutions. Some black veterans suggested that the movement should primarily be black organised and led. Even some staff who remained committed to nonviolence and integration, notably John Lewis, shared these views.

SNCC also developed links with black nationalist Malcolm X. Born Malcolm Little in Omaha, Nebraska, in 1925, as a young child he had attended UNIA meetings with his footloose, illiterate, self-ordained father. After his father died, supposedly the victim of a racist attack, and his mother entered an asylum, Little moved to Boston and into petty crime, hustling and drugs, until he was jailed for burglary. Encouraged by his siblings, Little joined the Nation of Islam, or Black Muslims, during his incarceration. Founded in 1930, the Black Muslims were led by Elijah Poole, a Georgia railway worker who had moved to Detroit and become a follower of Wallace D. Fard, an itinerant peddler, who fused orthodox Islam with black supremacy and then mysteriously disappeared in 1934. Shedding his 'slave' Anglo-name, Poole became Elijah Muhammad and propagated Fard's teachings that whites were an aberrant devil race whose rule a black Allah would eventually overturn before restoring the earth to blacks, its original possessors.

The Black Muslims followed an austere code of personal behaviour that emphasised self-discipline, hard work and devotion to Elijah Muhammad as the messenger of God. Little, now renamed Malcolm X to signify that his 'true African family name' was unknown, was a devoted convert.[34] A gifted minister, speaker and organiser, he contributed significantly to the growth of Black Muslim membership, located primarily in the urban North, from several hundred to as many as 15,000 or more during the 1950s and early 1960s. In line with Elijah Muhammad's teachings, Malcolm X called for a separate black state, emphasised racial pride and condemned whites as responsible for all the ills of the black community. A source of fear and fascination for the white media, Malcolm X gained ready access to its outlets, and displayed his sharp mind and polemical ability. Savagely critical of the integrationist goals, leaders and nonviolent methods of the civil rights movement, he asserted the right of black people to achieve freedom by any means necessary, and championed the right to armed self-defence and liberation. His militant rhetoric enthralled many ghetto dwellers, particularly black youth, who found the civil rights movement's message alien and its goals irrelevant to their lives.

According to biographer Bruce Perry, Malcolm X privately relinquished the white devil theory after a 1959 visit to the Middle East. He also chafed at Elijah Muhammad's instructions to avoid civil rights and political involvement, and for several years maintained a pained, but discreet, silence about his leader's serial womanising and high living. Publicly silenced in late 1963 by Elijah Muhammad, who felt threatened by his popularity, Malcolm X subsequently left the Muslims. After a visit to Mecca in 1964, he publicly rejected racist teachings, converted to orthodox Islam, taking the name El-Hajj Malik El-Shabazz, and gradually distanced himself from racial separatism. Without specifying means, he urged blacks to gain control of political, economic, educational and cultural institutions in their communities, and, in so doing, he anticipated the call for Black Power, which also borrowed heavily from his earlier emphasis on separatism, liberation through violence and denunciation of whites. In vain, he pressed African countries to internationalise the struggle against American racism by bringing the issue before the UN. He created two blacks-only religious and secular organisations, which recruited poorly and struggled financially. Nevertheless, after Malcolm X was shot dead by three Black Muslims in New York in February 1965, between 14,000 and 30,000 people viewed his coffin.[35] His bestselling autobiography appeared a few months later, and widened his influence.

In the last months of his life, Malcolm X had found some common ground with SNCC. He admired SNCC's radicalism, and the organisation's growing inclination towards self-defence, racial solidarity and Pan-Africanism accorded with his ideas. A SNCC delegation toured Guinea in September 1964 by invitation of its government. Two of the group extended their tour in Africa and had a chance encounter with

Malcolm X in Nairobi in October 1964. Thereafter, Malcolm X made overtures to SNCC, which resulted in him addressing an MFDP gathering in Harlem and, shortly before his death, black protesters in Selma.

As CORE became more involved in northern ghettoes, it also became increasingly influenced by black nationalism, the idea of black-community control of local institutions and the Nation of Islam. Primarily a white organisation, with a substantial Jewish presence, the character of CORE was changing not only with the growth of indigenous black CORE activists in the South, but also as CORE chapters in the North began focusing on ghetto issues, such as jobs, housing, education and racist policing, using direct-action techniques and civil disobedience. CORE's new direction attracted a growing African-American membership, with the result that by 1964 CORE's National Action Committee was 80 per cent black.[36]

While CORE began to move in a black nationalist direction, SNCC became increasingly divided and introspective after the disappointments of the Mississippi Summer Project. SNCC's staff were unsure of their future direction and some questioned whether desegregation and voting rights would in themselves transform the lives of rural black southerners. They also disagreed about polity. Floaters advocated SNCC's traditional decentralised, and often spontaneous, approach to organising. By contrast, hard-liners argued that SNCC, which had more than doubled its staff since 1963, needed discipline and centralised authority if it were to help African Americans achieve true equality. Bob Moses, who might have enabled the floaters to prevail by virtue of his intellectual capacity and legendary status as an organiser, withdrew from SNCC in 1965. Although the dispute between floaters and hard-liners remained unresolved, James Forman began to exert a growing influence in SNCC, supported by hard-liners Ruby Doris Smith Robinson, the group's administrative secretary, and Cleveland Sellers, its programme secretary. A skilled administrator who was also older than most SNCC staff, Forman had served in the Korean War and possessed a management degree. SNCC's executive secretary since 1961, he wanted to transform the group into a mass organisation, but many SNCC field workers continued to refuse direction from the centre.

Assisted by less than 200 white volunteers, SNCC undertook a second summer programme in Mississippi in 1965.[37] But internal racial tensions hampered the project. The state NAACP withdrew from COFO in 1965, anxious not to lose its identity and pre-eminence to the SNCC–MFDP dominated coalition. SNCC wound up COFO in July, and handed COFO's resources over to the MFDP. SNCC reasoned that the NAACP's withdrawal and the emergence of the indigenous MFDP had rendered COFO obsolete, but COFO's collapse also led SNCC and CORE to disengage from the state.

However, civil rights activity continued in Mississippi, primarily under the auspices of the NAACP, the MFDP and the Delta Ministry. Launched by the NCC in September 1964 as a ten-year programme to help the black poor, the Delta Ministry focused on voter registration, relief, health, economic development and community assistance in the Mississippi Delta, with shorter-lived projects in McComb and Hattiesburg. Staffed largely by northern white Protestant clergymen in its early years, the Ministry worked closely with the MFDP, but it also cooperated with the NAACP. The NCC project helped fill the void left by the gradual withdrawal of CORE and SNCC from Mississippi.

In 1965, the Ministry helped initiate the Child Development Group of Mississippi (CDGM), one of the first OEO-funded Head Start projects that were designed to help preschool children from deprived backgrounds. Open to but rejected by whites, CDGM provided thousands of African-American children with educational assistance, medical care and nutrition, and employed poor blacks as teacher aides. Speaking in Washington for Mississippi's conservative white politicians, Senator John Stennis sought to kill the programme. Vastly overstating the case, Stennis accused CDGM of fiscal mismanagement, but his real objection was to the presence of civil rights activists in CDGM and the programme's transference of several million dollars of federal funds, outside the control of white Mississippi, to African Americans. With Stennis's support needed for its domestic programmes and the war in Vietnam, in 1966 the Johnson administration began channelling Head Start grants primarily to Mississippi Action for Progress, a new group supported by the Mississippi NAACP and the state's moderate white Democrats. CDGM survived with diminished federal funding, but OEO slashed the national Head Start budget in 1968.

War on Poverty funds had a mixed impact on the civil rights movement. OEO's Community Action Program (CAP) was intended to allow the maximum feasible participation of the poor in local anti-poverty programmes. In some places, OEO funds fuelled activism, provided civil rights workers with employment, and gave blacks valuable political experience on CAP-governing boards. But in other places, rival black factions competed for federal funds in bruising internecine battles that retarded the progress of the black community. White political and business elites, in both urban and rural areas, sometimes exploited black divisions by coopting moderate blacks. In other cases, white elites secured control of anti-poverty funds directly by denying the poor representation on CAPS, notably in Atlanta, or by appealing to the Johnson administration, which proved unwilling to upset Democratic mayors. The War on Poverty had little effect, at least initially, in relieving black poverty in the rural Deep South. In Mississippi, the food stamp programme reduced the number of people receiving federal food aid by 63,915 between April 1966 and April 1967.[38] Many blacks who had previously received free surplus federal commodities in winter could not afford to buy the food stamps that replaced them and were redeemable for a value in goods substantially above their purchase price.

Poverty pervaded the Black Belt. Situated between Selma and Montgomery, Lowndes County, Alabama, typified the problem. A wealthy white planter elite wielded political and economic power in this majority black county, while most African-American residents remained impoverished. In March 1965, SNCC began a project in the county that was to bring its organiser Stokely Carmichael to the forefront of the group and mark another step towards SNCC's adoption of black nationalism and repudiation of nonviolence.

Born in the West Indies but raised in New York City, Carmichael had been beaten many times during his organising work in the South, which he had fitted around studies at Howard University in Washington before joining SNCC full time in 1964. Influenced by New York leftists, Carmichael was a socialist. Wary of the problems white volunteers could bring, he had tried to recruit an all-black staff for the district he organised during the Mississippi Summer Project.

Following meetings with a contingent from the SCLC during the Selma campaign, local black men and women had formed the Lowndes County Christian Movement for Human Rights (LCCMHR), led by John Hulett. A local man, Hulett had returned home in 1959 for personal reasons, having served as a foundry worker, union activist and NAACP member in Birmingham, Alabama. Like Hulett, many of the new organisation's members owned their own homes and had previous organising experience, often in churches or fraternal lodges.

Carmichael began a SNCC project in Lowndes County, shortly after the Selma to Montgomery March had passed through it. A gifted organiser and communicator, he established a good working relationship with the LCCMHR, while he and other SNCC workers undertook a voter registration campaign. Local black farmers often provided armed protection for rallies, but Carmichael, at first, remained personally committed to nonviolence. However, in August, a local white man murdered Jonathan Daniels. A white Episcopal seminary student from New Hampshire, Daniels had assisted SNCC as an unofficial volunteer, after Carmichael and the SNCC team had decided that Daniels's personal qualities outweighed concerns about his race. Angry at the murder, Carmichael declared: 'We're going to tear this county up. We're going to build it back, until it's a fit place for human beings.'[39]

At Carmichael's suggestion, Hulett and LCCMHR members formed the Lowndes County Freedom Organization (LCFO) in April 1966, because, potentially, the county's black majority could elect a black slate of candidates to office, and the Democratic Party of Alabama was publicly committed to white supremacy. Open to whites, the LCFO was, in practice, an independent all-black group. To signify its determination, the LCFO adopted a snarling black panther as its symbol. Aided by federal registrars, dispatched under the Voting Rights Act, SNCC and the LCFO soon registered enough African Americans to outnumber white voters. However, LCFO candidates did not win any posts until 1968 because of apathy and fear among some blacks, and intimidation and electoral fraud by whites. Although SNCC workers generally avoided making separatist appeals in the county during 1966, the LCFO was a sign of a growing orientation within SNCC ranks towards black consciousness and the creation of independent black community institutions.

Carmichael left the county after he became SNCC's chairman in May 1966. Carmichael's election in place of John Lewis, and also that of Ruby Doris Smith Robinson as executive secretary, reflected a growing militancy within SNCC. With its faith in white liberals exhausted by its experiences, SNCC immediately withdrew from the White House Conference on Civil Rights scheduled for June. The conference went ahead but had no impact on federal policy.

SNCC had criticised President Johnson's decision to escalate American involvement in Vietnam with bombing raids and mass deployment of troops in 1965. In April 1965, SNCC's executive committee endorsed the 'Spring Mobilization' in Washington, the first large-scale protest against the war. SNCC issued a stinging condemnation of the war in January

1966, linking the conflict with the struggle of the world's nonwhite peoples to free themselves from white oppression. In the same month, the Georgia legislature refused to seat Julian Bond, an Atlanta-based SNCC veteran, because of his anti-war position. Soon after, SNCC launched the Vine City project in Bond's black ghetto district. Racial separatists, half of them from the North, staffed the project and strengthened SNCC's increasingly nationalist direction.

Growing militancy in SNCC and CORE became readily and publicly apparent during the Meredith March in June 1966. James Meredith, who had desegregated the University of Mississippi in 1962, survived a murder attempt by a white segregationist, soon after beginning a lone march from Memphis, Tennessee, to Jackson, Mississippi, that he hoped would encourage black Mississippians to register and vote. Determined to continue the march, the national leaders of the SCLC, SNCC, CORE, the NAACP and the NUL converged on Memphis, where Meredith lay hospitalised. Roy Wilkins and Whitney Young wanted to use the march to generate support for the Johnson administration's civil rights bill, then under discussion in Congress. In what he later claimed was a calculated effort to force Wilkins and Young to withdraw, Carmichael launched a vigorous personal attack on the two men and insisted that the march should protest against the inadequate civil rights policy of their ally, the Johnson administration. He also demanded that the armed Deacons for Defense and Justice be included and whites barred from the demonstration. Disgusted, Wilkins and Young returned to New York.

As Carmichael had hoped, Martin Luther King opted to stay. King agreed a compromise with Carmichael and Floyd McKissick, a black nationalist who been elected CORE's leader in January 1966 after James Farmer resigned to join a War on Poverty literacy programme. The march included both the Deacons and whites, and it adopted a manifesto that called on the Johnson administration to enforce existing federal civil rights legislation, dispatch federal registrars to every Deep South county, increase spending on rural and urban poverty, and stiffen the civil rights bill by speeding up integration of southern juries and policing agencies.

The MFDP and the Delta Ministry assisted the march, which meandered through the Delta, and eventually registered 4,077 people along its route.[40] The protest proceeded untroubled, until Greenwood police arrested Carmichael and two other SNCC workers. On his release a few hours later, Carmichael declared that the state's courthouses should be burned and then, encouraged by SNCC worker Willie Ricks, persuaded an increasingly enthusiastic crowd to repeat his demand for Black Power. King feared that despite its popularity among blacks on the march route, Black Power would exacerbate the civil rights movement's problems. When McKissick supported Carmichael at a meeting of SCLC, SNCC and CORE staff in Yazoo City, King warned them to avoid a phrase 'that would confuse our allies, isolate the Negro community and give many prejudiced whites, who might otherwise be ashamed of their anti-Negro feeling, a ready excuse for self-justification'.[41] Although Carmichael had great personal respect for King, he refused to stop advocating Black Power.

The national press latched on to the Black Power slogan and condemned its use. White Mississippi opposition to the march also grew increasingly hostile. In Canton, state troopers attacked the marchers with tear gas and rifle butts, because they had defied an order not to pitch their tents at a local black school. Although the police riot in Canton was comparable to that at Selma a year before, the Johnson administration refused to act to protect those who had criticised its record. The march concluded in Jackson with an outward show of unity that barely masked the widening divisions within the movement revealed by the demand for Black Power.

In the months following the march, Carmichael began to define Black Power, which culminated in a book co-written with black political scientist Charles V. Hamilton, *Black Power: The Politics of Liberation in America*, in 1967. The book urged African Americans to unite by recognising their common culture and history, and called for black self-determination and control of community institutions.[42] The authors argued that blacks should close ranks, like white ethnic groups, and achieve bargaining power 'in a pluralistic society'.[43] Yet, at the same time, the book contended that black ghettoes constituted internal colonies that helped sustain the American economy by providing it with cheap labour and a market for products.[44] However, the ghettoes were of little economic importance to corporate America, especially with advancing automation, and the notion of oppressed internal colonies conflicted with a pluralistic conception of America.[45] *Black Power* rejected alliances with white liberals to tackle poverty, but, in their place, offered only the unlikely prospect of an eventual biracial alliance of the poor.[46]

Carmichael tended to tailor his message to his audience, redefining Black Power as it suited his purpose. Before ghetto audiences, Carmichael moved towards black separatism, and he was given to incendiary rhetoric. Shortly after a race riot in 1966, Carmichael told blacks in Cleveland that 'When you talk about black power, you talk about bringing this country to its knees. When you talk of black power, you talk of building a movement that will smash everything Western civilization has created.'[47]

However, Carmichael still saw a role for whites within SNCC, contending that they should work against racism in white communities. Consequently, Carmichael argued, along with Forman and Fannie Lou Hamer, against demands from the Atlanta staff in December 1966 that SNCC expel whites. However, the resolution was passed by nineteen votes to eighteen, with twenty-four abstentions.[48]

CORE followed a similar, albeit reformist, trajectory to SNCC. At its 1966 convention, CORE asserted the right to self-defence, condemned America's war in Vietnam, and endorsed Black Power, which it defined in terms of black capitalism and 'control of economic, political, and educational institutions and resources, from top to bottom, by black people in their own areas'.[49] By the end of the year, most whites had left the group. In 1968, CORE officially excluded the few whites who remained and adopted racial separatism under Roy Innis, its new national director.The adoption of Black Power cost CORE the white financial support on which it depended, and ensured the organisation's rapid decline.

SNCC's rapidly dwindling finances were a product not only of white opposition to Black Power but also of its white financial supporters focusing instead on opposing the Vietnam War. In 1968, a withered, ineffectual SNCC entered a brief, ill-fated merger with the Black Panther Party, founded in Oakland, California, in 1966 by violent petty criminal Huey P. Newton and Bobby Seale. Opposed to police brutality, the Panthers, who took their name from the LCFO's emblem, mounted armed surveillance of police patrols in Oakland. Heavily influenced by Malcolm X and by Robert Williams, who had been suspended by the national NAACP in 1959 for endorsing black armed self-defence and later called for guerilla warfare from exile abroad, the Panthers advocated armed self-defence, self-determination and economic justice for African Americans. Newton also organised a protection racket. He was jailed after killing a police officer in 1967. Party publicist and ex-convict Eldridge Cleaver organised a Free Huey campaign that turned Newton into a hero, enlarged the small group's membership and profile, and generated financial support from some rich white sympathisers.

Committed to racial pride, significant elements of the Panthers nevertheless opposed what they regarded as the distracting apolitical approach of cultural nationalism. Championed, among others, by Maulana Ron Karenga on the West Coast, who founded Us, and by poet LeRoi Jones on the East Coast, cultural nationalists sought to liberate blacks psychologically by giving them a positive sense of identity that included African art forms and dress, Afro hairstyles, and even learning Swahili. Historian William L. Van Deburg argues that Black Power made its greatest and most enduring contribution in the intellectual and cultural sphere by increasing black self-worth and identity, and fostering black studies in schools and universities.[50]

Van Deburg also notes that Black Power was multifaceted and ambiguous, which partly accounted for its appeal since blacks and their leaders could interpret it as they wished.[51] Black Power's rejection of integration, nonviolence and coalitions with white liberals marked a departure from the mainstream of the civil rights movement. However, as historian Richard King has noted, both 'the Southern civil rights movement and the (largely) Northern- and Western-based black pride and black consciousness movements which appeared in the late 1960s and early 1970s' shared 'the goal of constructing a new sense of self and of black culture'.[52] Van Deburg argues that the civil rights and Black Power movements were 'more compatible than contradictory', and that Black Power was 'a logical progression of the civil rights advocates' efforts to achieve dignity, equality, and freedom of choice in their adopted homeland'.[53] According to historian Clayborne Carson, 'many local activists' believed that 'a black freedom movement seeking generalized racial advancement evolved into a black power movement toward the unachieved goals of the earlier movement'.[54]

Citizenship education and freedom school classes had sought to engender black pride, identity and psychological freedom by teaching black history and culture. Martin Luther King and SNCC had linked the struggle of African Americans with that of nonwhites everywhere. Both civil rights and Black Power advocates wanted blacks to have freedom of thought and action. Furthermore, many southern blacks, particularly in the rural Deep South, considered armed self-defence essential to protect themselves and civil rights workers from racist attack.

However, they did not indulge in 'the rhetorical violence and racism of some black militants', that Carson concluded, prompted 'more effective repression' of the black struggle by the FBI in the late 1960s, and 'spurred the increasing popularity among whites of "law and order" politics', with the result that 'the black power movement … promised more than the civil rights movement but delivered less'.[55]

While most whites viewed Black Power negatively, a sizeable proportion of blacks supported it, and they often saw no contradiction between civil rights and Black Power. A 1967 survey in Detroit found that 57.8 per cent of whites and 16.5 per cent of blacks associated Black Power with black supremacy, racism, rioting and disorder, whereas 42.2 per cent of blacks and 10.7 per cent of whites interpreted Black Power favourably as meaning a 'fair share for black people' and 'racial (black) unity'.[56] Eighty-six per cent of Detroit's blacks supported integration, including many of those who viewed Black Power positively, and only 1 per cent of the city's African Americans favoured racial separatism.[57] Most southern blacks, raised in a Christian tradition of forbearance and forgiveness, rejected the anti-white, separatist connotations of Black Power. Southern activism for equality and justice continued through established means, such as protests, boycotts and legal challenges, and by using newly won opportunities for political participation.[58]

Although Roy Wilkins condemned Black Power as 'a reverse Mississippi, a reverse Hitler, a reverse Ku Klux Klan', the national NAACP also argued that it had long endorsed the right of self-defence.[59] Like Wilkins, Whitney Young continued to argue that African Americans could only advance with support from white liberal allies and the federal government. Nevertheless, in 1968 he endorsed Black Power in so far as it meant 'self-determination – pride – self respect – participation and control of one's destiny and community affairs', and the NUL's New Thrust programme focused on developing economic and political power in the ghetto.[60]

The Poor People's Campaign

Martin Luther King remained committed to nonviolence and integration. He criticised Black Power as implying separatism, violence and reverse racism. In essence, it was, he wrote, 'a nihilistic philosophy born out of the conviction that the Negro can't win'.[61] However, King agreed with Carmichael and Hamilton that blacks needed to develop group strength, as other ethnic groups had done, and thereby achieve bargaining power. King also regarded the ghettoes as internal colonies exploited by white capitalists. He recognised that Black Power addressed a psychological need for blacks to develop a full sense of their history, 'dignity and worth', after centuries of disparagement by white culture.[62] By 1966, King privately espoused democratic socialism. In 1967, he publicly called for a massive redistribution of wealth and power in America and advocated an interracial alliance of the poor. King died as he planned to bring that alliance to Washington DC in a Poor People's Campaign of civil disobedience.

King's increasing radicalism developed from his shocked realisation that racism deeply pervaded the entire nation, and from his opposition to the Vietnam War. In the Chicago campaign, King had experienced more virulent racism than he had in the South, and the long festering white backlash had revealed the depth of national white opposition to open housing, fair employment and fully integrated education. King had called for a negotiated end to the Vietnam War soon after America escalated its involvement in 1965, but he had muted his public criticism of the war after the SCLC failed to support him and President Johnson appealed for King's silence, citing secret peace negotiations. King feared upsetting patriotic blacks who otherwise supported him, rupturing his alliance with the federal government, and offending the NAACP and the NUL, which refused to look beyond domestic racial discrimination.

In 1966, Congress cut OEO's budget by half a billion dollars, reducing CAP funding by a third.[63] Washington increasingly channelled federal monies to supporting the conflict in southeast Asia. With justice, King argued that the war in Vietnam was destroying the War on Poverty. Recipient of a Nobel Peace Prize in 1964, King also felt he had a commitment to speak out against injustice everywhere. He was appalled by American violence in Vietnam on behalf of what he viewed as a corrupt regime that was opposed by a popular nationalist uprising led by Ho Chi Minh. King believed that in southeast Asia, as in Latin America and Africa, America supported dictatorships that allowed western capitalists exploitative access to resources and markets. He concluded that the needs of multinational companies underlay American and western support for racism, economic extortion and military force.

In February 1967, King focused an entire speech on criticising the war. At New York City's Riverside Church two months later, he argued that America had become 'the greatest purveyor of violence in the world today'.[64] King characterised leftist revolutionary movements in the developing world as legitimate responses to western colonialism and neocolonialism, and he urged his country to withdraw from Vietnam and offer reparations. By then, he had long since refused invitations to the

White House. Predictably, King's renewed criticism of the war infuriated Johnson, led the FBI to step up its long-standing efforts to discredit King, and brought condemnation from the NAACP and the NUL. The SCLC also suffered a large drop in donations, which, by the end of May, had cost the organisation a third of its staff.[65]

A loose amalgam of different groups that agreed on little except Vietnam, the anti-war movement lacked unity. King hoped to breach the divide by addressing the National Convention for New Politics, which sought to forge a popular alternative to the two major parties. In August 1967, 3,500 delegates, mainly from white leftist groups, met in Chicago. Many of them regarded King as a spent mainstream figure and greeted his speech with derision. The convention itself foundered after blacks insisted on taking a half-share of the conference votes and committee places, despite accounting for only 400 delegates.[66]

Despite his anti-war activities, King remained committed to civil rights and searched for a new approach in place of the now ruptured national civil rights coalition. In early 1968, the SCLC began organising a campaign to bring an interracial group of America's poor to Washington DC. Once there, they would create a shanty town on the Mall, and, if need be, engage in nonviolent civil disobedience to exert pressure on the federal government to reverse its continued scaling down of the War on Poverty. The campaign, as many of King's aides warned him, had little prospect of success.

In February 1968, President Johnson received the report of the National Advisory Commission on Civil Disorders, which he had appointed under the chairmanship of Otto Kerner during the 1967 riots. The report argued that America was 'moving toward two societies, one black, one white – separate and unequal', blamed the riots and ghettoes on white racism, and called for massive remedial federal spending.[67] Johnson rejected the recommendations as politically unfeasible, and, faced with growing anti-war opposition, he declined to run for re-election.

King interrupted ongoing preparations for the Poor People's Campaign to assist African-American garbage workers in their campaign for union recognition and higher wages in Memphis, Tennessee. He was murdered by a white racist on 4 April. African Americans participated in riots and disturbances in more than one hundred locations across the nation in the week after his assassination, resulting in 46 deaths, more than 3,000 people injured, 27,000 arrests, and $45 million of destruction.[68] King's death ensured the passage of a civil rights bill on 10 April, which also owed much to the lobbying efforts of the NAACP's Clarence Mitchell. The act incorporated a fair housing section, which Johnson had sought for over two years, and included renting and house sales that involved real estate agents. The legislation also gave federal protection for civil rights workers, and, to placate conservatives, increased penalties for rioters. However, the act lacked the enforcement powers needed to tackle housing discrimination. Following Johnson's successful nomination of Thurgood Marshall to the Supreme Court less that a year earlier, it was the president's last contribution to civil rights.

Ralph Abernathy, King's successor as head of the SCLC, led the Poor People's Campaign. Beset by poor organisation, internal disagreement, ethnic tensions, violence, criminality and FBI harassment, the campaign failed. After a few weeks, the authorities dismantled what remained of the shanty town near the Lincoln Memorial in June 1968. Deprived of King's unifying leadership and beset by internal wrangling and staff departures, the SCLC's decline accelerated.

To some extent, the national civil rights coalition was a casualty of its own success. Together, the SCLC, SNCC, CORE and the NAACP had overturned legal segregation and black disfranchisement in the South, although NAACP lawyers, local groups and black voters would have to engage in a continuing struggle to turn rights into realities. But years of southern white violence and federal government unreliability, and an influx of northern black members, had eroded the commitment of SNCC and CORE to nonviolence, integration and working with the national Democratic party and its allies. White resistance to black demands for an end to *de facto* discrimination in housing, employment and education revealed complex problems, rooted in deeply embedded inequalities in wealth and power, that were beyond the movement's capacity to resolve. Riots bore witness to the frustration of northern ghetto blacks with inequality, but they only fuelled a pre-existing white backlash against black demands for a fair share of America's prosperity and opportunities. A new wave of black nationalism within and without the movement's ranks, Johnson's escalation of American involvement in the Vietnam War and consequent downgrading of the War on Poverty, and the diversion of many movement supporters and their energies into the anti-war movement ensured the final breakup of the national civil rights coalition. The African-American struggle for equality would continue, but it would do so in a new era of political conservatism and rising economic problems.

Notes

1. John Dittmer, *Local People: The Struggle for Civil Rights in Mississippi* (Urbana and Chicago: University of Illinois Press, 1994), p. 205.
2. Adam Fairclough, *Race and Democracy: The Civil Rights Struggle in Louisiana, 1915– 1972* (Athens and London: University of Georgia Press, 1995), p. 309.
3. Dittmer, *Local People*, p. 244.
4. Ibid. p. 264.
5. Ibid. pp. 264–5.
6. Allen J. Matusow, 'From Civil Rights to Black Power: The Case of SNCC, 1960– 1966', in Barton J. Bernstein and Allen J. Matusow (eds), *Twentieth-Century America: Recent Interpretations* (New York: Harcourt, Brace, and World, 1969), p. 539; Emily Stoper, 'The Student Nonviolent Coordinating Committee: Rise and Fall of a Redemptive Organization', *Journal of Black Studies* 8 (September 1977), pp. 22–3.
7. Dittmer, *Local People*, p. 259.
8. Clayborne Carson, *In Struggle: SNCC and the Black Awakening of the 1960s* (Cambridge, MA, and London: Harvard University Press, 1981), p. 117.
9. August Meier and Elliott Rudwick, *CORE: A Study in the Civil Rights Movement 1942–1968* (1973; Urbana, Chicago, and London: University of Illinois Press, 1975), p. 268.
10. Dittmer, *Local People*, p. 251; Doug McAdam, *Freedom Summer* (1988; New York and Oxford: Oxford University Press, 1990), p. 96.
11. Dittmer, *Local People*, p. 418.
12. Kay Mills, *The Little Light of Mine: The Life of Fannie Lou Hamer* (1993; New York: Plume, 1994), p. 121.
13. Hugh Davis Graham, 'On Riots and Riot Commissions: Civil Disorders in the 1960s', *Public Historian* 2 (Summer 1980), p. 12.
14. Gerald Horne, *Fire This Time: The Watts Uprising and the 1960s* (1995; New York: Da Capo Press, 1997), p. 3.
15. Graham, 'On Riots and Riot Commissions', p. 12.
16. Robert Weisbrot, *Freedom Bound: A History of America's Civil Rights Movement* (New York and London: W. W. Norton, 1990), p. 161.
17. M. J. Heale, *The Sixties in America: History, Politics and Protest* (Edinburgh: Edinburgh University Press, 2001), p. 64.
18. Richard Polenberg, *One Nation Divisible: Class, Race, and Ethnicity in the United States Since 1938* (New York: Penguin, 1980), p. 202.
19. Ibid. p. 198.
20. Fairclough, *To Redeem the Soul of America*, p. 303.
21. 'Agreement of the Subcommittee to the Conference on Fair Housing Convened by the Chicago Conference on Religion and Race', in Clayborne Carson, David J. Garrow, Gerald Gill, Vincent Harding, and Darlene Clark Hine (eds), *The Eyes on the Prize Civil Rights Reader* (New York: Penguin, 1991), p. 305.
22. Ibid.
23. Fairclough, *To Redeem the Soul of America*, pp. 279–307, 349–50.
24. James J. Ralph, Jr, *Northern Protest: Martin Luther King, Jr., Chicago, and the Civil Rights Movement* (Cambridge, MA, and London: Harvard University Press, 1993), p. 233.

25. Ibid. p. 3.
26. Ibid. pp. 5–6.
27. Thomas J. Sugrue, *The Origins of the Urban Crisis: Race and Inequality in Postwar Detroit* (Princeton: Princeton University Press, 1996), p. 233.
28. Arnold R. Hirsch, *Making the Second Ghetto: Race and Housing in Chicago, 1940–1960* (1983; Chicago and London: University of Chicago Press, 1998), pp. 41, 46, 52–3; Arnold R. Hirsch, 'Massive Resistance in the Urban North: Trumbull Park, Chicago, 1953–1966', *Journal of American History* 88 (September 1995), pp. 522–3, 527, 529, 530, 534, 540–1, 548.
29. Stephen Grant Meyer, *As Long As They Don't Move Next Door: Segregation and Racial Conflict in American Neighborhoods* (Lanham, Boulder, New York and Oxford: Rowman and Littlefield, 2001), pp. 6, 47.
30. Allen J. Matusow, *The Unraveling of America: A History of Liberalism in the 1960s* (New York: Harper and Row, 1984), p. 139.
31. Hazel Erskine, 'The Polls: Negro Housing' *Public Opinion Quarterly* 31 (Fall 1967), p. 491.
32. Robert Dallek, *Flawed Giant: Lyndon Johnson and His Times 1961–1973* (New York and Oxford: Oxford University Press, 1998), p. 323.
33. Weisbrot, *Freedom Bound*, p. 220.
34. Malcolm X with Alex Haley, *The Autobiography of Malcolm X* (1965; London: Penguin, 1968), p. 296.
35. Bruce Perry, *Malcolm: The Life of a Man Who Changed Black America* (Barrytown, NY: Station Hill, 1992), pp. 205–7, 264, 374. The *New York Times* estimated that 22,000 people saw the body. Charles M. Payne, *I've Got the Light of Freedom: The Organizing Tradition and the Mississippi Freedom Struggle* (Berkeley, Los Angeles and London: University of California Press, 1995), p. 435.
36. Meier and Rudwick, *CORE*, p. 292.
37. Dittmer, *Local People*, p. 344.
38. 'Hunger in the Mississippi Delta', n.d., folder 289, box 6, Edwin King Collection, Tougaloo College, Mississippi.
39. Charles W. Eagles, *Outside Agitator: Jon Daniels and the Civil Rights Movement in Alabama* (Chapel Hill and London: University of North Carolina Press, 1993), p. 181.
40. *Lexington (Mississippi) Advertiser*, 30 June, 1966, p. 1.
41. Carson, *In Struggle*, p. 210.
42. Stokely Carmichael and Charles V. Hamilton, *Black Power: The Politics of Liberation in America* (New York: Vintage, 1967), pp. viii, 34–56.
43. Ibid. p. 44.
44. Ibid. pp. 5–6, 16–23.
45. Richard H. King, *Civil Rights and the Idea of Freedom* (1992; Athens and London: University of Georgia Press, 1996), pp. 154–5.
46. Carmichael and Hamilton, *Black Power*, pp. 60–84.
47. Carson, *In Struggle*, p. 221.
48. Ibid. p. 240.
49. Meier and Rudwick, *CORE*, pp. 415–16.
50. William L. Van Deburg, *New Day in Babylon: The Black Power Movement and American Culture, 1965–1975* (Chicago and London: University of Chicago Press, 1992), pp. 17–18, 294, 304, 306–7.

51. Ibid. p. 9.
52. King, *Civil Rights and the Idea of Freedom*, p. 5.
53. Van Deburg, *New Day in Babylon*, p. 24.
54. Clayborne Carson, 'Civil Rights Reform and the Black Freedom Struggle', in Charles W. Eagles (ed.), *The Civil Rights Movement in America* (Jackson and London: University Press of Mississippi, 1986), pp. 27–8.
55. Clayborne Carson, 'Rethinking African-American Political Thought in the Post-Revolutionary Era', in Brian Ward and Tony Badger (eds), *The Making of Martin Luther King and the Civil Rights Movement* (Basingstoke: Macmillan, 1996), p. 122.
56. A further 11.7 per cent of whites and 6.5 per cent of blacks made negative comments about Black Power, including 'ridicule, obscenity [and] abhorrence'. Joel D. Aberbach and Jack L. Walker, 'The Meanings of Black Power: A Comparison of White and Black Interpretations of a Political Slogan', *American Political Science Review* 64 (June 1970), p. 370.
57. Ibid. p. 383.
58. Dittmer, *Local People*, p. 411; King, *Civil Rights and the Idea of Freedom*, p. 169; Adam Fairclough, *Better Day Coming: Blacks and Equality, 1890–2000* (2001; New York and London: Penguin, 2002), p. 316.
59. Fairclough, *Better Day Coming*, p. 314 (quotation); Roy Wilkins with Tom Mathews, *Standing Fast: The Autobiography of Roy Wilkins* (New York: Viking, 1982), p. 316.
60. Nancy J. Weiss, *Whitney M. Young, Jr., and the Struggle for Civil Rights* (Princeton: Princeton University Press, 1989), p. 183.
61. Martin Luther King, Jr., *Where Do We Go From Here: Chaos or Community?* (1967; Toronto, New York, and London: Bantam, 1968), p. 51.
62. Ibid. p. 47.
63. Adam Fairclough, 'Martin Luther King, Jr., and the War in Vietnam', *Phylon* 45 (March 1984), p. 27.
64. Ibid. p. 29.
65. Ibid. p. 31.
66. Simon Hall, 'On the Tail of the Panther: Black Power and the 1967 Convention of the National Conference for New Politics', *Journal of American Studies* 37 (April 2003), pp. 58, 64–6, 68–70, 73; Fairclough, *To Redeem the Soul of America*, p. 344.
67. *Report of the National Advisory Commission on Civil Disorders* (Toronto, New York, and London: Bantam, 1968), p. 1.
68. Harvard Sitkoff, *The Struggle for Black Equality, 1954–1992*, rev. edn (New York: Hill and Wang, 1993), p. 208.

CHAPTER 5

Civil Rights in a Conservative Era

After the disintegration of the national civil rights coalition, the NAACP and the NUL, and the Leadership Conference on Civil Rights, to which they belonged, continued to exert pressure on the federal government to support the African-American struggle for equality. Despite the withering of SNCC and CORE, and the decline of the SCLC, the southern civil rights movement persisted at the local level. By the mid-1970s, direct action had largely ended in the region, but voter registration and litigation continued. Sometimes assisted by outside organisations, local groups, voters' leagues and, above all, NAACP chapters worked to implement civil rights legislation, and to achieve school desegregation, quality education, fair policing, economic development and black political representation.

In both sections of the country, increasing numbers of African Americans secured elective office, but below the proportion of the black share of the voting-age population. African-American officeholders were often unable to effect significant change because many held relatively minor posts, needed white allies or acquiescence, and operated in the context of significant local and national economic problems. In the 1970s, attempts to establish a durable National Black Political Assembly failed. Intra- and intergroup rivalries and feuds, and police and government repression, destroyed many black nationalist groups, while midway through the decade the Nation of Islam switched to orthodox Islam after the death of Elijah Muhammad. Although the black consciousness movement enjoyed success on the cultural level, by 1974 many cultural nationalists had turned to Marxism-Leninism, which had little appeal for most African Americans since they wanted to be included in the prosperity generated by American capitalism and looked to the Democratic Party to redress discrimination.

However, the presidential election of 1968 marked the end of Democratic ascendancy in presidential politics. Furthermore, the nation experienced recurrent economic difficulties, marked by rising inflation and growing unemployment, that persisted into the 1980s. While increased educational opportunities and affirmative action programmes expanded the African-American middle class, one-third of blacks lived in poverty, and, by the 1980s, social scientists identified an alienated black under-class in America's inner cities, which were plagued by poverty, crime, family breakdown and drugs. In that decade, the Reagan administration implemented severe cuts in federal welfare programmes that particularly hurt African Americans since poverty afflicted them disproportionately. Many schools resegregated in the 1980s, and outside the workplace, *de facto* segregation existed across America. The civil rights acts of the 1960s remained in force during the Reagan years, but the persistence of black poverty provided a reminder of the failure of the civil rights movement to find viable solutions for African-American economic problems.

Nixon's 'Southern Strategy'

A three-way contest between vice president Hubert Humphrey, Republican Richard Nixon and Independent George Wallace, the presidential election of 1968 revealed growing antipathy among many white voters towards the African-American struggle for equality. Humphrey laboured to free himself from an administration that many voters associated with a failed and divisive war in Vietnam, ghetto riots and federal programmes that supposedly benefited the undeserving poor, especially blacks. Both Nixon and Wallace called for law and order, and attacked the busing of children to achieve school desegregation. Bidding for national lower-class white support, Wallace lambasted federal officials and judges for interfering in people's everyday lives and mollycoddling criminals, and he savagely attacked anti-war protesters as unpatriotic. In more measured tones, Nixon promised to bring domestic peace and end America's war in Vietnam with honour.

Effectively conceding the Deep South to Wallace, Nixon courted the peripheral South, and with the help of Senator Strom Thurmond, who had defected to the Republicans in 1964, South Carolina. In May 1968, the Supreme Court outlawed 'freedom of choice' plans in *Green* v. *New Kent County Board of Education* and required school boards to devise plans that would achieve desegregation. Adopted by the vast majority of southern school districts in order to remain eligible for federal funds under the 1964 Civil Rights Act, 'freedom of choice' had ostensibly allowed parents to choose their children's school. In practice, whites did not apply to black schools. African-American parents, who were not deterred from sending their children to white schools by the fear of losing their jobs or suffering other forms of white intimidation, faced many obstacles from local white education officials. By 1968, only 18 per cent of southern black children were enrolled in majority white schools.[1] To attract southern white support, Nixon called for the retention of 'freedom of choice' and championed neighbourhood schools, while avoiding overt racial appeals.[2]

Although Humphrey won 42.7 per cent of the popular vote and Wallace 13.5 per cent, Nixon received 43.4 per cent and, more importantly, a comfortable margin in the electoral college.[3] Union publicity about Wallace's anti-labour record damaged him among erstwhile northern white supporters, and he carried only Arkansas, and the Deep South states of Alabama, Georgia, Louisiana and Mississippi. Nixon's 'southern strategy' succeeded in winning him five southern states, including South Carolina. Aware that he would also need southern white votes to secure a second term in 1972, Nixon maintained the strategy after the election.

Before his inaugural, Nixon promised Thurmond, a long-standing opponent of civil rights, that he would pressure the Department of Health, Education and Welfare (HEW) not to cut off federal funds from school districts that failed to integrate. Nixon also appointed Harry Dent, a Thurmond aide, as his deputy counsel. During the early months of the Nixon administration, HEW reversed its policy since 1965 by attempting to slow down desegregation in some South Carolina and Mississippi school districts. In the federal court, the US Justice Department argued for school desegregation in Mississippi to be delayed. However, in October 1969, the Supreme Court ruled in *Alexander* v. *Holmes County Board of Education* that school segregation should end immediately. As a result, by 1970 39.4 per cent of African-American children attended white majority schools in the South and even the Deep South had begun large-scale desegregation.[4]

In February 1970, Leon E. Panetta, the liberal integrationist director of HEW's Office for Civil Rights, resigned under pressure from Nixon, and HEW ceased withholding funds from recalcitrant school districts. Unable to restrict desegregation by the judiciary, Nixon declared in March 1970 that school districts should obey the courts. But he urged the judiciary to tread lightly regarding *de facto* segregation. In an attempt to limit judicial activism, Nixon nominated conservatives to the Supreme Court. The Democratic-controlled Congress accepted Warren Burger, but rejected two southerners, Clement F. Haynsworth, Jr, and G. Harrold Carswell, both of whom had sided with segregationists in court proceedings. To enhance his southern standing, Nixon characterised the rejections as attacks on the South, before successfully nominating Minnesotan Harry A. Blackmun. Nixon repeatedly declared his opposition to busing, but, despite his conservative appointments, the Supreme Court unanimously sanctioned its use in *Swann* v. *Charlotte-Mecklenburg Board of Education* (1971).

Nixon employed the 'southern strategy' when the Voting Rights Act came up for renewal in 1970. Although he did not oppose the act outright, Nixon argued that, to avoid stigmatising the South, the ban on literacy tests should apply nationwide. He also opposed preclearance under section five, which provided a mechanism to challenge a move by several Deep South states from ward to at-large elections in order to weaken the impact of African-American votes. Whereas African-American candidates might be elected from a ward with a large black population, they had less chance of being elected in at-large elections, which encompassed a wider geographical area and generally many more white voters. Clarence Mitchell, the Leadership Conference on Civil Rights, and black congressmen, who would form the Congressional Black Caucus (CBC) in 1971, lobbied hard for the act's renewal. Liberal Democrats and northern Republicans succeeded in extending the act for a further five years with preclearance intact, while Nixon secured a national prohibition of literacy tests and ensured that the legislation applied across the country.

The president sought to exploit divisions among his political opponents. Eager to set working-class and lower-middle-class white northerners against the Democratic Party, and to splinter the alliance between organised labour and the NAACP and the NUL, Nixon supported affirmative action under the Philadelphia Plan. Devised by the Labor Department's Office of Federal Contract Compliance (OFCC) between 1966 and 1967, the plan required construction companies with federal contracts to ensure representative minority employment. Nixon's Secretary of Labor George P. Shultz revived the plan, after Johnson's comptroller general had rejected the measure as reverse discrimination that violated the colour-blind approach of the 1964 Civil Rights Act. As Nixon anticipated, organised labour opposed the Philadelphia Plan as a threat to seniority rights, while northern Democrats divided over the proposal. Although Nixon soon lost interest in the Philadelphia Plan, the Labor Department extended its provisions to all federal contractors. However, the OFCC lacked enforcement powers.

The EEOC, which spearheaded federal action against employment discrimination, suffered from a rapid turnover in staff and accumulated a vast backlog of cases. Consequently, the NAACP Legal Defense and Educational Fund and other private lawyers' groups turned to the courts. In March 1971, the Supreme Court ruled in *Griggs* v. *Duke Power Co.* that employers would have to prove that racial discrimination did not account for an inadequate level of minority employment. With support from the Leadership Conference on Civil Rights and women's groups, Congress passed the Equal Employment Opportunity Act in 1972, which widened the EEOC's purview to include state and local government, and enabled the commission to file suit against discriminatory employers or unions. Nixon, who had successfully opposed giving the EEOC the power to issue cease-and-desist orders, signed the bill into law. Employers increasingly adopted affirmative action programmes, rather than face the prospect of litigation before unsympathetic federal courts.

In private, Nixon was dismissive of the ability of African Americans. Nevertheless, he supported black capitalism and created the Office of Minority Business Enterprise to help black entrepreneurs gain federal contracts. Minority-owned businesses also received fixed per centages of federal contracts, known as set-asides. By 1974, federal minority set-asides had increased to $242.2 million.[5] Opposed to the social welfare bureaucracy, Nixon sponsored a Family Assistance Plan which would have given the poor a guaranteed federal minimum income and work incentives. However, the plan ran into opposition from conservatives who regarded it as too costly, and liberals who considered its support levels to be too low. Unwilling to fight for the plan's adoption, Nixon soon lost interest in the proposal.

As the 1972 election approached, Nixon sought to cover his flank against George Wallace, who campaigned once more against busing and federal bureaucracy and interference. Nixon called for a constitutional amendment against busing, but Wallace's strong candidacy for the Democratic Party nomination, which eventually won him victories in five primaries and strong support in several others, was effectively ended by an attempted assassination that left him paralysed. In the November election, Nixon gained 60.7 per cent of the popular vote and easily defeated Senator George S. McGovern of South Dakota, a strong critic of the Vietnam War who ran a poor campaign and was widely perceived as radical.[6]

Cut short by his resignation in August 1974 during the Watergate crisis, Nixon's second term saw him eliminate OEO and scale down elements of the Great Society. Nevertheless, spending on Social Security and welfare doubled during the Nixon years, and the food stamp programme was liberalised and extended to twenty million Americans. Nixon also increased expenditure for civil rights enforcement by federal agencies to $66.3 million in 1973.[7] The OFCC more than doubled its compliance monitoring between 1971 and 1973 to 52,000, and by 1974, the EEOC had a $43 million budget and a greatly expanded staff.[8]

Nixon believed in equal employment opportunities, but he opposed forced integration outside the workplace and accepted voluntary separatism. Committed to neighbourhood schools by personal conviction and by political opportunism, Nixon correctly discerned growing nationwide white opposition to busing. By his second term, he had appointed four conservatives to the Supreme Court. In June 1974, the court ruled in *Milliken* v. *Bradley* against the use of interdistrict busing to achieve school desegregation. The decision effectively exempted suburban children from busing to inner cities, and deprived the courts of one of the most effective means of achieving school desegregation. Many cities had too few white children to desegregate largely black urban schools. After *Milliken*, schools began to resegregate since whites and blacks mostly lived in different neighbourhoods.

In South Boston, working-class Irish Americans resented the fact that their children, unlike those of wealthier suburbanites, were subject to federal court-ordered busing to the Roxbury ghetto. South Boston residents organised a campaign of resistance that began with the onset of busing in 1974 and lasted for three years. They borrowed such civil rights movement tactics as prayer vigils and marches, and staged a march on Washington. A minority also engaged in violent resistance. Historian Ronald Formisano characterises the struggle in Boston as a product of 'the interplay of race and class, in admixture with ethnicity and place, or "turf"', rather than just racism.[9]

Nixon often stated his opposition to busing, and many contemporaries regarded him as hostile to civil rights. Ralph Abernathy accepted an invitation to the White House in May 1969, but Abernathy's overbearing manner and his demands for welfare, job creation and fair employment initiatives alienated Nixon, who became reluctant to meet with civil rights leaders. Roy Wilkins claimed that Nixon wanted to 'turn the clock back on everything' and condemned the president's attempt to dilute the Voting Rights Act and retard school desegregation.[10] Bishop Stephen G. Spottswood, the NAACP's national chairman, accused the Nixon administration of being 'anti-Negro'.[11] However, Nixon gradually developed a positive relationship with Whitney Young, based on their mutual interest in developing minority businesses and job opportunities, and the administration directed $21 million of federal subsidies to the NUL.[12]

Many historians, such as William H. Chafe, have condemned the Nixon administration's record on civil rights, especially the 'southern strategy'.[13] However, in recent years historians Joan Hoff and Dean J. Kotlowski have presented a more positive assessment. Although she condemns its attempts to delay southern school desegregation, Hoff argues that 'the Nixon administration desegregated southern schools' and claims that Nixon's achievements for 'women and minorities far outweighed those of his predecessors'.[14] Kotlowski contends that 'Nixon compiled a creditable record on civil rights' by implementing 'affirmative action and set-aside programs for minority-owned companies' and desegregating southern schools.[15]

However, Hugh Davis Graham makes a convincing case that school desegregation should be credited to the judiciary and that it was the Democratic Congress that 'repeatedly forced Nixon's hand in major civil rights legislation'. Nixon exploited busing and affirmative action for political advantage, and, in private, he repeatedly made racist statements. Graham attributes much greater enforcement efforts by the EEOC to pressure from NAACP suits. He does not regard the Nixon record as entirely negative. Nixon, Graham argues, supported black capitalism from conviction, and his administration helped ensure a peaceful transition to school desegregation in the South. Furthermore, Graham notes that Nixon sanctioned budgets that greatly increased federal civil rights enforcement.[16]

A New South? Protest and Politics

The story of civil rights was, of course, played out at the local, as well as the national, level. Adam Fairclough argued that after the Selma campaign in 1965, 'Confused, divided, and weary from battle fatigue, the black movement in the South ground to a halt. Within a year, it had virtually disintegrated.'[17] But recent state and local studies show that the civil rights movement endured in the region for at least a decade after Selma. Fairclough later concluded that 'the evidence of Louisiana contradicts the notion that the civil rights movement suddenly collapsed after Black Power supposedly split it asunder'.[18] He contends that the movement continued in the South 'albeit in an attentuated form, in the states, cities, and rural areas, where blacks continued to struggle for jobs, integrated schools, and political representation'.[19] More recently, Stephen Tuck has argued that the movement 'in Georgia followed this pattern, with continuity of protest at the local level as much as change'.[20] Noting that protest carried on in Mississippi, supported after 1964 by African-American paramilitary protection, Akinyele Omowale Umoja contends that 'Between 1965 and 1979, economic boycotts were a principal form of insurgency for Black activists' in the state.[21]

Assisted by outside support, independent local movements continued in the post-Selma South. Local voters' leagues and the NAACP received grants from the SRC, which funded a second VEP between 1966 and 1968 that supported 200 registration campaigns across the region.[22] The Lawyers' Constitutional Defense Committee, which several civil rights organisations had formed in 1964, the American Civil Liberties Union (ACLU) and sympathetic religious groups continued to help local movements in both Louisiana and Mississippi, particularly in voting rights cases. The ACLU also supported legal challenges against discrimination in Georgia. The CORE Scholarship, Educational and Defense Fund, which had financed much of CORE's legal programme and voter registration work in the 1960s, objected to CORE's nationalist direction and became an independent organisation in 1967. The Fund continued its community organising work and provided thousands of local activists with training in the functioning of the political system as they sought to advance black political representation in the wake of the Voting Rights Act.

The dispatch of federal registrars to parts of the South under the act, and extensive citizenship education and voter registration campaigns by NAACP chapters, the Scholarship, Educational and Defense Fund, the Delta Ministry and local groups brought a huge rise in black voter registration. By 1968, 62 per cent of voting age African Americans were registered in the eleven southern states. The gains were particularly impressive in Mississippi, where black registration rose from 6.7 per cent in 1964 to 59.4 per cent four years later.[23]

The Supreme Court ruled in *Allen* v. *State Board of Elections* (1969) that the Voting Rights Act applied to racial discrimination in all aspects of the electoral process. Consequently, civil rights groups challenged a wide range of discriminatory mechanisms, as well as fraud and intimidation at the ballot box that particularly plagued rural areas. Federal War on Poverty funds supported local black organisations, and groups, such as the Delta Ministry, helped local communities apply for federal grants to improve the dilapidated infrastructure of small, largely black towns and fund small-business development.

As African Americans entered the political system, protest continued. Direct action revived between 1966 and 1970 as the state and local civil rights struggle continued in the South and extended to areas previously untouched by the movement. The protesters targeted school desegregation, jobs, policing and student rights. African Americans sought access to, and a fair share of, public services. They adopted nonviolent means and most sought integration.

Between 1972 and 1980, when the acquittal of white policemen for killing an African American led to a riot in Miami that brought eighteen deaths, there were few major racial disturbances in the South. A more conservative political climate and repressive policing had a deterrent affect. When African Americans in Augusta, Georgia, rioted in May 1970 and left fifty stores ablaze, the police killed six blacks, by shooting some repeatedly in the back. In the same month, police and Mississippi highway patrolmen shot dead two African Americans and wounded twelve others during a peaceful protest for greater student autonomy at all-black Jackson State College. In 1971, the National Guard quelled a riot in Chattanooga, Tennessee, in which one black died and many more suffered injuries.

The NAACP helped fill the void left by the departure of SNCC and CORE workers from the South. In Louisiana, Fairclough notes, the NAACP became 'more militant, more confrontational, and more oriented towards direct action' in the late 1960s. NAACP Youth Councils recruited young African Americans, who had been radicalised by the call for Black Power. At the same time, white leaders became increasingly willing to negotiate and work with the NAACP.[24] The Association's expansion was greatest in parts of the state that had seen little previous civil rights activity as African Americans sought to overturn decades of discrimination.[25] In Arkansas, the NAACP's 'Branch membership started to grow again in precisely those areas where SNCC had been active.'[26] By 1965, the NAACP had shrunk to sixteen chapters in Georgia, but the Savannah and Brunswick branches 'inspired and organized protests in the surrounding counties'.[27]

In the late 1960s and 1970s, NAACP branches and NAACP Legal Defense and Educational Fund lawyers helped African-American workers in the South file class action lawsuits and make complaints to the EEOC under the Civil Rights Act of 1964. Such local activism played a significant role in integrating the region's textile and paper industries.[28]

The SCLC neglected the South after its lacklustre Summer Community Organizational and Political Education programme had added few African Americans to the voter registration rolls in 1965. However, between 1968 and 1971, the SCLC enjoyed 'a minor revival of its work in the South'.[29] The organisation led demonstrations in Alabama and Georgia for school integration, and against desegregation schemes that resulted in the firing of African-American teachers and principals as black schools closed and their pupils were transferred to formerly white schools. The protests brought hundreds of arrests and forced significant concessions. The SCLC also ran some successful voter registration drives in the two states. Tuck argues that the SCLC 'became the driving force in the development of small town protests across Georgia', which continued into the mid-1970s as African Americans pressured local whites to obey federal civil rights legislation, desegregate schools, hire African Americans and end police brutality.[30]

In 1969, the SCLC helped striking hospital workers in Charleston, South Carolina, win their demands for union recognition, higher wages and the rehiring of activist union members whose firing had sparked the protests. The authorities' heavy handedness united the black community behind the SCLC's efforts. Over 1,000 people were jailed during the protest, which enjoyed supported from the UAW. However, by 1972, the SCLC's dwindling contributions forced it to cut its staff from sixty-one to forty, and by 1973 to seventeen.[31] Demoralised, Abernathy tried to relinquish the SCLC's presidency in 1973, but, urged to continue, he served another four years.

Financial problems also dogged the Delta Ministry. Support for civil rights and other forms of social activism had brought a decline in the membership of the NCC's major denominations, and weakened their finances and contributions to the National Council. In 1971, the NCC cut the Delta Ministry's budget by more than half and reduced its staff to four.[32]

Mississippi witnessed racial violence in August 1971, when the FBI and Jackson police initiated a gun battle with the black nationalist Republic of New Africa (RNA) by firing on the group's state headquarters during a raid. One police officer died. Arrested on charges that included murder, assault and waging war on Mississippi, several RNA members were convicted and jailed. Formed in 1968 following a meeting of black nationalists in Detroit, the RNA sought to create an independent black nation in the five states of the Deep South and demanded reparations for slavery from the federal government. In 1970, the small organisation concentrated on establishing a base in Jackson, but by constantly publicising its demands the RNA made itself a target for white authorities. Few African-American Mississippians supported the group, which had little prospect of success, and, like most other black southerners, they sought change through existing structures.

By the early 1970s, the African-American struggle for equality had made some significant gains. Between 1964 and 1970, the number of southern black elected officials had increased from fewer than twenty-five to over 700.[33] Racist demagoguery declined in southern elections, and white candidates increasingly sought to attract black voters. In 1970, African Americans in Arkansas, Florida, Georgia and South Carolina helped elect moderate governors, and by 1972 most southern states had moderate executives. Andrew Young, who had resigned from the SCLC in 1970 to enter politics, was elected to the US House of Representatives in 1972. A year later, Maynard Jackson became Atlanta's first African-American mayor.

However, many black elected officials held minor local offices, located predominantly in small towns and rural areas that had a black population of at least 60 per cent.[34] Engrained patterns of deference led some blacks to vote for white candidates, while whites also resorted to fraud. Whites and white officials, particularly in the rural Deep South, discouraged African Americans from voting or pressured them into choosing white candidates by using intimidation and violence. During the 1970s, membership in the Ku Klux Klan tripled, and in the late 1970s and early 1980s Klan violence increased significantly.[35] The US Commission on Civil Rights surveyed the Deep South in 1981 and reported 'white resistance and hostility by some State and local officials to increased minority participation in virtually every aspect of the electoral process'.[36]

As African Americans entered the political system, southern whites registered and voted in ever greater numbers. By 1985, nearly 80 per cent of eligible whites were registered to vote, compared to 66 per cent of eligible blacks.[37] Whites also proved far less willing than blacks to vote for candidates of a different race. By calling for limited federal government, and adopting code words for racial issues such as law and order, neighbourhood schools and opposition to welfare dependants, Republicans began to make significant inroads in the South.

To reduce the impact of black votes, southern white officials and legislators switched from district to at-large elections, made elective offices appointive, redrew electoral boundaries, adopted multimember legislative districts, and annexed areas with large white populations. Enforcement of the preclearance requirement of the Voting Rights Act eliminated some of these discriminatory devices and acted as a deterrent, but the act did not apply to measures adopted before 1965. In the 1970s and 1980s, the Legal Defense and Educational Fund, the ACLU and other lawyers' groups filed suits that gradually overturned at-large electoral systems and many other discriminatory measures, and increased black representation. African-American officeholders more than doubled in Georgia during the 1980s, but there, as elsewhere across the South, blacks continued to be underrepresented.[38] African Americans comprised 19 per cent of the southern population in 1986, but only 3 per cent of the region's elected officials.[39]

Many African Americans held local offices in poor rural areas that gave them little scope to tackle poverty or improve education and infrastructure. Even black mayors of large cities, such as Atlanta, were restricted by declining tax bases, caused by white flight to the suburbs to evade school and residential desegregation. Black politicians were often middle class, and many had not been involved in the civil rights movement. Although they believed in racial equality, they were often more concerned with balancing budgets and attracting low-wage industries with tax breaks, than with social programmes for the poor. Between 1973 and 1978, Mayor Maynard Jackson used affirmative action to increased black employment in public professional jobs from 19.2 per cent to 42.2 per cent in Atlanta.[40] However, Jackson also sacked 900 predominantly black garbage workers in 1977 for striking.[41]

Affirmative action and the postwar growth of the southern economy led to nearly 30 per cent of African Americans holding middle-class jobs by 1980, up from 4 per cent in 1940.[42] Attracted by employment opportunities, the end of *de jure* discrimination and by family ties, blacks began migrating to the South in the 1970s. However, black poverty persisted in city ghettoes and much of the rural South. The proportion of southern blacks living below the federal poverty level declined by 5 per cent between 1970 and 1982, but in 1983 40 per cent of black Mississippians lived below the poverty line.[43]

For many years neglectful of poverty and economic issues and never able to devise an effective approach towards them, the civil rights movement seemed to have greater success in desegregating southern schools. By 1972, 46 per cent of southern black pupils attended predominantly white schools, compared with 28 per cent of African-American children outside the region.[44] Surveys also found an unprecedented change in southern white opinion. By 1970, 16 per cent of southern white parents did not object to token school desegregation, compared to 61 per cent in 1963.[45] However, school desegregation led many whites to enrol their children in private schools in rural areas that had large African-American populations, and, in both the urban and rural South, white parents tended to abandon integrated schools when blacks constituted more than 30 per cent of school enrolment.[46] School desegregation accelerated white flight to the suburbs, which was also a product of growing white affluence and a long-standing response to black urban migration.

African Americans became increasingly disillusioned with school integration, which occurred at the expense of black schools and black educators, produced racial tensions within desegregated formerly white schools, and did not necessarily improve black educational achievement and opportunity as the NAACP had anticipated. Many black communities regretted the closure of schools that had been at the centre of local life, the busing of black children to often hostile environments and the displacement of staff who had served as role models. According to a 1974 survey conducted by Walter De Vries, 69.3 per cent of southern blacks favoured greater spending to improve African-American schools, instead of busing.[47]

Some blacks resisted school integration, which invariably occurred on terms determined by whites. African Americans in rural Hyde County, North Carolina, began a successful protest in 1968 against a desegregation plan that would have closed two black high schools. The campaign included a year-long school boycott, demonstrations and marches. When white voters rejected a tax rise to fund the proposed enrolment of blacks in white schools, the school board agreed to maintain the black schools.

In some locations, such as Charlotte-Mecklenburg, North Carolina, and Nashville, Tennessee, busing worked well despite initial difficulties. However, ongoing white flight to the suburbs and private schools made racial balance in schools impractical in many cities. The Atlanta school system was 83 per cent black, when the city's NAACP reached an agreement in 1973 that excluded substantial busing, guaranteed that each school would have at least 30 per cent black enrolment, and ensured that African Americans would hold at least half of all administrative positions in the Atlanta school system, including the superintendency.[48] Roy Wilkins condemned the agreement for its acceptance of segregation, but Lonnie King, head of the Atlanta NAACP, believed that busing would undermine black neighbourhood schools and only spur further white withdrawal from the school system.

In 1984 historian Raymond Wolters evaluated the long-term experience of the five school districts that the Supreme Court had ordered to desegregate thirty years before. Wolters concluded that *Brown* had failed to improve the academic underperformance of black children relative to whites, harmed education overall, and led both white and black middle-class parents to seek alternatives to these school districts for their children. He traced the problem to the *Green* ruling, which abandoned *Brown*'s colour-blind rejection of racial segregation in favour of racial balance in schools. Enforced mass school integration, Wolters contended, led to mixed-ability teaching and reduced educational standards in order to accommodate poorly-prepared and poorly-behaved lower-class black children who suffered from a variety of social problems.[49] David Garrow accused Wolters of clothing 'biases and political agendas' in the 'garb of careful scholarship' and maintained that 'this book suffers fatally from a multiplicity of some of the most serious failings that a purported work of scholarship can offer'.[50] Education issues also generated controversy in the North.

The Struggle in the North

Frustrated by the failure to overcome *de facto* school segregation, by the mid-1960s minority groups in New York City sought community control of local schools. The result was a bitter dispute in the poor Ocean Hill–Brownsville section of Brooklyn that undermined race relations across the city. Local residents elected a governing school board in 1967 that reflected Ocean Hill's mostly black and Puerto Rican population. To increase minority representation in the schools, the board sought to appoint some black and Puerto Rican principals, which meant overlooking civil service lists of candidates which were dominated by whites who had passed mandatory qualifying examinations. In May, the board tried to reassign nineteen white teachers. Their union, the white-majority United Federation of Teachers (UFT), responded with a series of strikes. Almost the city's entire workforce of school teachers joined the action in support of the union's demand that their colleagues be reinstated.

After months of acrimony, the UFT secured the teachers' reinstatement. The city also terminated the governing board. However, the New York State Court of Appeals upheld the appointment of principals from outside civil service lists, and in 1971 a federal court outlawed the examination requirement for principals as racially discriminatory. In the meantime, white suburban flight had increased, violence permeated the city's schools and racial divisions in New York had intensified. Many whites who supported equality of opportunity proved far less willing to accept the costs involved to achieve equality of result.

In the late 1960s, racial tension was an escalating national phenomenon. SNCC and the Black Panthers adopted revolutionary rhetoric and publicly advocated violence. In 1967 Rap Brown, SNCC's newly-elected chairman, declared 'don't be trying to love that honky to death. Shoot him to death.'[51] Brown's incendiary rhetoric and carrying of firearms earned him several spells in jail in the late 1960s. By the time Brown was convicted of robbery in 1973, SNCC had disappeared. With some success, the FBI directed its counterintelligence programme, COINTELPRO, to infiltrating and disrupting radical and nationalist groups. The FBI disseminated misinformation that exacerbated tensions within and between different nationalist groups. Its efforts helped destroy a merger between SNCC and the Panthers, and encouraged conflict between the Panthers and Us that resulted in bombings, shootings and murders.

Reacting more to their rhetoric than their capabilities, in 1968 the FBI claimed that the Panthers posed the greatest internal threat to American security. The police also targeted the Panthers, who, for their part, routinely engaged in robbery and other petty crime, advocated killing police officers, and sought confrontations with the police. Between late 1967 and the end of 1969, clashes between the police and the Panthers left nine police officers and ten Panthers dead.[52]

However, FBI and police repression and media attention helped boost the Panthers' membership by 1,000 during 1968 and gained the party twelve additional chapters.[53] By the end of 1969, the Panthers' newspaper had a circulation of 140,000, and in January 1970 a national Lou Harris survey found that 64 per cent of African Americans took pride in the Panthers, even if many did not share the Marxist-Leninism perspective that the party now espoused.[54] Although the Panthers' militancy and victimisation by the authorities generated black admiration and sympathy, the party's membership peaked at 2,000.[55] By 1970, the Panthers were divided by violent factional conflict, and many of the party's leading figures were either dead, in prison, or, in the case of Eldridge Cleaver, living abroad to avoid jail. Released from prison in 1970, after his murder conviction had been overturned on a technicality, Huey Newton became addicted to cocaine. By 1972, the party had only 150 members.[56] Newton's biographer, Hugh Pearson, concludes that the Panthers were 'little more than a temporary media phenomenon'.[57] Roy Wilkins dismissed them as 'mouth power'.[58]

Following SNCC's failed merger with the Panthers and as SNCC disintegrated, James Forman sought other means to advance the black struggle. In April 1969, Forman appeared at the National Black Economic Development Conference in Detroit, which was sponsored primarily by the Interreligious Foundation for Community Organization, an interfaith group that sought to channel church money to black community groups. He insisted successfully that the conference adopt his proposal for a Black Manifesto, which excoriated white Christians and Jews for complicity in centuries of racial oppression and demanded that white churches and Jewish synagogues pay reparations of $500 million.[59]

Forman took his demands to the nation's major denominations. In May 1969, he interrupted services at New York City's prestigious Riverside Church, across from the offices of the NCC, to present the Black Manifesto. Forman's visits attracted widespread publicity, but a Gallup poll found that only 2 per cent of whites and 21 per cent of African Americans supported his idea, although 27 per cent of blacks were undecided.[60] Although Forman's proposal led some major denominations to increase their support for black groups, a year later the Black Economic Development Conference had received only $300,000, despite Forman raising his demand to $3 billion.[61] The conference spent most of the money publishing militant black literature. Forman spent the early 1970s writing his memoirs. He also helped the League of Revolutionary Black Workers, which developed from the Dodge Revolutionary Union Movement (DRUM).

Formed in 1968 by black car workers in Detroit to protest against racist practices by their employer and the UAW, DRUM staged strikes and pickets. African-American workers formed parallel organisations in several other northern and western industrial plants that coalesced in the League. Within a few years, the League and its member groups disappeared, undermined by UAW concessions to secure the loyalty of black workers and the UAW's depiction of the League as dominated by dangerous radicals.

Many leftist black organisations failed to sustain themselves, but African Americans made increasing progress in electoral politics. In 1967, Carl Stokes, a former city prosecutor, became the first African-American mayor of a large city by winning the first of two terms in Cleveland, Ohio. In the same year, Richard Hatcher, who had participated in the local civil rights movement, became mayor of Gary, Indiana. Over the next decade, blacks won mayoralty elections in several other northern cities, just as they were also doing in the South. In both regions, their success reflected well-organised campaigns, but also resulted from black migration to the cities and white flight to the suburbs.

Hatcher convened a meeting of African-American political and civil rights leaders in September 1971 at Northlake, Illinois, which led to the meeting of the National Black Political Convention in March 1972. Held in Gary, the convention attracted 3,000 delegates (and 9,000 other attenders), who represented virtually every stripe of black opinion.[62] Amiri Baraka (formerly LeRoi Jones), Hatcher and Representative Charles Diggs, Jr, a Detroit Democrat who had organised the CBC, chaired the convention. Although some NAACP leaders, such as Wilkins, refused to attend, participants included Martin Luther King's widow, Coretta, and Jesse Jackson, who had left the SCLC in December after being disciplined by Ralph Abernathy for financial irregularities in Operation Breadbasket. Jackson had recently begun Operation PUSH (People United to Save Humanity), which incorporated Operation Breadbasket, and thereby deprived the SCLC of its main beachhead outside the South.

The convention called for proportional representation, reparations, a guaranteed national income, national health insurance and a range of other measures to assist the poor. It also established the National Black Political Assembly that was designed to help African Americans achieve elective office and influence at all levels of the political system. According to historian Manning Marable, 'the political tone of black nationalism ...

filled the convention hall', and the meeting marked 'the zenith not only of black nationalism, but of the entire black movement' during the civil rights era.[63]

Marable's enthusiastic account of the convention glosses over differences of opinion within it, and, judged by its results, the meeting had much less impact than such milestones of the civil rights movement as the Birmingham and Selma campaigns. Most black politicians were unwilling to abandon working through the two-party system by creating an independent black political party. Meetings of the National Black Political Assembly in 1974 and 1976 drew fewer and fewer politicians and delegates. By 1977, the assembly's national membership had dwindled to less than 300.[64]

Baraka, one of the assembly's main supporters, had abandoned cultural nationalism by 1974, and he, like many other of its former proponents, such as Maulana Karenga, had become a Marxist-Leninist. Frustrated by their failure to generate a revolutionary consciousness among African Americans, many former cultural nationalists now argued that the key to black progress lay in overturning capitalism and ending class exploitation. However, few African Americans shared their perspective.

Black nationalism was in decline by the mid-1970s. Never a unified group, nationalists remained divided. They were also increasingly unsure of which direction to take. Committed to working through conventional politics, especially as African Americans gained greater influence in Congress and municipal government, black elected officials distanced themselves from nationalists. Universities began to cut back black studies programmes, while many African Americans (and even some whites) absorbed elements of African art and culture, without adopting a nationalist or Pan-Africanist perspective.

Following the death of Elijah Muhammad in 1975, Wallace D. Muhammad, his son and successor, repudiated his father's racial doctrines and steered the Nation of Islam, renamed the World Community of Al-Islam in the West, towards adoption of nonracial orthodox Islam. Muslims could now participate in politics and even serve in the American military. Disgruntled by these changes, minister Louis Farrakhan broke with Wallace Muhammad in 1977, and subsequently led a re-created Nation of Islam that added anti-Semitism to its traditional belief in black supremacy. However, most Muslims retained their allegiance to Wallace Muhammad.

Although black nationalism was in decline, conventional politics proved to be far less rewarding than many African Americans had anticipated. By 1976, African Americans beyond the South held fewer offices, in relative and absolute terms, than blacks in the South.[65] As in the South, black mayors in the North took control of cities that were suffering from declining tax bases as whites fled to the suburbs, and inflation also ate away at city budgets for basic services. Furthermore, by the mid-1970s, the North was experiencing deindustrialisation as a result of foreign competition and the relocation of industry from the northern rust belt to the low-tax, low-wage and less unionised sun belt of the South and West. Both the Nixon and Ford administrations were unwilling to provide significant aid to cities facing budget crises.

The Federal Government and Civil Rights: From Ford to Reagan

Gerald R. Ford, the Republican vice president who succeeded Nixon after Watergate, declared his opposition to busing and welcomed congressional passage of a Nixon measure that urged the courts to preserve neighbour-hood schools and restrict the use of busing. However, Ford, unlike Nixon, five years before, supported the renewal of the Voting Rights Act in 1975 with preclearance intact. Sixty-nine of the 105 southern white legislators voted for the act's seven-year extension.[66] Ford was a conservative president, apt to veto proposals by the Democratic Congress, and unwilling to support measures that would have helped poor Ameri-cans. Stagflation, a combination of rising inflation and unemployment, afflicted the economy, with African Americans and other minorities worst affected. By 1975, 7.8 per cent of whites were unemployed, compared to 13.8 per cent of nonwhites.[67]

America's economic problems and Ford's pardoning of Nixon for Watergate presented him with significant difficulties as he sought election as president in his own right. Ford faced former Georgia governor Jimmy Carter in the 1976 election. Despite courting segrega-tionists in the 1970 Georgia gubernatorial primary, Carter had denounced racial discrimination in his inaugural, doubled black employment in state government and supported an open housing bill. Andrew Young and members of Martin Luther King's family endorsed Carter in 1976, but Julian Bond refused because of Carter's fiscal conservatism. Opposed to the Nixon–Ford record on economics and race, 5.2 million black voters supported Carter and ensured his victory over Ford by 1.7 million votes in the popular election. Carter beat Ford by just fifty-seven electoral college votes, the narrowest margin since 1916.[68]

Carter made several high-level black appointments, including Andrew Young as UN Ambassador and Patricia R. Harris as secretary of housing and urban development. Twelve per cent of Carter's appointees were African American, slightly ahead of the black share of the population.[69] The Carter administration supported government set-aside programmes for minorities and declared its support for affirmative action to rectify the effects of past discrimination, but Carter rejected rigid imposition of employment quotas for minorities. In this, Carter was in line with mainstream white opinion. According to a 1972 poll, 77 per cent of whites favoured African-American job-training programmes, but 82 per cent rejected affirmative action measures in cases in which blacks and whites held commensurate qualifications.[70]

Affirmative action came before the Supreme Court in 1978, after white applicant Alan Bakke sued the University of California at Davis for denying him admission to its medical school, while admitting less qualified black applicants under an affirmative action programme. After considerable internal debate, the US Justice Department filed a brief with the Supreme Court that endorsed the university's inclusion of race in admission decisions. Affected by Nixon's conservative judicial appointments, in *University of California Regents* v. *Bakke* the court ordered Bakke's admission, and rejected quotas for minorities, but it permitted race to be taken into account in admissions to promote diversity in the student body. The decision thereby approved affirmative action within tight constraints.

A year later, in *United Steelworkers of America* v. *Weber*, the Supreme Court upheld a voluntary affirmative action programme agreed by Kaiser Aluminium and the union to ensure representative black employment in skilled jobs. In 1980, the court considered a congressional programme which required that 10 per cent of federally-funded state and local public works projects be set aside for minority-owned businesses. In *Fullilove* v. *Klutznick*, the court approved the measure by six votes to three.[71] However, in the same year, the court weakened the Voting Rights Act by ruling five to four in *City of Mobile* v. *Bolden* that plaintiffs challenging voting laws had to prove such laws had been adopted with intent to discriminate against minorities.[72]

Although Carter supported set-asides, he lacked either the desire or the mandate to undertake social reform or large-scale government programmes to alleviate worsening unemployment. He offered only token support for the Humphrey-Hawkins 'full employment' bill in 1978, sponsored by Democrats Senator Hubert Humphrey of Minnesota, the former vice president, and Representative Augustus Hawkins, an African American from California. Carter acted with justified confidence that the bill's congressional opponents would weaken its provisions.[73] As enacted, the legislation disappointed the CBC by offering little more than a rhetorical federal commitment to tackling unemployment, and leaving job creation to the private sector. The economic position of blacks worsened under the Carter administration. The median income of African Americans relative to whites slipped from 61.5 to 57.9 per cent between 1975 and 1980.[74] While adult black employment remained high at 14 per cent in 1980, twice the white level, African-American teenage joblessness stood at 40 per cent, more than double the white teenage rate.[75] Poverty afflicted 10 per cent of whites and 33 per cent of African Americans, and inflation reached 12.4 per cent.[76]

Carter's detractors chided him for failing to tackle economic problems effectively, and his African-American critics were further disappointed when Carter forced Young to resign after the ambassador had met with representatives of the Palestine Liberation Organisation in breach of administration policy. Young was popular among African Americans, who welcomed his outspoken support for civil rights causes at home and abroad. The appointment of another African American, Donald F. McHenry, in Young's place did not fully restore Carter's reputation among blacks, whose votes he needed as he faced a tough re-election campaign against Ronald Reagan in 1980.

A conservative Republican, Reagan believed in states' rights, low taxes and limited federal government in domestic affairs. He opposed affirmative action and promised a tough policy against the Soviet Union. Although Carter received the overwhelming bulk of African-American votes, some registered black voters stayed home, dismayed by the choices on offer. Associated with economic decline and ineptitude in foreign policy, epitomised by the taking of American embassy staff hostage in Iran, Carter received only 41 per cent in the popular vote, with Reagan taking 51 per cent and John Anderson, a liberal Republican, 8 per cent. However, Reagan achieved a large majority in the electoral college, and his party also gained control of the Senate, helped by the election of four new southern Republican legislators.[77]

Reagan appointed a black secretary of housing and urban development,

Samuel Pierce, but he made far fewer African-American appointments at all levels of government (4 per cent) during his presidency than Carter.[78] Furthermore, Reagan appointed conservatives to enforce civil rights. William Bradford Reynolds, the new assistant attorney general for civil rights, opposed race-based remedies to compensate for past discrimination. Clarence Pendleton, a black former Democrat, took over the chairmanship of the US Commission on Civil Rights and dismissed affirmative action and busing as 'bankrupt' approaches.[79]

Committed to federal noninterference in private bodies and opposed to racial guidelines in education, Reagan ordered the Internal Revenue Service to reverse its policy since 1970, and restore tax-exempt status to racially-discriminatory private educational institutions, among them Bob Jones University in South Carolina, which prohibited interracial dating. Under intense pressure from civil rights advocates within and outside Congress, the administration reversed itself. In 1983, the Supreme Court affirmed the right of the Internal Revenue Service to apply its long-standing policy.

Aware that extension of the Voting Rights Act enjoyed widespread political support, the Reagan administration did not oppose the act's renewal. However, the administration opposed efforts led by the Leadership Conference on Civil Rights and the CBC to pass a renewal bill that eliminated the intent test stipulated by *Mobile*. Reagan cautioned that renewal on such terms would create a quota system for minority representation. However, he had to accept defeat when Congress voted in 1982 to extend the Voting Rights Act for twenty-five years and require the courts to take discriminatory results into account in electoral practice cases. The importance of the southern black electorate ensured that most of the region's senators did not oppose renewal. Even Strom Thurmond supported a civil rights measure for the first time.

Although African Americans remained able to protect their voting rights, they suffered disproportionately from Reagan's policy of cutting budgets to reduce inflation, and during an economic recession between 1981 and 1982. The administration reduced spending by $18 billion during its first two years on a broad range of programmes that assisted low-income people, including food stamps, which aided twenty million people, one-third of them African American.[80] By 1982, more than 17 per cent of blacks were unemployed, and 35.7 per cent of black families lived in poverty. Fifty-six per cent of black female-headed families were impoverished.[81] By 1984, there were over a quarter more young blacks in prison than in college.[82] Drugs and gang warfare increasingly afflicted ghetto neighbourhoods.

By the mid-1980s, social scientists began to argue that a ghetto underclass had developed, whose members were cut off from mainstream society, and prone to unemployment, criminality, violence, promiscuity and family breakdown. African-American sociologists William Julius Wilson and Charles Murray agreed that the phenomenon existed but differed over its causes. Wilson focused primarily on structural economic factors, such as deindustrialisation, which had created mass ghetto unemployment and thereby reduced the number of 'marriageable men', while the outmigration of the black middle and sturdy working class had removed employment and community networks, and role models, from the ghetto.[83] Murray blamed a liberal elite for advocating too generous welfare benefits to the black (and white) poor which undermined their motivation to work and create stable families, tolerated educational decline and condoned anti-social conduct.[84] A third view, advanced by white sociologist Christopher Jencks, maintained that the whole of American society had been affected by growing family breakdown, illegitimacy and disrespect for authority since the late 1960s. These phenomena were more marked in the ghetto, Jencks argued, because African Americans there already suffered from fewer educational and employment opportunities and greater social problems.[85]

Although the inner-city poor were often regarded as politically apathetic, aided by a coalition of civil rights groups that included the NAACP, the NUL and Jesse Jackson's PUSH, Harold Washington succeeded in mobilising more than 80 per cent of Chicago's black poor in his successful bid in 1983 to become the city's first African-American mayor.[86] Inspired by Washington's success, Jackson ran for the Democratic presidential nomination in 1984.

Reminiscent of the Poor People's Campaign of 1968, Jackson tried to fashion an interracial alliance of America's poor. Like, King, Jackson opposed high military spending, and favoured more equitable wealth distribution, but, unlike the martyred civil rights leader, Jackson sought to make capitalism work for the poor, rather than replace it. He received the support of many black clergy and endorsement by the National Baptist Convention, the nation's largest black denomination, but many black political leaders remained loyal to established national Democratic leaders, such as Walter F. Mondale. Jackson damaged his limited appeal among whites by courting Farrakhan and maligning New York City as

'Hymietown', an anti-Semitic slur.[87] Jackson's campaign helped boost black voter registration, and he finished third among eight candidates, with 3.5 million primary votes. Mondale, the nominee, lost in a Reagan landslide.[88]

Jackson came second in the Democratic race four years later. By focusing on broad economic issues and hiring seasoned white advisers, he nearly doubled his overall support, and his share of the white vote rose from 4 to 10 per cent.[89] However, using a race-based law and order appeal, George Bush defeated Democrat Michael Dukakis in the November election and ensured another four years of Republican presidential rule.

Reagan left office in January 1989. While a lame duck president, his veto of the 1988 Civil Rights Restoration Act had been overridden by Congress. The act effectively reversed a four-year-old Supreme Court ruling, *Grove City College* v. *Bell*, by ensuring that institutions had to be fully compliant with anti-discrimination legislation if any of their pro- grammes received federal funding. The *Grove* ruling had only required the recipient programme, rather than the host institution, to be non- discriminatory.[90] In the same month as Reagan left the White House, his legacy of conservative appointments to the Supreme Court was reflected in *City of Richmond* v. *Croson*, which severely restricted the use of minority set-aside programmes by state and local government.

Years of conservatism had blunted the African-American struggle for equality, but by 1990 blacks formed 11.2 per cent of registered voters, and 12.3 per cent of the total population.[91] By 1993, there were over 7,000 black elected officials, including forty in Congress.[92] Martin Luther King's birthday had become a national holiday. By 1990, 30 per cent of black families had annual incomes in excess of $35,000, up from 23.8 per cent in 1970, and 80 per cent of blacks finished high school, double the percentage twenty years earlier.[93] However, African Americans comprised less than 2 per cent of elected officials in 1992, schools in the North and urban South had resegregated, and *de facto* residential segregation was the norm across America.[94] Black median income was only 58 per cent of white income in 1990, down from 61.3 per cent in 1970.[95] A majority of African Americans lived in inner cities, and 31.9 per cent of blacks were trapped in poverty, many of them living in female-headed families, which comprised 56.2 per cent of all black families in 1990.[96] African Americans were six times more likely than whites to suffer violent crime, and blacks comprised more than 45 per cent of US prison inmates in 1990.[97]

African Americans had preserved many gains from the civil rights movement, such as the Voting Rights Act, and they continued to challenge discrimination in electoral laws. Many blacks had entered the middle class, and affirmative action was embattled but largely intact. However, there was little white sympathy for and growing fear of poor African Americans. Perhaps only a new social movement could have led to effective action against poverty, but with whites largely indifferent and blacks increasingly divided by class and ideology, there was little prospect of change as the last decade of the century approached. Nevertheless, the achievements of the civil rights movement should not be belittled, or the contributions of many otherwise ordinary men and women to the movement forgotten.

Notes

1. Donald G. Nieman, *Promises to Keep: African-Americans and the Constitutional Order, 1776 to the Present* (New York and Oxford: Oxford University Press, 1991), p. 179.
2. Dean J. Kotlowski, *Nixon's Civil Rights: Politics, Principle, and Policy* (Cambridge, MA, and London: Harvard University Press, 2001), pp. 18–19.
3. Allen J. Matusow, *The Unraveling of America: A History of Liberalism in the 1960s* (New York: Harper and Row, 1984), p. 437.
4. Alvy L. King, 'Richard M. Nixon, Southern Strategies, and Desegregation of Public Schools', in Leon Friedman and William F. Levantrosser (eds), *Richard M. Nixon: Politician, President, Administrator* (New York, Greenwood, CT, and London: Greenwood Press, 1991), p. 142.
5. Hugh Davis Graham, *The Civil Rights Era: Origins and Development of National Policy 1960–1972* (New York and Oxford: Oxford University Press, 1990), p. 448.
6. Paul S. Boyer, Clifford E. Clark, Jr, Joseph F. Kett, Neal Salisbury, Harvard Sitkoff and Nancy Woloch, *The Enduring Vision: A History of the American People*, 5th edn (Boston and New York: Houghton Mifflin, 2004), p. A–26.
7. Graham, *Civil Rights Era*, p. 448.
8. Graham, *Civil Rights Era*, p. 448; Joan Hoff, *Nixon Reconsidered* (New York: Basic Books, 1994), p. 93.
9. Ronald P. Formisano, *Boston Against Busing: Race, Class, and Ethnicity in the 1960s and 1970s* (Chapel Hill and London: University of North Carolina Press, 1991), pp. xi–xii. White participation in Boston's state schools declined from 54 per cent of the total enrolment in 1974 to 27 per cent in 1985. James T. Patterson, *Brown v. Board of Education: A Civil Rights Milestone and Its Troubled Legacy* (Oxford and New York: Oxford University Press, 2001), p. 176.
10. Hugh Davis Graham, 'Richard Nixon and Civil Rights: Explaining an Enigma', *Presidential Studies Quarterly* 26 (Winter 1996), p. 94.
11. Kotlowski, *Nixon's Civil Rights*, p. 174.
12. Ibid. p. 183.
13. William H. Chafe, *The Unfinished Journey: America since World War II*, 5th edn (New York and London: Oxford University Press, 2003), pp. 371–4.

14. Hoff, *Nixon Reconsidered*, p. 113.
15. Kotlowski, *Nixon's Civil Rights*, pp. 1 (second quotation), 3 (first quotation).
16. Graham, 'Richard Nixon and Civil Rights', pp. 93–106 (quotation on p. 97); Graham, *Civil Rights Era*, pp. 320, 383–6, 448.
17. Adam Fairclough, *To Redeem the Soul of America: The Southern Christian Leadership Conference and Martin Luther King, Jr.* (Athens and London: University of Georgia Press, 1987), p. 253.
18. Adam Fairclough, *Race and Democracy: The Civil Rights Struggle in Louisiana, 1915–1972* (Athens and London: University of Georgia Press, 1995), p. 384.
19. Ibid.
20. Stephen G. N. Tuck, *Beyond Atlanta: The Struggle for Racial Equality in Georgia, 1940–1980* (Athens and London: University of Georgia Press, 2001), p. 195.
21. Akinyele Omowale Umoja, '"We Will Shoot Back": The Natchez Model and Paramilitary Organization in the Mississippi Freedom Movement', *Journal of Black Studies* 32 (January 2002), p. 271.
22. Stephen F. Lawson, *Running for Freedom: Civil Rights and Black Politics in America Since 1941*, 2nd edn (New York: McGraw-Hill, 1997), p. 112.
23. David J. Garrow, *Protest at Selma: Martin Luther King, Jr., and the Voting Rights Act of 1965* (New Haven and London: Yale University Press, 1978), pp. 19, 189.
24. Fairclough, *Race and Democracy*, p. 385.
25. Ibid. p. 384.
26. John A. Kirk, *Redefining the Color Line: Black Activism in Little Rock, Arkansas, 1940–1970* (Gainesville: University Press of Florida, 2002), p. 169.
27. Tuck, *Beyond Atlanta*, p. 198.
28. Timothy J. Minchin, *Hiring the Black Worker: The Racial Integration of the Southern Textile Industry, 1960–1980* (Chapel Hill and London: University of North Carolina Press, 1999); Timothy J. Minchin, *The Color of Work: The Struggle for Civil Rights in the Southern Paper Industry, 1945–1980* (Chapel Hill and London: University of North Carolina Press, 2001).
29. Fairclough, *To Redeem the Soul of America*, p. 394.
30. Tuck, *Beyond Atlanta*, pp. 198–200 (quotation on p. 199).
31. Fairclough, *To Redeem the Soul of America*, pp. 396–7.
32. Mark Newman, *Divine Agitators: The Delta Ministry and Civil Rights in Mississippi* (Athens and London: University of Georgia Press, 2004), pp. 180, 192, 197.
33. Lawson, *Running for Freedom*, p. 122.
34. Ibid. p. 152.
35. David R. Goldfield, *Black, White, and Southern: Race Relations and Southern Culture 1940 to the Present* (Baton Rouge and London: Louisiana State University Press, 1990), pp. 211, 274–5.
36. Ibid. p. 238.
37. Ibid. p. 241.
38. Tuck, *Beyond Atlanta*, p. 227.
39. Goldfield, *Black, White, and Southern*, p. 228.
40. Tuck, *Beyond Atlanta*, p. 223.
41. Goldfield, *Black, White, and Southern*, p. 192.
42. Ibid. p. 244.
43. Ibid. pp. 245, 247.
44. Nieman, *Promises to Keep*, p. 179.

45. John Shelton Reed and Merle Black, 'Jim Crow, R.I.P.', in John Shelton Reed, *Surveying the South: Studies in Regional Sociology* (Columbia and London: University of Missouri Press, 1993), p. 98.

46. Fairclough, *Race and Democracy*, p. 453.

47. Jack Bass and Walter De Vries, *The Transformation of Southern Politics: Social Change and Political Consequence since 1945* (1976; Athens and London: University of Georgia Press, 1995), pp. 16 n. 16, 17.

48. Tuck, *Beyond Atlanta*, p. 212.

49. Raymond Wolters, *The Burden of Brown: Thirty Years of School Desegregation* (Knoxville: University of Tennessee Press, 1984), pp. 7–8, 273, 274–5, 281–9.

50. David J. Garrow, 'Segregation's Legacy', *Reviews in American History* 13 (September 1985), p. 432.

51. Harvard Sitkoff, *The Struggle for Black Equality, 1954–1992*, rev. edn (New York: Hill and Wang, 1993), p. 203.

52. Hugh Pearson, *The Shadow of the Panther: Huey Newton and the Price of Black Power in America* (Reading, MA: Addison-Wesley, 1994), p. 206. Kenneth O'Reilly estimates that 'at least two policemen' and ten Panthers died in armed confrontations during this period. Kenneth O'Reilly, *'Racial Matters': The FBI's Secret File on Black America, 1960–1972* (New York: Free Press, 1989), p. 297.

53. Herbert H. Haines, *Black Radicals and the Civil Rights Mainstream, 1954–1970* (Knoxville: University of Tennessee Press, 1988), p. 68.

54 Pearson, *Shadow of the Panther*, pp. 196, 210.

55. Ibid. p. 173.

56. Ibid. p. 247.

57. Ibid. p. 347.

58. Ibid. p. 210.

59. 'Manifesto to the White Christian Churches and the Jewish Synagogues in the United States of America and all other racist institutions', 26 April 1969, p. 6, folder 298, box 4, Wendell R. Grigg Papers, Wake Forest University, North Carolina.

60. George H. Gallup, *The Gallup Poll: Public Opinion 1935–1971, Vol. 3: 1959–1971* (New York: Random House, 1972), p. 2200.

61. 'Black Manifesto's Birthday: Frosting on the Cake?', *Christianity Today* 14 (22 May 1970), p. 37.

62. Manning Marable, *Race, Reform, and Rebellion: The Second Reconstruction in Black America, 1945–1990*, 2nd edn (Basingstoke: Macmillan, 1991), p. 122.

63. Ibid. pp. 122–3 (first quotation on p. 122; second quotation on p. 123).

64. Ibid. pp. 133, 137.

65. Lawson, *Running for Freedom*, pp. 156, 179, 200; Goldfield, *Black, White, and Southern*, p. 228.

66. Lawson, *Running for Freedom*, p. 185.

67. William Julius Wilson, *The Truly Disadvantaged: The Inner City, the Underclass, and Public Policy* (Chicago and London: University of Chicago Press, 1987), p. 31.

68. Lawson, *Running for Freedom*, p. 191.

69. John Dumbrell, *The Carter Presidency: A Re-evaluation*, 2nd edn (Manchester and New York: Manchester University Press, 1995), p. 89; Boyer et al., *Enduring Vision*, p. A–19.

70. Lawson, *Running for Freedom*, p. 195.

71. Nieman, *Promises to Keep*, pp. 211–12.

72. Lawson, *Running for Freedom*, p. 205.
73. Ibid. p. 198.
74. Lawson, *Running for Freedom*, p. 285. According to Iwan W. Morgan, average African-American income stood at 63 per cent of average white income in 1975. Iwan W. Morgan, *Beyond the Liberal Consensus: A Political History of the United States since 1965* (London: Hurst, 1994), p. 256.
75. Lawson, *Running for Freedom*, pp. 199–200.
76. Lawson, *Running for Freedom*, p. 200; Robert Weisbrot, *Freedom Bound: A History of America's Civil Rights Movement* (New York and London: W. W. Norton, 1990), p. 300.
77. Lawson, *Running for Freedom*, p. 201.
78. Dumbrell, *Carter Presidency*, p. 89.
79. Lawson, *Running for Freedom*, p. 203.
80. Weisbrot, *Freedom Bound*, p. 302.
81. Lawson, *Running for Freedom*, p. 207.
82. Weisbrot, *Freedom Bound*, p. 311.
83. William Julius Wilson, *The Declining Significance of Race: Blacks and Changing American Institutions*, 2nd edn (Chicago and London: University of Chicago Press, 1980), pp. 129–34, 142, 151–2, 156–7, 158, 160–1, 166, 169–70, 171–2; Wilson, *The Truly Disadvantaged*, pp. ix, 7–8, 20, 22–9, 36–62, 82–4, 91 (quotation), 95–6, 100–6, 135–6, 137, 138, 143–6.
84. Charles Murray, *Losing Ground: American Social Policy, 1950–1980* 2nd edn (1984; New York: Basic Books, 1994), pp. 9, 42–3, 46–7, 50, 92, 133, 135, 145–53, 159–91, 219–20, 222–3.
85. Christopher Jencks, *Rethinking Social Policy: Race, Poverty, and the Underclass* (1992; New York: HarperPerennial, 1993), pp. 133–6, 194–8.
86. Robert Cook, *Sweet Land of Liberty? The African-American Struggle for Civil Rights in the Twentieth Century* (London and New York: Longman, 1998), p. 274.
87. Lawson, *Running for Freedom*, p. 227.
88. Ibid. p. 228.
89. Ibid. p. 247.
90. William T. Martin Riches, *The Civil Rights Movement: Struggle and Resistance* (Basingstoke and New York: Palgrave, 1997), p. 119.
91. Sitkoff, *Struggle for Black Equality*, p. 220; Boyer, et al., *Enduring Vision*, p. A-19.
92. Sitkoff, *Struggle for Black Equality*, p. 221; Lawson, *Running for Freedom*, p. 271.
93. Sitkoff, *Struggle for Black Equality*, pp. 223, 225.
94. Ibid. p. 221.
95. Lawson, *Running for Freedom*, p. 285. Morgan gives a figure of 56 per cent. Morgan, *Beyond the Liberal Consensus*, p. 256.
96. Weisbrot, *Freedom Bound*, p. 306; Morgan, *Beyond the Liberal Consensus*, p. 256; Sitkoff, *Struggle for Black Equality*, pp. 225, 227.
97. Sitkoff, *Struggle for Black Equality*, p. 227.

CHAPTER 6

Conclusion

Although the civil rights movement was unable to end racial inequality in America, it had an enormous impact on the lives and prospects of many African Americans, whether they were movement contemporaries or belonged to a later generation. The destruction of *de jure* segregation and voter disfranchisement in the South, and the opening up of economic opportunities to many African Americans across the country had manifold practical advantages, even though desegregation undermined black schools and many black businesses that had thrived in black communities. And while many African Americans did not necessarily wish to associate with whites, they resented the everyday indignities and discourtesies of Jim Crow, and their exclusion from the quality of public accommodations enjoyed by whites. Although the movement never developed or implemented an effective economic agenda, neither its benefits nor its membership should be seen as simply confined to the black middle class. As activist Julian Bond points out, 'Black professionals in Baton Rouge and Montgomery did not ride the city buses, but blue-collar blacks did. Blacks in the middle class in Oklahoma City and Greensboro did not eat at Woolworths and Kresge's, but blue-collar blacks did'.[1] Many of those involved in the movement arrived at what Richard King describes as 'a new sense of themselves as neither beleagured, isolated individuals nor as oppressed masses'.[2] Participants gained a greater sense of self-respect by acting collectively against oppression. The African-American struggle for equality boosted black pride and cultural awareness, while also enabling some whites to overcome their racism. What follows are some reflections on the movement.

The civil rights movement, at least in the South, began to emerge in the 1930s and early 1940s. A case can also be made for dating the movement to the founding of the NAACP, or more importantly to its first major successes during the time of the First World War and its postwar expansion in membership and branches across the country.

However, the NAACP had to weather financial problems and a membership decline during the Depression. Although the national NAACP continued to campaign against lynching in the 1930s, and began also to focus on economic and education issues, the Association did not recover and expand in the South until the 1940s. The late 1930s and 1940s saw the formation of NAACP state conferences in the region to coordinate branch activities. In many southern states, there was continuity between voter registration campaigns by NAACP chapters and other local groups, which local NAACP leaders and members often controlled or influenced, and the movement in the 1950s and 1960s.

The Great Migration of blacks to the urban South and North in the twentieth century, and the transformation of the South's agricultural system from tenancy and sharecropping to agribusiness were essential prerequisites for the development of the southern civil rights movement. These circumstances allowed a more educated and concentrated black community to develop in southern towns and cities that provided the movement with crucial support, and, in the larger cities, began to register to vote in the 1940s. Migration also created a black vote concentrated in the industrial North's major cities, which Democratic presidential candidates needed to win in order to secure election. The federal government, which expanded its function and budget during the New Deal, the Second World War and the Cold War, increasingly, if not always consistently or enthusiastically, supported the movement's objectives.

Adam Fairclough contends that the civil rights movement was 'a two-act play', with the first act occurring between the late 1930s and 1955, and the second act marked by protests during the second half of the 1950s and the 1960s.[3] More recently, Stephen Tuck has argued that there was 'a third act' that began as local people, assisted by outside organisations, tried to secure implementation of the federal civil rights legislation of 1964–5.[4] That struggle continued in Georgia and other parts of the South during the 1970s, and, in terms of challenging discrimination in the electoral process, into the 1980s.

The NAACP played a crucial role throughout the civil rights movement, and not simply by winning important legal cases and lobbying the president and Congress. Although suppressed in parts of the South during massive resistance, NAACP branches sometimes formed the basis of new alternative local groups that continued the struggle, and they created networks that subsequent activists used. Without the assistance of NAACP branch leaders, Bob Moses claimed that he could not have begun and developed SNCC's work in Mississippi. Although the NAACP's national office generally held aloof from direct action in the early 1960s, the NAACP often furnished crucial legal representation and bail money to people arrested in direct-action protests, and, unlike Roy Wilkins, some board members praised the protesters. While the NAACP's national board was committed to litigation and lobbying, it sanctioned local initiatives in 1959 and four years later the Association's annual convention endorsed mass protest.

NAACP chapters defy easy classification. They ranged from being cautious and conservative to becoming fully engaged in direct action during the 1960s. Aaron Henry, the president of the Mississippi NAACP, led a direct-action campaign in Clarksdale, and the South Carolina NAACP, led by president I. DeQuincey Newman, organised direct-action protests and dominated the state's civil rights movement. Even when NAACP branches in some states frowned on direct action, their Youth Councils sometimes participated. In the second half of the 1960s, NAACP branches and Youth Councils in Louisiana became more militant and confrontational, and the same was true of many of their northern counterparts. NAACP youths in Milwaukee joined in fair-housing protests headed by Catholic priest Father James Groppi, while Cecil B. Moore, the head of the Philadelphia NAACP, endorsed self-defence and black nationalism.

Although many NAACP branches were largely middle class, it was also the case that many others, like the civil rights movement overall, involved members from all classes, and drew upon a wide range of sources, beyond simply the church. While there was class conflict within the movement, notably in Mississippi, it is more striking how often the struggle against the common enemy of racial discrimination enabled black communities to set aside class and other divisions.

Labour unions, Masonic lodges, high school and college students, teachers' organisations, neighbourhood groups, women's associations, independent farmers, businesspeople and black newspapers all contributed to the movement. A broad cross-section of the African-American community joined in the Albany, Georgia, protests in the early 1960s.

Charles M. Payne argues in his study of the movement in the Delta and southwest of Mississippi that 'in the most dangerous moments of the rural movement, sustained militant leadership came from the working class and the poor, while the better classes temporized'.[5] Many African Americans, of course, did not participate in the movement. Fear of white economic and violent retaliation, careerism, apathy, disdain for direct-action tactics and a preference for segregation either from a nationalist perspective or simply acquiesence in Jim Crow, all kept blacks outside the movement.

While important, the church provided only one of the movement's building blocks. Fairclough notes that 'The church emerged as a distinct force only when the NAACP came under state persecution in the late 1950s, and only in Alabama, where the organisation was suppressed altogether, did ministerial leadership entirely supplant that of the NAACP.'[6] Although individual ministers, such as Ralph Mark Gilbert in Georgia, James Hinton and Newman in South Carolina, Fred Shuttles-worth in Birmingham, C. K. Steele in Tallahassee, Wyatt Walker in Petersburg, Virginia, and most famously of all Martin Luther King, played active roles in local, state and broader movement activity, they were exceptional. Most black clergy, particularly outside the ranks of educated pastors who led the larger urban churches, held aloof from the movement altogether. Some other clergymen performed a secondary, supportive role by urging their congregants to register to vote, and Charles F. Golden, the African-American Bishop of the Nashville-Carolina Area of the Methodist Church, ordered black churches under his authority in Mississippi to allow civil rights meetings.

Studies of Georgia, Louisiana and Mississippi find little movement involvement by black ministers, although until the advent of massive resistance clergymen led, albeit rather poorly, about a third of Louisiana's NAACP's chapters. Robert Cook notes that in many instances, such as the Montgomery bus boycott, the sit-ins, the Freedom Rides and the Mississippi Summer Project, civil rights campaigns were not launched by the church. Black ministers had little influence in some local movements, such as that in Cambridge, Maryland.[7] Dismissing Aldon Morris's emphasis on the role of the black church in protest activity, historian August Meier argues that 'There is little if any evidence of a broad church-based organizational network on which the movement of the 1960s was built.'[8]

However, religion clearly mattered a great deal in the movement. Despite its early organisational deficiencies, the SCLC had several vigorous local affiliates, and, in its southern campaigns, the organisation exploited local church networks, which provided meeting places, finan-cial support, contacts and volunteers. Local affiliates sometimes influenced the SCLC's direction, notably by inviting the organisation to campaign in Birmingham in 1963. Although most churches did not participate in the movement, members of their congregations sometimes pressured and shamed their reluctant pastors into opening them to movement meetings. Many SNCC and CORE activists were not themselves devout, but they were often careful to incorporate religious language and metaphors into civil rights meetings, to respect religion, and to hold meetings in churches.

Black southerners were overwhelmingly a religious people. Evangelical Protestantism taught forbearance, love and forgiveness, and provided comfort with the assurance that how ever hard life was in the present, the just would be rewarded in the hereafter. Although, like many movement activists, most black southerners did not fully comprehend the philosophy of Gandhian nonviolence, their religious beliefs enabled them to participate in nonviolent protest and to share the aspiration of a beloved community. Even though southern blacks, particularly in rural areas, were prepared to protect and defend themselves with arms, most rejected calls by nationalists for armed struggle and separatism in the mid and late 1960s. While northern blacks turned to rioting in disappointment at lack of progress, many black southerners found that the pace of change around them had exceeded their expectations.

Religion also helps to explain the disproportionate presence of women in the civil rights movement, aside from their greater number in many southern rural black communities, traditional assertiveness and extensive community networks. The movement's emphasis on issues beyond simply the workplace, such as segregated transportation and schools, also increased the scope for female involvement. Women formed the bulk of church congregations, played active roles in church life, and gained organising and leadership experience as Sunday school teachers and church secretaries. Women's clubs and female voters leagues often developed from church-based networks.

Men predominated in prominent leadership roles in the civil rights movement, but some women held leadership positions, such as Ruby Doris Smith Robinson in SNCC, Lucille Black, the NAACP's national membership secretary, Daisy Lampkin, a national field worker for the NAACP, and Ella Baker and Ruby Hurley who helped organise the NAACP's southern recuitment. At the state level, Lula B. White served as director of state branches of the Texas NAACP, and Daisy Bates as president of the Arkansas NAACP. Women were often NAACP branch secretaries, and, despite male chauvinism, SNCC had significant female involvement. Crucial as teachers in citizenship education classes, women were also more apt than men to enrol in them as students, to go to mass meetings and to try to register to vote. Historian Anne Standley concludes that 'Black women directed voter registration drives, taught in freedom schools, and provided food and housing for movement volunteers.'[9]

While Baker and Septima Clark criticised male domination and hierarchy in the SCLC, and the organisation's eulogising of Martin Luther King, both King and his organisation had a unique position in the movement. Raised in the black Baptist church, King excelled at inspiring black southerners using the religious language with which they and he were both familiar. However, the civil rights movement developed before King emerged. He did not initiate the Montgomery bus boycott, played no significant part in the sit-ins or Freedom Rides, and became involved in Albany, Birmingham, St Augustine, Selma and Chicago at the invitation of local leaders. Nevertheless, King played a crucial role in the movement, and many ordinary blacks and whites considered him to be its leader. As Meier has argued, King communicated black aspirations to whites 'more effectively than anyone else', and his emphasis on Christianity, redemption and nonviolence helped reassure those whites who were prepared to listen to him.[10]

Although nationwide white majorities in the 1960s frequently opposed the movement's tactics and tempo, civil rights protests helped persuade white majorities to support the movement's goals, and less supportive whites to accept change if only to maintain or restore social order. Elizabeth Jacoway contends that 'in the 1950s and 1960s, white businessmen across the South found themselves pushed – by the federal government and civil rights forces as well as by their own economic interests and values – into becoming reluctant advocates of a new departure in southern race relations'.[11] However, William H. Chafe has shown that in Greensboro, North Carolina, businessmen conceded as little change as they could, while cultivating an image of civility that masked continued racial discrimination.[12] Other local studies suggest that businessmen did not act in racial crises, such as St Augustine, when they did not feel that their economic interests were endangered.[13]

King and the SCLC tailored their strategies to influence northern white opinion and the federal government positively and to exploit divisions among white southerners. Meier describes King as a 'conservative militant', who occupied a position at the vital centre of the movement.[14] In the first half of the 1960s, King was able to keep ties open with the

White House and to help maintain the national civil rights coalition. King forged a consensus among strong-willed SCLC lieutenants and moulded their ideas together. Without King's binding presence, the SCLC's leading staff fell out among themselves after his death. Broadly speaking, in the early 1960s the national NAACP represented the moderate wing of the movement, CORE and SNCC its radical wing, and the SCLC a position somewhere between the two that enabled King to liaise between the coalition's different groups. A. Philip Randolph, rather than King, originated the March on Washington in 1963, but it was King who made the march a memorable event, and it was his presence which helped ensure that all the major civil rights groups were represented. King's powerful oratory, restrained leadership of civil rights demonstrations and thoughtful interviews also played well in the black and white media until he spoke out against the Vietnam War. Part of King's power within the movement derived from the sympathetic media portrayal he received.

Although each civil rights group engaged to some extent in voter registration, direct action and lobbying, their different emphases were mutually reinforcing in the early 1960s. The national NAACP focused on litigation and lobbying, the NUL on employment, CORE and SNCC on organising in the rural Deep South, and the SCLC on using local campaigns to create pressure for federal civil rights legislation. To some extent, competition and rivalry between the major civil rights groups also drove the movement forward. However, such conflict could be debilitating. Local movements sometimes found that the national groups brought their detrimental rivalries with them and could spend as much time fighting each other as they did Jim Crow. The NAACP, in particular, often engaged in turf wars. SNCC resented the SCLC's tendency to override SNCC's patient organising efforts and use local campaigns to influence national opinion.

There is nothing to be gained from trying to privilege either local or national movements; both were clearly important to the movement's development and progress. While some local movements were relatively independent of national groups and events, others were more obviously influenced by them and sometimes the local and national movements came directly together, as in Selma and Birmingham. Local movements operated within a framework that was influenced by state, regional and national phenomena, and they have to be seen in context. Except for the Johnson administration, the federal government was largely a reluctant suitor, but presidential, congressional and Supreme Court and lower federal court actions were crucial in the movement's growth and success. Disillusionment with white liberals and the federal government, and their experiences in the rural Deep South, made SNCC and CORE increasingly radical. King remained committed to nonviolence, but he urged a massive redistribution of the nation's resources and a reorientation of American foreign policy away from militarism. Black Power was primarily, but not exclusively, a northern and western phenomenon, which had antecedents in the beliefs of Malcolm X. In the South, local black people saw voter registration and political representation as a route to power and equality, and many had always believed in armed self-defence as a last resort. The movement continued in the South after 1965 to register voters, and to ensure the implementation of federal legislation and court rulings outlawing segregation, disfranchisement and discrimination in employment and political representation. Whether a new movement will emerge to mount an effective challenge against poverty and *de facto* segregation remains to be seen.

Notes

1. Julian Bond, 'The Politics of Civil Rights History', in Armstead L. Robinson and Patricia Sullivan (eds), *New Directions in Civil Rights Studies* (Charlottesville and London: University Press of Virginia, 1991), p. 15.
2. Richard H. King, *Civil Rights and the Idea of Freedom* (1992; Athens and London: University of Georgia Press, 1996), p. 7.
3. Adam Fairclough, *Race and Democracy: The Civil Rights Struggle in Louisiana, 1915–1972* (Athens and London: University of Georgia Press, 1995), p. xii.
4. Stephen G. N. Tuck, *Beyond Atlanta: The Struggle for Racial Equality in Georgia, 1940–1980* (Athens and London: University of Georgia Press, 2001), p. 2.
5. Charles M. Payne, *I've Got the Light of Freedom: The Organizing Tradition and the Mississippi Freedom Struggle* (Berkeley, Los Angeles and London: University of California Press, 1995), p. 434.
6. Fairclough, *Race and Democracy*, p. xvi.
7. Robert Cook, *Sweet Land of Liberty? The African-American Struggle for Civil Rights in the Twentieth Century* (London and New York: Longman, 1998), p. 237.
8. August Meier, 'Epilogue: Toward a Synthesis of Civil Rights History', in Robinson and Sullivan (eds), *New Directions in Civil Rights Studies*, p. 215.
9. Anne Standley, 'The Role of Black Women in the Civil Rights Movement', in Vicki L. Crawford, Jacqueline Anne Rouse, and Barbara Woods (eds), *Women in the Civil Rights Movement: Trailblazers and Torchbearers, 1941–1965* (1990; Bloomington and Indianapolis: Indiana University Press, 1993), p. 184.
10. August Meier, 'On the Role of Martin Luther King', *New Politics* 4 (Winter 1965), p. 53.
11. Elizabeth Jacoway, 'An Introduction: Civil Rights and the Changing South', in

Elizabeth Jacoway and David R. Colburn (eds), *Southern Businessmen and Desegregation* (Baton Rouge and London: Louisiana State University Press, 1982), p. 1.

12. William H. Chafe, *Civilities and Civil Rights: Greensboro, North Carolina, and the Black Struggle for Freedom* (1980; Oxford and New York: Oxford University Press, 1981), pp. 8, 34–9, 46–7, 92–3, 107–8, 121, 146–7, 155–6, 235, 240–1.

13. David R. Colburn, *Racial Change and Community Crisis: St. Augustine, Florida, 1877–1980* (1985; Gainesville: University of Florida Press, 1991), pp. 213–14; Tony Badger, 'Segregation and the Southern Business Elite', *Journal of American Studies* 18 (1984), pp. 108–9.

14. Meier, 'On the Role of Martin Luther King', p. 53.

Suggestions for Further Reading

There is a vast and ever-growing literature about the civil rights movement. The readings suggested below are necessarily very selective.

Introductions to key issues in the movement's history are provided by leading scholars in Charles W. Eagles (ed.), *The Civil Rights Movement in America* (Jackson and London: University Press of Mississippi, 1986), Armstead L. Robinson and Patricia Sullivan (eds), *New Directions in Civil Rights Studies* (Charlottesville and London: University Press of Virginia, 1991), and Jeffrey Ogbar (ed.), *Problems in American Civilization: The Civil Rights Movement* (Boston and New York: Houghton Miflin, 2003). For an overview of the South in the civil rights era see David R. Goldfield, *Black, White, and Southern: Race Relations and Southern Culture, 1940 to the Present* (1990; Baton Rouge and London: Louisiana State University Press, 1991). On the relative importance of national leaders and local activism see Steven F. Lawson and Charles Payne, *Debating the Civil Rights Movement, 1945–1968* (Lanham, Boulder, New York and Oxford: Rowman and Littlefield, 1998). On ideas and the movement see Richard H. King, *Civil Rights and the Idea of Freedom* (1992; Athens and London: University of Georgia Press, 1996), and Ted Ownby (ed.), *The Role of Ideas in the Civil Rights South* (Jackson: University Press of Mississippi, 2002). Useful historiographical studies include Adam Fairclough, 'State of the Art: Historians and the Civil Rights Movement', *Journal of American Studies* 24 (December 1990), pp. 387–98, Steven F. Lawson, 'Freedom Then, Freedom Now: The Historiography of the Civil Rights Movement', *American Historical Review* 96 (April 1991), pp. 456–71, Charles M. Payne, 'Bibliographic Essay: The Social Construction of History', in Payne, *I've Got the Light of Freedom: The Organizing Tradition and the Mississippi Freedom Struggle* (Berkeley, Los Angeles and London: University of California Press, 1995), pp. 413–41, Charles W. Eagles, 'Toward New Histories of the Civil Rights Era', *Journal of Southern History* 66 (November 2000), pp. 815–48, and Charles W. Eagles, 'The Civil Rights Movement', in John B. Boles (ed.), *A Companion to the American South* (Malden, MA, and Oxford: Blackwell, 2002), pp. 461–73. Among the best collections of scholarly essays and documents are Raymond D'Angelo, *The American Civil Rights Movement Readings and Interpretations* (New York:

McGraw-Hill/Dushkin, 2001) and Jack E. Davis (ed.), *The Civil Rights Movement* (Malden, MA, and Oxford: Blackwell, 2001).

For an understanding of the development of segregation in the South see C. Vann Woodward, *The Strange Career of Jim Crow*, 3rd edn (New York: Oxford University Press, 1974), Howard N. Rabinowitz, *Race Relations in the Urban South, 1865–1890* (1978; Athens and London: University of Georgia Press, 1996) and Grace Elizabeth Hale, *Making Whiteness: The Culture of Segregation in the South, 1890–1940* (New York: Pantheon Books, 1998). On the First World War and the postwar era see Mark I. Solomon, *The Cry Was Unity: Communists and African Americans, 1917–1936* (Jackson: University Press of Mississippi, 1998), Mark Ellis, *Race, War, and Surveillance: African Americans and the United States Government during World War I* (Bloomington: Indiana University Press, 2001) and Mark Robert Schneider, *'We Return Fighting': The Civil Rights Movement in the Jazz Age* (Boston: Northeastern University Press, 2002).

On the 1930s see Barton J. Bernstein, 'The New Deal: The Conservative Achievements of Liberal Reform', in Barton J. Bernstein (ed.), *Towards a New Past: Dissenting Essays in American History* (New York: Pantheon, 1968), pp. 244–64, August Meier and Elliott Rudwick, *Along the Color Line: Explorations in the Black Experience* (Urbana, Chicago and London: University of Illinois Press, 1976), Harvard Sitkoff, *A New Deal for Blacks: The Emergence of Civil Rights as a National Issue – Volume I: The Depression Decade* (New York: Oxford University Press, 1978), John B. Kirby, *Black Americans in the Roosevelt Era: Liberalism and Race* (Knoxville: University of Tennessee Press, 1980), Nancy J. Weiss, *Farewell to the Party of Lincoln: Black Politics in the Age of FDR* (Princeton: Princeton University Press, 1983), and Patricia Sullivan, *Days of Hope: Race and Democracy in the New Deal Era* (Chapel Hill and London: University of North Carolina Press, 1996).

Analytical interpretations of the movement's origins appear in Aldon D. Morris, *The Origins of the Civil Rights Movement: Black Communities Organizing for Change* (New York: Free Press, 1984) and Doug McAdam, *Political Process and the Development of Black Insurgency, 1930–1970*, 2nd edn (Chicago and London: University of Chicago Press, 1999). On key early movement organisations and leaders see August Meier and Elliott Rudwick, *CORE: A Study of the Civil Rights Movement* (1973; Urbana, Chicago and London: University of Illinois Press, 1975), Robert L. Zangrando, *The NAACP Crusade against Lynching, 1909–1950* (Philadelphia: Temple University Press, 1980), Mark Tushnet, *The NAACP's Legal Strategy against Segregated Education, 1925–1950* (Chapel Hill and London: University of North Carolina Press, 1987), August Meier and John H. Bracey, Jr, 'The NAACP as a Reform Movement, 1909–1965: "To reach the conscience of America''', *Journal of Southern History* 59 (February 1993), pp. 3–30, Denton L. Watson, 'Assessing the Role of the NAACP in the Civil Rights Movement', *The Historian* 55 (1993), pp. 453–68, Linda A. Reed, *Simple Decency and Common Sense: The Southern Conference Movement, 1938–1963* (1991; Bloomington and Indianapolis: Indiana University Press, 1994), John Egerton, *Speak Now against the Day: The Generation before the Civil Rights Movement in the South* (1994; Chapel Hill and London: University of North Carolina Press, 1995), Paula F. Pfeffer, *A. Philip Randolph, Pioneer of the Civil Rights Movement* (1990; Baton Rouge and London: Louisiana State University Press, 1996), Solomon, *The Cry Was Unity*, and Beth Tompkins Bates, *Pullman Porters and the Rise of Protest Politics in Black America, 1925–1945* (Chapel Hill and London: University of North Carolina Press, 2001).

State and local studies demonstrate that local movements often had their own distinct origins and momentum, although many also interacted with and were affected by regional and national developments and organisations. Increasingly numerous, they include William H. Chafe, *Civilities and Civil Rights: Greensboro, North Carolina, and the Black Struggle for Freedom* (1980; Oxford and New York: Oxford University Press, 1981), David R. Colburn, *Racial Change and Community Crisis: St. Augustine, Florida, 1877–1980* (1985; Gainesville: University of Florida Press, 1991), Earl Lewis, *In Their Own Interests: Race, Class, and Power in Twentieth-Century Norfolk, Virginia* (Berkeley, Los Angeles and Oxford: University of California Press, 1991), John Dittmer, *Local People: The Struggle for Civil Rights in Mississippi* (Urbana and Chicago: University of Illinois Press, 1994), Adam Fairclough, *Race and Democracy: The Civil Rights Struggle in Louisiana, 1915–1972* (Athens and London: University of Georgia Press, 1995), Glenn T. Eskew, *But for Birmingham: The Local and National Movements in the Civil Rights Struggle* (Chapel Hill and London: University of North Carolina Press, 1997), Robert J. Norrell, *Reaping the Whirlwind: The Civil Rights Movement in Tuskegee* (1985; Chapel Hill and London: University of North Carolina Press, 1998), Glenda Alice Rabby, *The Pain and the Promise: The Struggle for Civil Rights in Tallahassee, Florida* (Athens and London: University of Georgia Press, 1999), Stephen G. N. Tuck, *Beyond Atlanta: The Struggle for Racial Equality in Georgia, 1940–1980* (Athens and London: University of Georgia Press, 2001), John A. Kirk, *Redefining the Color Line: Black Activism in Little Rock, Arkansas, 1940–1970* (Gainesville: University Press of Florida, 2002), and Mark Newman, *Divine Agitators: The Delta Ministry and Civil Rights in Mississippi* (Athens and London: University of Georgia Press, 2004).

Local civil rights efforts were sometimes connected with labour struggles. On labour and the civil rights movement see Robert J. Norrell, 'Caste in Steel: Jim Crow Careers in Birmingham, Alabama', *Journal of American History* 73

(December 1986), pp. 669–94, Robert Korstad and Nelson Lichtenstein, 'Opportunities Found and Lost: Labor, Radicals, and the Early Civil Rights Movement', *Journal of American History* 75 (December 1988), pp. 786–811, Michael Honey 'Operation Dixie: Labor and Civil Rights in the Postwar South', *Mississippi Quarterly* 45 (Fall 1992), pp. 439–52, Steve Rosswurm (ed.), *The CIO's Left-Led Unions* (New Brunswick, NJ: Rutgers University Press, 1992), Michael Honey, *Southern Labor and Black Civil Rights: Organizing Memphis Workers* (Urbana and Chicago: University of Illinois Press, 1993), Robin D. G. Kelley, '"We Are Not What We Seem": Rethinking Black Working-Class Opposition in the Jim Crow South', *Journal of American History* 80 (June 1993), pp. 75–112, Bruce Nelson, 'Organized Labor and the Struggle for Black Equality in Mobile during World War II', *Journal of American History* 80 (December 1993), pp. 952–88, Alan Draper, *Conflict of Interests: Organized Labor and the Civil Rights Movement in the South, 1954–1968* (Ithaca: ILR Press, 1994), Robin D. G. Kelley, *Race Rebels: Culture, Politics, and the Black Working Class* (New York: Free Press, 1994), Robert H. Zieger (ed.), *Southern Labor in Transition, 1940–1995* (Knoxville: University of Tennessee Press, 1997), Timothy J. Minchin, *Hiring the Black Worker: The Racial Integration of the Southern Textile Industry, 1960–1980* (Chapel Hill and London: University of North Carolina Press, 1999), Eric Arnesen, *Brotherhoods of Color: Black Railroad Workers and the Struggle for Equality* (Cambridge, MA, and London: Harvard University Press, 2001), Timothy J. Minchin, *The Color of Work: The Struggle for Civil Rights in the Southern Paper Industry, 1945–1980* (Chapel Hill and London: University of North Carolina Press, 2001), Bruce Nelson, *Divided We Stand: American Workers and the Struggle for Black Equality* (Princeton: Princeton University Press, 2001), and Robert Rodgers Korstad, *Civil Rights Unionism: Tobacco Workers and the Struggle for Democracy in the Mid-Twentieth-Century South* (Chapel Hill and London: University of North Carolina Press, 2003).

Much of the scholarship on labour and the civil rights movement focuses on the Second World War and its aftermath, which also profoundly affected many African Americans in other ways. On wartime and early postwar developments see Richard M. Dalfiume, 'The "Forgotten Years" of the Negro Revolution', *Journal of American History* 55 (June 1968), pp. 90–106, Richard M. Dalfiume, *Desegregation of the U.S. Armed Forces: Fighting on Two Fronts, 1939–1953* (Columbia: University of Missouri Press, 1969), Harvard Sitkoff, 'Racial Militancy and Interracial Violence in the Second World War', *Journal of American History* 58 (December 1971), pp. 661–81, Lee Finkle, 'The Conservative Aims of Militant Rhetoric: Black Protest during World War II', *Journal of American History* 60 (December 1973), pp. 692–713, Peter J. Kellogg, 'Civil Rights Consciousness in the 1940s', *The Historian* 18 (November 1979), pp. 18–

41, John Modell, Marc Goulden, and Sigurdur Magnusson, 'World War II in the Lives of Black Americans: Some Findings and an Interpretation', *Journal of American History* 76 (December 1989), pp. 838–48, Pete Daniel, 'Going among Strangers: Southern Reactions to World War II', *Journal of American History* 77 (December 1990), pp. 886–911, Merl E. Reed, *Seedtime for the Modern Civil Rights Movement: The President's Committee on Fair Employment Practice, 1941–1946* (Baton Rouge and London: Louisiana State University Press, 1991), Neil A. Wynn, *The Afro-American and the Second World War*, rev. edn (New York and London: Holmes and Meier, 1993), Neil R. McMillen, 'Fighting for What We Didn't Have: How Mississippi's Black Veterans Remember World War II', in Neil R. McMillen (ed.), *Remaking Dixie: The Impact of World War II on the American South* (Jackson: University Press of Mississippi, 1997), pp. 93–110, Harvard Sitkoff, 'African American Militancy in the World War II South: Another Perspective', in McMillen (ed.), *Remaking Dixie*, pp. 70–92, Sherie Mershon and Steven Schlossman, *Foxholes and Color Lines: Desegregating the U.S. Armed Forces* (Baltimore: Johns Hopkins University Press, 1998), and Daniel Kryder, *Divided Arsenal: Race and the American State during World War II* (New York: Cambridge University Press, 2000).

In recent years, historians have investigated the connections between civil rights and US foreign policy. See Brenda Gayle Plummer, *Rising Wind: Black Americans and U.S. Foreign Affairs, 1935–1960* (Chapel Hill and London: University of North Carolina Press, 1996), 'Symposium: African Americans and U.S. Foreign Relations', *Diplomatic History* 20 (Fall 1996), pp. 531–650, Penny M. Von Eschen, *Race Against Empire: Black Americans and Anticolonialism, 1937–1957* (Ithaca and London: Cornell University Press, 1997), Mary L. Dudziak, *Cold War Civil Rights: Race and the Image of American Democracy* (Princeton and Oxford: Princeton University Press, 2000), Azza Salama Layton, *International Politics and Civil Rights Policies in the United States, 1941–1960* (Cambridge: Cambridge University Press, 2000), Thomas Borstelmann, *The Cold War and the Color Line: American Race Relations in the Global Arena* (Cambridge, MA, and London: Harvard University Press, 2001), and Carol Anderson, *Eyes Off the Prize: The United Nations and the African American Struggle for Human Rights, 1944–1955* (Cambridge: Cambridge University Press, 2003).

Aside from coverage in the foreign policy works above, the response of the Truman and Eisenhower administrations to civil rights is also examined in William C. Berman, *The Politics of Civil Rights in the Truman Administration* (Columbus: Ohio State University Press, 1970), Harvard Sitkoff, 'Harry Truman and the Election of 1948: The Coming of Age of Civil Rights in American Politics', *Journal of Southern History* 37 (November 1971), pp. 597–616, Donald R. McCoy and Richard T. Ruetten, *Quest and Response: Minority Rights and the Truman Administration* (Lawrence: University Press of Kansas,

1973), Barton J. Bernstein, 'The Ambiguous Legacy: The Truman Administra-
tion and Civil Rights', in Barton J. Bernstein (ed.), *Politics and Policies of the
Truman Administration* (1970; Chicago: Quadrangle Books, 1974), pp. 269–314,
Robert Fredrick Burk, *The Eisenhower Administration and Black Civil Rights*
(Knoxville: University of Tennessee Press, 1984), Michael S. Mayer, 'With
Much Deliberation and Some Speed: Eisenhower and the *Brown* Decision',
Journal of Southern History 52 (February 1986), pp. 43–76, and Michael R.
Gardner, *Harry Truman and Civil Rights: Moral Courage and Political Risks*
(Carbondale and Edwardsville: Southern Illinois University Press, 2002).

In addition to Neil R. McMillen, *The Citizens' Council: Organized Resistance to
the Second Reconstruction, 1954–64* (1971; Urbana and Chicago: University of
Illinois Press, 1994) and Numan V. Bartley, *The Rise of Massive Resistance: Race
and Politics in the South During the 1950's* (1969; Baton Rouge: Louisiana State
University Press, 1999), southern white resistance to desegregation is explored
in Michael J. Klarman, 'How *Brown* Changed Race Relations: The Backlash
Thesis', *Journal of American History* 81 (June 1994), pp. 81–118, and Kari
Frederickson, *The Dixiecrat Revolt and the End of the Solid South, 1932–1968*
(Chapel Hill and London: University of North Carolina Press, 2001). On the
broad response of southern whites to the civil rights movement and its demands
see Elizabeth Jacoway and David R. Colburn (eds), *Southern Businessmen and
Desegregation* (Baton Rouge and London: Louisiana State University Press,
1982), David L. Chappell, *Inside Agitators: White Southerners in the Civil Rights
Movement* (Baltimore and London: Johns Hopkins University Press, 1994), and
Mark Newman, *Getting Right with God: Southern Baptists and Desegregation,
1945–1995* (Tuscaloosa and London: University of Alabama Press, 2001).

On northern white resistance to African Americans see James J. Ralph, Jr,
Northern Protest: Martin Luther King, Jr., Chicago, and the Civil Rights Movement
(Cambridge, MA, and London: Harvard University Press, 1993), Arnold R.
Hirsch, 'Massive Resistance in the Urban North: Trumbull Park, Chicago,
1953–1966', *Journal of American History* 88 (September 1995), pp. 522–50,
Thomas J. Sugrue, *The Origins of the Urban Crisis: Race and Inequality in
Postwar Detroit* (Princeton: Princeton University Press, 1996), Arnold R.
Hirsch, *Making the Second Ghetto: Race and Housing in Chicago, 1940–1960*
(1983; Chicago and London: University of Chicago Press, 1998), and Stephen
Grant Meyer, *As Long As They Don't Move Next Door: Segregation and Racial
Conflict in American Neighborhoods* (Lanham, Boulder, New York and Oxford:
Rowman and Littlefield, 2001).

The literature on Martin Luther King, Jr, is enormous. Among the best and
most influential works are August Meier, 'On the Role of Martin Luther King',
New Politics 4 (Winter 1965), pp. 52–9, David J. Garrow, *Protest at Selma:*

Martin Luther King, Jr., and the Voting Rights Act of 1965 (New Haven and London: Yale University Press, 1978), David J. Garrow, *The FBI and Martin Luther King, Jr.: From 'Solo' to Memphis* (New York: Norton, 1981), David J. Garrow, *Bearing the Cross: Martin Luther King, Jr., and the Southern Christian Leadership Conference* (New York: William Morrow, 1986), Adam Fairclough, *To Redeem the Soul of America: The Southern Christian Leadership Conference and Martin Luther King, Jr.* (Athens and London: University of Georgia Press, 1987), Taylor Branch, *Parting the Waters: America in the King Years, 1954–63* (New York: Simon and Schuster, 1988), Keith D. Miller, *Voice of Deliverance: The Language of Martin Luther King, Jr., and Its Sources* (New York: Free Press, 1992), Peter J. Albert and Ronald Hoffman (eds), *We Shall Overcome: Martin Luther King, Jr., and the Black Freedom Struggle* (1990; New York: Da Capo Press, 1993), Ralph, Jr, *Northern Protest*, Richard Lischer, *The Preacher King: Martin Luther King, Jr., and the Word that Moved America* (New York and Oxford: Oxford University Press, 1995), Taylor Branch, *Pillar of Fire: America in the King Years, 1963–65* (New York: Simon and Schuster, 1998), and Peter J. Ling, *Martin Luther King, Jr.* (London and New York: Routledge, 2002).

On SNCC see Clayborne Carson, *In Struggle: SNCC and the Black Awakening of the 1960s* (Cambridge, MA, and London: Harvard University Press, 1981). The long-neglected role of women in the movement is examined in Vicki L. Crawford, Jacqueline Anne Rouse and Barbara Woods (eds), *Women in the Civil Rights Movement: Trailblazers and Torchbearers, 1941–1965* (1990; Bloomington and Indianapolis: Indiana University Press, 1993), Belinda Robnett, *How Long? How Long? African-American Women in the Struggle for Civil Rights* (New York and Oxford: Oxford University Press, 1997), Bettye Collier-Thomas and V. P. Franklin (eds), *Sisters in the Struggle: African American Women in the Civil Rights-Black Power Movement* (New York and London: New York University Press, 2001), and Lynne Olson, *Freedom's Daughters: The Unsung Heroines of the Civil Rights Movement from 1830 to 1970* (New York: Scribner, 2001).

On the response of Presidents Kennedy and Johnson to civil rights see Victor S. Navasky, *Kennedy Justice* (New York: Atheneum, 1971), James C. Harvey, *Black Civil Rights During the Johnson Administration* (Jackson: University and College Press of Mississippi, 1973), Carl M. Brauer, *John F. Kennedy and the Second Reconstruction* (New York: Columbia University Press, 1977), Bruce Miroff, 'Presidential Leverage over Social Movements: The Johnson White House and Civil Rights', *Journal of Politics* 43 (February 1981), pp. 2–23, Mark Stern, *Calculating Visions: Kennedy, Johnson, and Civil Rights* (New Brunswick, NJ: Rutgers University Press, 1992), and Dudziak, *Cold War Civil Rights*.

On Black Power and black nationalism see Stokely Carmichael and Charles V. Hamilton, *Black Power: The Politics of Liberation in America* (New York:

Vintage, 1967), Herbert H. Haines, *Black Radicals and the Civil Rights Mainstream, 1954–1970* (Knoxville: University of Tennessee Press, 1988), Manning Marable, *Race, Reform, and Rebellion: The Second Reconstruction in Black America, 1945–1990*, 2nd edn (Basingstoke: Macmillan, 1991), Bruce Perry, *Malcolm: The Life of a Man Who Changed Black America* (1991; Barrytown, NY: Station Hill, 1992), William L. Van Deburg, *New Day in Babylon: The Black Power Movement and American Culture, 1965–1975* (Chicago and London: University of Chicago Press, 1992), Hugh Pearson, *The Shadow of the Panther: Huey Newton and the Price of Black Power in America* (Reading, MA: Addison-Wesley, 1994), King, *Civil Rights and the Idea of Freedom*, Rod Bush, *We Are Not What We Seem: Black Nationalism and Class Struggle in the American Century* (New York and London: New York University Press, 1999), and Timothy B. Tyson, *Radio Free Dixie: Robert F. Williams and the Roots of Black Power* (Chapel Hill and London: University of North Carolina Press, 1999).

On the Nixon administration see Hugh Davis Graham, *The Civil Rights Era: Origins and Development of National Policy, 1960–1972* (New York and Oxford: Oxford University Press, 1990), Joan Hoff, *Nixon Reconsidered* (New York: Basic Books, 1994), Hugh Davis Graham, 'Richard Nixon and Civil Rights: Explaining an Enigma', *Presidential Studies Quarterly* 26 (Winter 1996), pp. 93–106, and Dean J. Kotlowski, *Nixon's Civil Rights: Politics, Principle, and Policy* (Cambridge, MA, and London: Harvard University Press, 2001), and more generally on federal policy Hanes Walton, Jr, *When the Marching Stopped: The Politics of Civil Rights Regulatory Agencies* (Albany: State University of New York Press, 1988).

The long-term impact of the movement is considered in Raymond Wolters, *The Burden of Brown: Thirty Years of School Desegregation* (Knoxville: University of Tennessee Press, 1984), Abigail M. Thernstrom, *Whose Votes Count? Affirmative Action and Minority Voting Rights* (Cambridge, MA, and London: Harvard University Press, 1987), Thomas Byrne Edsall and Mary D. Edsall, *Chain Reaction: The Impact of Race, Rights, and Taxes on American Politics* (New York and London: Norton, 1991), Goldfield, *Black, White, and Southern*, John Shelton Reed with Merle Black, 'Jim Crow, R.I.P.', in John Shelton Reed, *Surveying the South: Studies in Regional Sociology* (Columbia and London: University of Missouri Press, 1993), pp. 96–106, John Shelton Reed, 'Up From Segregation: The American South and the Promise of Racial Justice', in Reed, *Surveying the South*, pp. 107–20, Chandler Davidson and Bernard Grofman (eds), *Quiet Revolution in the South: The Impact of the Voting Rights Act, 1965–1990* (Princeton: Princeton University Press, 1994), Fairclough, *Race and Democracy*, J. Morgan Kousser, *Colorblind Injustice: Minority Voting Rights and the Undoing of the Second Reconstruction* (Chapel Hill and London: University of North Carolina Press, 1999), James T. Patterson, *Brown v. Board of Education:*

A Civil Rights Milestone and Its Troubled Legacy (Oxford and New York: Oxford University Press, 2001), Tuck, *Beyond Atlanta*, and Newman, *Divine Agitators*.

On African Americans and politics see three books by Steven F. Lawson, *Black Ballots: Voting Rights in the South, 1944–1969* (New York: Columbia University Press, 1976), *In Pursuit of Power: Southern Blacks and Electoral Politics, 1965–1982* (New York: Columbia University Press, 1985), and *Running for Freedom: Civil Rights and Black Politics in America Since 1941*, 2nd edn (New York: McGraw-Hill, 1997), and Robert C. Smith, *We Have No Leaders: African Americans in the Post-Civil Rights Era* (Albany: State University of New York, 1996).

Key works on the underclass debate include William Julius Wilson, *The Declining Significance of Race: Blacks and Changing American Institutions*, 2nd edn (Chicago and London: University of Chicago Press, 1980), William Julius Wilson, *The Truly Disadvantaged: The Inner City, the Underclass, and Public Policy* (Chicago and London: University of Chicago Press, 1987), Christopher Jencks, *Rethinking Social Policy: Race, Poverty, and the Underclass* (1992; New York: HarperPerennial, 1993), Michael B. Katz (ed.), *The 'Underclass' Debate: Views from History* (Princeton: Princeton University Press, 1993), and Charles Murray, *Losing Ground: American Social Policy, 1950–1980* (1984; New York: Basic Books, 1994).

On the federal government and civil rights in the late 1970s and 1980s see Lawson, *In Pursuit of Power*, Norman C. Amaker, *Civil Rights and the Reagan Administration* (Washington, DC: Urban Institute Press, 1988), Walton, *When the Marching Stopped*, Steven A. Shull, *A Kinder, Gentler Racism? The Reagan-Bush Civil Rights Legacy* (New York: M. E. Sharpe, 1993), and John Dumbrell, *The Carter Presidency: A Re-evaluation*, 2nd edn (Manchester and New York: Manchester University Press, 1995).

Index